Reviews

'Ha-Joon Chang has produced a provocative critique of mainstream economists' sermons directed to developing countries, amounting to 'Do as I say, not as I did.' It demands attention.'

Charles Kindleberger, Emeritus Professor of Economics, MIT, USA

'Ha-Joon Chang has examined a large body of historical material to reach some very interesting and important conclusions about institutions and economic development. Not only is the historical picture re-examined, but Chang uses this to argue the need for a changing attitude to the institutions desired in today's developing nations. Both as historical reinterpretation and policy advocacy, *Kicking Away the Ladder* deserves a wide audience among economists, historians, and members of the policy establishment.'

Stanley Engermann, Professor of Economic History,
Rochester University, USA

'People have 'always known' that leading economies used directed policies to industrialize when they were less affluent and then told poorer countries NOT to do the same, i.e. the incumbent rich always tell the poor to adopt a liberal policy stance. But this common knowledge had never been adequately documented until Ha-Joon Chang took on the task. *Kicking Away the Ladder* is a scholarly tour-de-force and essential reading for industrial policy-makers in the 21st century.'

Lance Taylor, Professor of Economics, New School University, USA

'In this lively, knowledgeable and original contribution to international political economy, Ha-Joon Chang puts economic history at the centre of the current trade liberalization debate, arguing that developing countries should not be denied policy instruments used by Europe and America for their own development. He deserves our thanks for making this argument with rare force and skill.'

John Toye, Professor of Economics, University of Oxford, UK

'This is an original and provocative work, an immensely valuable contribution to current debates on development. No one will agree with all of Chang's arguments. Indeed, many will disagree with most of what he has to say. Nonetheless, the book is far too carefully grounded and cogently argued to be dismissed, even by those who disagree with it. It will become the focus of a broad and lively debate that will enrich development theory and challenge contemporary policy.'

Peter Evans, Professor of Sociology, University of California, Berkeley, USA

Anthem Studies in Development and Globalization

Kicking Away the Ladder

Development Strategy in Historical Perspective

To the students of
Charterhouse

with best wishes

Ha-Joon Chang

Anthem Press
London

Anthem Press
An imprint of Wimbledon Publishing Company
75-76 Blackfriars Road, London SE1 8HA, UK
or
PO Box 9779, London SW19 7ZG, UK
and
9415 Bay Colony Dr 1W, Des Plaines, IL 60016, USA
www.anthempress.com

This edition first published by Anthem Press 2003
Reprinted 2003, 2004, 2005, 2006

British Library Cataloguing in Publication Data
A catalogue record for this book is available from the British Library.

Library of Congress Cataloging in Publication Data
A catalog record for this book has been requested.

5 7 9 10 8 6 4

ISBN 1 84331 027 9 (Pbk)

Cover illustration: Mark Bennington

Printed in Great Britain

Acknowledgments

Three names deserve special mention as key catalysts for the birth of this book. The first is Erik Reinert, who, through his incredible knowledge of economic history and history of economic thoughts, has directed me to many sources which I would not otherwise have even known about. The second is James Putzel; through his support for my undertaking a project on the history of institutional development, which forms the basis of the second of the main chapters (chapter 3), he provided the critical impetus to get this book going. Last but not least, I must mention Charles Kindleberger, who, despite his disagreements, provided me with exceptionally detailed and knowledgeable critical comment on an earlier version of the manuscript. He also drew my attention to the passage from Friedrich List, from which the phrase that forms the title of this book is taken.

I owe special thanks to Wolfgang Drechsler, Michael Ellman, Stanley Engerman, Peter Evans, Ben Fine, Ilene Grabel, William Milberg, Eyüp Özveren, Peter Nolan, Howard Stein, Lance Taylor and Larry Westphal, who read various earlier versions of the book with great care and provided many important comments, not all of which I was able to incorporate into the final version of the book. Van Anantha-Nageswaran, Ashwini Deshpande, Jacob Gulman, SunMok Ha, Irfan ul Haque, John Grieve Smith, Haider Khan, Tony Miller, Leon Montes, Gabriel Palma, John Sender, Jang-Sup Shin, Judith Tendler, John Toye and Tianbiao Zhu also made many helpful suggestions. Jonathan Pincus gave me not only important intellectual comments but also provided me with a lot of useful editorial advice. Duncan Green, Jonathan di John, Richard Kozul-Wright, Sandra Pepera, Bob Rowthorn, Peter Temin and Roger Wilson all provided useful comments on the paper that eventually became chapter 3. The financial support for the research behind chapter 3 from the UK

Government's Department for International Development is gratefully acknowledged.

The research for the book would have not been possible with the help of three extremely able and dedicated research assistants. Elaine Tan provided brilliant research assistance for chapter 3 and also made helpful comments on various parts of an early draft. Bente Molenaar was a very creative and careful assistant for all parts of the book, and also translated sources in Scandinavian languages for me. Edna Armendariz located and translated sources in Spanish, Portugese and French. I must also thank Daniel Hahn, my personal editor, who has done a wonderful editorial job.

Kamaljit Sood, Noel McPherson and their team at Anthem Press have allowed an experience of publication which is beyond expectation in today's sluggish and impersonal publishing world. Tom Penn, my editor at Anthem, gave me not only valuable editorial inputs but also important advice on substantive matters, especially on Tudor History.

The concentrated effort that was required for writing the book would not have been possible without a stable and loving family life. My parents and parents-in-law have always been the bedrock for our little English outpost. I finally wish to thank the members of this outpost, my wife, Hee-Jeong, daughter Yuna and son Jin-Gyu for their love and affection, in particular for putting up with my mad bouts of writing at irregular hours and my neglect of family duties.

Contents

Chapter 1

Introduction:
How did the Rich Countries *Really* Become Rich?

1.1. Introduction

There is currently great pressure on developing countries from the developed world, and the international development policy establishment that it controls, to adopt a set of 'good policies' and 'good institutions' to foster their economic development.[1] According to this agenda, 'good policies' are broadly those prescribed by the so-called Washington Consensus. They include restrictive macroeconomic policy, liberalization of international trade and investment, privatization and deregulation.[2] The 'good institutions' are essentially those that are to be found in developed countries, especially the Anglo-American ones. The key institutions include: democracy; 'good' bureaucracy; an independent judiciary; strongly protected private property rights (including intellectual property rights); and transparent and market-oriented corporate governance and financial institutions (including a politically independent central bank).

As we shall see later in the book, there have been heated debates on whether or not these recommended policies and institutions are in fact appropriate for today's developing countries. Curiously, however, many of those critics who question the applicability of these recommendations nevertheless take it for granted that these 'good' policies and institutions were used by the developed countries when they themselves were in the process of developing.

For example, it is generally accepted that Britain became the world's first industrial superpower because of its *laissez-faire* policy, while France fell behind as a result of its interventionist policies. Similarly, it is widely believed that that the USA's abandonment of free trade in favour of the protectionist Smoot-Hawley Tariff at the outset of the Great Depression

(1930) was, in the words of the famous free-trade economist Bhagwati, 'the most visible and dramatic act of anti-trade folly'.[3] Yet another example of the belief that developed countries attained their economic status through 'good' policies and institutions is the frequent claim that, without patents and other private intellectual property rights, these countries would not have been able to generate the technologies that made them prosperous. The US-based National Law Center for Inter-American Free Trade claims that '[t]he historical record in the industrialized countries, which began as developing countries, demonstrates that intellectual property protection has been one of the most powerful instruments for economic development, export growth, and the diffusion of new technologies, art and culture'.[4] And so on.

But is it really true that the policies and institutions currently recommended to the developing countries are those that were adopted by the developed countries when they themselves were developing? Even at a superficial level, there seem to be bits and pieces of historical evidence that suggest otherwise. Some of us may know that, in contrast to its eighteenth or twentieth-century nature, the French state in the nineteenth century was quite conservative and non-interventionist. We may also have read about the high tariffs in the USA, at least after the Civil War. A few of us have heard somewhere that the US central bank, the Federal Reserve Board, was set up as late as 1913. One or two of us may even know that Switzerland became one of the world's technological leaders in the nineteenth century without a patent law.

In light of such counter-evidence to the orthodox view of capitalism's history, it is fair to ask whether the developed countries are somehow trying to hide the 'secrets of their success'. This book pieces together various elements of historical information which contradict the orthodox view of the history of capitalism, and provides a comprehensive but concise picture of the policies and institutions that the developed countries used when they themselves were developing countries. In other words, what this book is asking is: 'How did the rich countries *really* become rich?'

The short answer to this question is that the developed countries did not get where they are now through the policies and the institutions that they recommend to developing countries today. Most of them actively used 'bad' trade and industrial policies, such as infant industry protection and export subsidies – practices that these days are frowned upon, if not actively banned, by the WTO (World Trade Organisation). Until they were quite developed (that is, until the late nineteenth to early twentieth century), they had very few of the institutions deemed essential by developing countries today, including such 'basic' institutions as central banks and limited liability companies. | LLC ⇒ entrepreneurship ? entrepreneurship ?

If this is the case, aren't the developed countries, under the guise of recommending 'good' policies and institutions, actually making it difficult for the developing countries to use policies and institutions which they themselves had used in order to develop economically in earlier times? This is the question that this book hopes to address.

1.2. Some Methodological Issues: Drawing Lessons from History

The nineteenth-century German economist Friedrich List (1789–1846) is commonly known as the father of the infant industry argument, namely, the view that in the presence of more developed countries, backward countries cannot develop new industries without state intervention, especially tariff protection. His masterpiece, *The National System of Political Economy*, was originally published in 1841.[5]

List starts the book with a lengthy historical discussion. In fact he devotes the first 115 pages of his 435-page text to a review of trade and industrial policies in the major countries of the western world up to his time. Included in his survey were the experiences of Venice (and other Italian states), the Hanseatic cities (led by Hamburg and Lübeck), the Netherlands, England, Spain and Portugal, France, Germany and the USA.

Many of these accounts go almost completely against what most of us know (or think we know) about the economic histories of these countries.[6] Particularly striking to the contemporary reader are List's analyses of Britain and the USA – the supposed homes of liberal economic policy.

List argues that Britain was actually the first country to perfect the art of infant industry promotion, which in his view is the principle behind most countries' journey to prosperity. He goes as far as saying that we should 'let [whoever is not convinced of the infant industry argument] first study the history of English industry'.[7] His summary of the British road to industrial success is worth quoting at length.

> [H]aving attained to a certain grade of development by means of free trade, the great monarchies [of Britain] perceived that the highest degree of civilisation, power, and wealth can only be attained by a combination of manufactures and commerce with

agriculture. They perceived that their newly established native manufactures could never hope to succeed in free competition with the old and long-established manufactures of foreigners [the Italians, the Hansards, the Belgians, and the Dutch] ... Hence they sought, by a system of restrictions, privileges, and encouragements, to transplant on to their native soil the wealth, the talents, and the spirit of enterprise of foreigners.[8]

This is a characterization of British industrial development which is fundamentally at odds with the prevailing view of Britain as a valiant free-trade, free-market economy fighting against the *dirigiste* countries on the Continent, eventually proving the superiority of its policies with an industrial success unprecedented in human history.

List then goes on to argue that free trade is beneficial among countries at similar levels of industrial development (which is why he strongly advocated a customs union among the German states – *Zollverein*), but not between those at different levels of development. Like many of his contemporaries in countries that were trying to catch up with Britain, he argues that free trade benefits Britain but not the less developed economies. To be sure, he acknowledges that free trade benefits agricultural exporters in these economies, but this is to the detriment of their national manufacturers and thus of their national economic prosperity in the long run. To him, therefore, the preachings on the virtues of free trade by British politicians and economists of his time were done for nationalistic purposes, even though they were cast in the generalistic languages of what he calls 'cosmopolitical doctrine'. He is worth quoting at length on this point:

It is a very common clever device that when anyone has attained the summit of greatness, he *kicks away the ladder* by which he has climbed up, in order to deprive others of the means of climbing up after him. In this lies the secret of the cosmopolitical doctrine of Adam Smith, and of the cosmopolitical tendencies of his great contemporary William Pitt, and of all his successors in the British Government administrations.

Any nation which by means of protective duties and restrictions on navigation has raised her manufacturing power and her navigation to such a degree of development that no other nation can sustain free competition with her, can do nothing wiser than to *throw away these ladders* of her greatness, to preach to other nations the benefits of free trade, and to declare in penitent tones that she has hitherto wandered in the paths of error, and has now for the first time succeeded in discovering the truth. [my italics][9]

As for the USA, List points out that the country had previously been misjudged by the great economic theorists Adam Smith and Jean Baptiste Say as being 'like Poland', namely, destined to rely on agriculture.[10] Indeed, Adam Smith in his *Wealth of Nations* sternly warned the Americans against any attempt at infant industry promotion:

> Were the Americans, either by combination or by any other sort of violence, to stop the importation of European manufactures, and, by thus giving a monopoly to such of their own countrymen as could manufacture the like goods, divert any considerable part of their capital into this employment, they would retard instead of accelerating the further increase in the value of their annual produce, and would obstruct instead of promoting the progress of their country towards real wealth and greatness.[11]

Two generations later, when List was writing his book, many Europeans still shared Smith's view. Fortunately for them, List argues, the Americans firmly rejected Smith's analysis in favour of 'common sense' and 'the instinct of what was necessary for the nation', proceeding to protect their infant industries with great success after 1816.[12]

List's observation was more than vindicated subsequently, as the USA remained the most ardent practitioner – and the intellectual home – of protectionism for a century after he wrote those passages but also became the world's industrial leader by the end of that period (see section 2.2.2 of Chapter 2). List was also proven right by subsequent historical events with regard to his comment on 'kicking away the ladder'. When its industrial supremacy became absolutely clear after the Second World War, the USA was no different from nineteenth-century Britain in promoting free trade, despite the fact that it acquired such supremacy through the nationalistic use of heavy protectionism.

These are important historical facts that we will establish in greater detail in the next chapter. For the moment, however, I would like to draw the reader's attention to List's methodology, that is, his historical approach to economics.

This approach, if applied appropriately, does not limit itself to the collection and cataloguing of historical facts in the hope that some pattern will naturally emerge. Rather, it involves searching for persistent historical patterns, constructing theories to explain them, and applying these theories to contemporary problems, while taking into account changes in technological, institutional and political circumstances.

This approach, which is concrete and inductive, contrasts strongly with the currently dominant Neoclassical approach based on abstract and deductive methods. This sort of methodology was in fact the staple of the German Historical School, which was the dominant school of economics in many continental European countries before the Second World War, and can be found in works written in English by authors such as Polanyi and Shonfield.[13] The School included among its leading members the likes of Wilhelm Roscher, Bruno Hildebrand, Karl Knies, Adolph Wagner (of Wagner's Law fame)[14], Gustav Schmoller, Werner Sombart and (contentiously) Max Weber. Weber, these days mistakenly known only as a sociologist, was in fact a professor of economics in the Universities of Freiburg and Heidelberg.[15]

It is today rarely acknowledged that the German Historical School's influence before the Second World War went well beyond Continental Europe. Yet the school strongly impressed one of the founding fathers of Neoclassical economics, Alfred Marshall, who remarked that its work has 'done more than almost anything else to broaden our ideas, to increase our knowledge of ourselves, and to help us to understand the central plan, as it were, of the Divine government of the world'.[16]

In the late nineteenth and early twentieth centuries, many leading American economists were directly and indirectly influenced by this School.[17] Although he eventually drifted away from its influence, the patron saint of American Neoclassical economics John Bates Clark, in whose name the most prestigious award for young American economists is given today, went to Germany in 1873 and studied under Roscher and Knies.[18] Richard Ely, one of the leading American economists of the time, also studied under Knies. Ely subsequently influenced the American Institutionalist School through his disciple, John Commons.[19] Ely was one of the founding fathers of the American Economic Association(AEA); to this day, the biggest public lecture at the Association's annual meeting is given in Ely's name, although few of the present AEA members would know who he was.

After the Second World War, when the development of post-colonial countries became a major issue, the historical approach was deployed very successfully by many founding fathers of 'development economics'.[20] The likes of Arthur Lewis, Walt Rostow and Simon Kuznets formulated their theories of the 'stages' of economic development on the basis of their extensive knowledge of the history of industrialization in developed countries.[21] Also influential was the 'late development' thesis of the Russian-born American economic historian, Alexander Gerschenkron, who, drawing on European experiences of industrialization, argued that the continuously increasing scale of technology would make it necessary for countries embarking on industrialization to deploy more powerful institutional vehicles in order to mobilise industrial financing. Gerschenkron's work provides an important backdrop to Hirschman's pioneering work in development economics. Kindleberger's classic textbook on development economics makes extensive reference to historical experiences of the developed countries, once again with numerous references to Gerschenkron.[22]

In the 1960s, the heyday of development economics, there were even some collections of essays intended explicity to derive lessons for currently-developing countries from the historical experiences of developed countries.[23] As late as 1969, Gustav Ranis, a leading neoclassical development economist (although of an older, gentler vintage), wrote an article entitled 'Economic Development in Historical Perspective' for the key mainstream journal *American Economic Review*.[24]

Unfortunately, during the last couple of decades, even development economics and economic history – two sub-fields of economics for which the historical approach is most relevant – have been dominated by mainstream neoclassical economics, which categorically rejects this sort of inductive reasoning. The unfortunate result of this has been that the contemporary discussion on economic development policy-making has been peculiarly ahistorical.

The development literature is certainly full of theoretically-based propositions (e.g., free trade benefits all countries) and may also draw extensively on contemporary experiences (e.g., the literature on the East Asian 'developmental state'). However, we rarely now see discussions that are based on the historical experiences of the now-developed countries (hereafter NDCs). To be sure, there are some scattered historical references, but these are often based on highly-stylized characterizations of historical experiences, and moreover tend to refer only to Britain and the USA. The supposed free-trade, free-market histories of these countries are held up as examples for developing countries. Yet these discussions of the British and US experiences are extremely selective and thus misleading, as will become clearer later in this book.

The upshot is that, unfortunately, with a few notable exceptions, there have been few serious studies over the last few decades which deploy the historical approach in the study of economic development.[25] This is why one of the aims of this book is to reaffirm the usefulness of the historical approach by applying it to the critique of the current popular discourses on 'good policies' and 'good governance'. Saying this, however, may give the reader the mistaken impression that the book's main aim is to prove the validity of an approach, using a policy issue as the raw material. That is not the main aim of this book. It is rather to discuss a contemporary problem with the help of history. I would further argue that, given current debates on 'good' policies and institutions, this approach is particularly relevant at the moment.

The book will naturally focus on the nineteenth and the early twentieth centuries, roughly between the end of the Napoleonic Wars (1815) and the beginning of the First World War (1914), the period when most of the now-developed countries were going through their Industrial Revolutions. However, in some cases, we will extend our time-frame. Britain, for example, deserves attention from the fourteenth century onwards, given its pioneer status in many areas of economic policy and of institutional development. Eighteenth-century Prussia is another special case that deserves attention, given its bureaucratic reforms and development of new methods of state-led industrial promotion. Other exceptions that merit discussion here are the post-Second World War experiences of countries like Japan and France, who were able to generate impressive economic growth on the basis of radical institutional transformation following the war.

An effort has been made to cover as many countries as possible. Although this attempt to bring in a wide range of evidence reinforces our main findings, it also necessarily invites criticism from specialists in the economic histories of these countries. This is to be expected and is very welcome. For not only do we hope to encourage development economists to reconsider the historical basis of their theories, we would also like to see economic historians take greater cognizance of the theoretical implications of their work. If this book succeeds in generating debate over the generalities and particulars discussed in the pages that follow, then it will have achieved its main aim.

Special effort is made to incorporate in the book examples from outside the more 'important', and thus better-known, countries (that is, Britain, the USA, Germany, France, and Japan) so that more general lessons can be drawn. However, coverage of other countries necessarily remains less extensive due to the sheer paucity of English-language studies on them. I have tried in part to overcome this problem with the help of research assistants who speak other languages, but the limitations of such methods are patent. In addition, it should be pointed out that there is still great value in looking at the experiences of the supposedly better-known countries, particularly because there exist many myths and misconceptions about their histories.

The distinction between policies and institutions that I adopt in the book is necessarily arbitrary. In common-sense usage, we might say that institutions are more permanent arrangements while policies are more easily changeable. For example, raising tariffs for certain industries would constitute a 'policy', whereas the tariff itself could be regarded as an 'institution'. However, such simple distinctions quickly break down. For example, patent law might be regarded as an 'institution', but a country could adopt a 'policy' of not recognizing patents – as indeed Switzerland and the Netherlands did until the early twentieth century. Similarly, when we examine competition law we will do so in the context of corporate governance institutions, but also as a part of industrial policy.

1.3. The Chapters

Chapter two deals mainly with what these days are called industrial, trade and technology policies (or ITT policies for short). This is because, in my view, differences in these policies separate the countries that have been more successful in generating growth and structural change from the others. ITT policies have for a few hundred years stood at the centre of controversies in the theory of economic development. This does not imply, of course, that other policies are unimportant for development.[26] Nor does it imply that economic growth (still less industrial growth) is all that matters, although I do believe that growth is a key to more broadly-defined economic development.

Chapter two focuses on a smaller number of countries than the following chapter on institutions. This is above all because policies are more difficult to characterize than institutions, given that they are, as I have defined them, more variable. For example, we can easily date the formal legislation of limited liability or central banking (although it may be more difficult to define the exact point when the institution in question became widely accepted and effective), but it is much more difficult to establish that, say, France had a free-trade policy during the late nineteenth century. Because of the difficulty involved in clearly identifying the existence and the intensity of particular policies, I felt that more country-based narratives were necessary, which in turn meant that I could not cover as many countries in the chapter on policies as in that on institutions (Chapter 3).

Chapter 3 ranges more widely both geographically and conceptually. Partly because of the institutional complexity of modern societies, and also because we have a limited understanding of which institutions are really critical for economic development, a relatively large number of institutions are covered in this chapter. They include: democracy; bureaucracy; judiciary; property rights (especially intellectual property rights); corporate governance institutions (limited liability, bankruptcy law, auditing/disclosure requirements, competition law); financial institutions (banking, central banking, securities regulation, public finance institutions); social welfare and labour institutions (child labour laws, institutions regulating adult working hours and conditions). As far as I am aware, this book is unique in providing information on such a wide range of institutions over a large number of countries.

Chapter 4, the final chapter of the book, returns to the central question: are the developed countries trying to 'kick away the ladder' by which they have climbed up to the top, by preventing developing countries from adopting policies and institutions that they themselves used?

I will argue that the current policy orthodoxy does amount to 'kicking away the ladder'. Infant industry promotion (but not just tariff protection, I hasten to add) has been the key to the development of most nations, and the exceptions have been limited to small countries on, or very close to, the world's technological frontiers, such as the Netherlands and Switzerland. Preventing the developing countries from adopting these policies constitutes a serious constraint on their capacity to generate economic development.

In the case of institutions, the situation is more complex. My main conclusion is that many of the institutions that are these days regarded as necessary for economic development were actually in large part the outcome, rather than the cause, of economic development in the now-developed countries. This is *not* to say that developing countries should not adopt the institutions which currently prevail in developed countries (although conversely they should not adopt the industrial and trade policies now in place in developed countries). Some of these institutions may even be beneficial for most, if not necessarily all, developing countries, although the exact forms that they should take is a matter of controversy. For example, central banking is necessary to manage systemic financial risk, but it is debatable whether the central bank should have near-absolute political independence and focus exclusively on inflation control, as the current orthodoxy has it. Indeed, given that many potentially beneficial institutions have only developed after painful economic lessons and political struggle, it would be foolish for developing countries to forego the advantages of being the latecomer which stem from the possibility of 'institutional catch-up'.

However, the benefits of institutional catch-up should not be exaggerated, as not all 'global standard' institutions are beneficial or necessary for all developing countries. To refer to some examples that I will discuss in depth later, stringent intellectual property rights may not be beneficial for most developing countries. Equally, some other institutions, such as anti-trust regulations, may not be all that necessary for them, which means that the net result of adopting such institutions may even be negative, given that the establishment and maintenance of these institutions demand resources, in particular skilled human resources, which are often scarce. There is also the question of whether introducing 'advanced' institutions in countries that are not ready for them implies that these institutions might not function as well as they should. Moreover, we should not lose sight of the fact that the currently developing countries actually have much higher levels of institutional development when compared to the NDCs when they were at equivalent stages of development (see section 3.3.3 of Chapter 3). If this is indeed the case, there may actually be relatively little room for effective improvement in institutions for these countries in the short run.

From this perspective, we could also say that there is an element of 'kicking away the ladder' in the dominant development discourse on institutional upgrading, in so far as some of the institutions demanded of the developing countries are irrelevant or harmful given their stage of development, and to the extent that they are costly to run.

1.4. A 'Health Warning'

What this book is about to say will undoubtedly disturb many people, both intellectually and morally. Many of the myths that they have taken for granted or even passionately believed in will be challenged, in the same way that many of my own assumptions were challenged in the process of researching it. Some of the conclusions may be morally uncomfortable for some readers. Of course, I claim no moral superiority for the arguments put forward. I hope, however, to reveal some of the complexities surrounding these issues which have long been obscured by ahistorical and often moralistic arguments.

Chapter 2

Policies for Economic Development: Industrial, Trade and Technology Policies in Historical Perspective

2.1. Introduction

In the previous chapter, I pointed out that there have been surprisingly few attempts to apply lessons learned from the historical experiences of developed countries to problems of contemporary development. Also, as will become clearer further on, the few references to these historical experiences tend to be full of myths that support the orthodox version of the history of economic policy in the NDCs, which emphasize the benefits of free trade and *laissez-faire* industrial policy. The story, which underlies virtually all recommendations for Washington Consensus-type policies, goes something like the following.[1]

From the eighteenth century onward, the industrial success of *laissez-faire* Britain proved the superiority of free-market and free-trade policies. Through such policies, which unleashed the entrepreneurial energy of the nation, it overtook interventionist France, its main competitor at the time, establishing itself as the supreme world economic power. Britain was then able to play the role of the architect and hegemon of a new 'Liberal' world economic order, particularly once it had abandoned its deplorable agricultural protection (the Corn Laws) and other remnants of old mercantilist protectionist measures in 1846.

In its quest for this Liberal world order, Britain's ultimate weapon was its economic success based on a free-market/free-trade system; this made other countries realize the limitations of their mercantilist policies and start to adopt free (or at least freer) trade from around 1860. However, Britain was also greatly helped in its project by the works of its classical economists such as Adam Smith and David Ricardo, who theoretically proved the superiority of *laissez-faire* policy, in particular free trade. According to Willy de Clercq, the European Commissioner for External Economic Relations during the early days of the Uruguay Round (1985–9):

> Only as a result of the theoretical legitimacy of free trade when measured against widespread mercantilism provided by David Ricardo, John Stuart Mill and David Hume, Adam Smith and others from the Scottish Enlightenment, and as a consequence of the relative stability provided by the UK as the only and relatively benevolent superpower or hegemon during the second half of the nineteenth century, was free trade able to flourish for the first time [in the late nineteenth century].[2]

This Liberal world order, perfected around 1870, was based on: *laissez-faire* industrial policies at home; low barriers to the international flows of goods, capital and labour; and the macroeconomic stability, both nationally and internationally, which was guaranteed by the Gold Standard and the principle of balanced budgets. A period of unprecedented prosperity followed.

Unfortunately, according to this story, things started to go wrong with the onset of the First World War. In response to the ensuing instability of the world economic and political system, countries once again started to erect trade barriers. In 1930, the USA abandoned free trade and enacted the infamous Smoot–Hawley tariff. According to de Clercq, this tariff 'had disastrous effects on international trade and after a while . . . on American economic growth and employment. Nowadays, some economists even believe that the Great Depression was caused primarily by these tariffs'.[3] The likes of Germany and Japan erected high trade barriers and also started creating powerful cartels, which were closely linked with fascism and these countries' external aggression in the following decades.[4] The world free trade system finally ended in 1932, when Britain, hitherto its champion, succumbed to temptation and reintroduced tariffs. The resulting contraction and instability in the world economy, and then the Second World War, destroyed the last remnants of the first Liberal world order.

After the Second World War, so the story goes, some significant progress was made in trade liberalization through the early GATT (General Agreement on Trade and Tariffs) talks. However, *dirigiste* approaches to economic management dominated the policy-making scene until the 1970s in the developed world, and until the early 1980s in developing countries (as well as the Communist world until its collapse in 1989). According to Sachs and Warner, a number of factors contributed to the pursuit of protectionism and interventionism in developing countries.[5] 'Wrong' theories, such as the infant industry argument, the 'big push' theory of Rosensetin-Rodan (1943), and Latin American structuralism, not to speak of various Marxist theories, prevailed. Protectionist policies were also motivated by political requirements, such as the need for nation building and the need to 'buy off' certain interest groups. There were also legacies of wartime control that persisted into peacetime.

Fortunately, it is held, interventionist policies have been largely abandoned across the world since the 1980s with the rise of Neo-Liberalism, which emphasizes the virtues of small government, *laissez-faire* policies and international openness. By the late 1970s economic growth had begun to falter in most countries in the developing world, with the exception of those in East and Southeast Asia, which were already pursuing 'good' policies. This growth failure, which often manifested itself in the economic crises of the early 1980s, exposed the limitations of old-style interventionism and protectionism.

As a result, most developing countries have come to embrace Neo-Liberal policy reform. The most symbolic of these conversions, according to Bhagwati, are: Brazil's embrace of Neo-Liberal doctrine under the presidency of Fernando Henrique Cardoso, a leading Dependency theorist until the 1980s; the entry of traditionally anti-US Mexico into the NAFTA (North American Free Trade Agreement); and the move towards an open, liberal economy by India, once the bastion of protectionism and regulation.[6] The crowning glory of this trend towards liberalization and opening-up was the fall of Communism in 1989, which finally ended the 'historical anomaly' of a closed world trading system that had prevailed in the early postwar years.[7]

When combined with the establishment of new global governance institutions represented by the WTO, these policy changes at the national level have created a new global economic system, which is comparable in its potential prosperity only to the earlier 'golden age' of Liberalism (1870–1914).[8] Renato Ruggiero, the first Director-General of the WTO, argues that thanks to this new world order we now have 'the potential for eradicating global poverty in the early part of the next [21st] century – a utopian notion even a few decades ago, but a real possibility today'.[9]

As we shall see later, this story paints a powerful but fundamentally misleading picture. Indeed, it should be accepted that there are also some senses in which the late nineteenth century can indeed be described as an era of *laissez-faire*.

To begin with, as we can see in table 2.1, there was a period in the late nineteenth century, albeit a brief one, when liberal trade regimes prevailed in large parts of the world economy. Starting in 1846 with the repeal of the Corn Laws, Britain made a decided shift to a unilateral free trade regime (which was accomplished by the 1860s), although this move was based on its then unchallenged economic superiority and was intricately linked with its imperial policy. Between 1860 and 1880, many European countries reduced tariff protection substantially. At the same time, most of the rest of the world was forced to practice free trade through colonialism (see section 2.3.1) and, in the cases of a few nominally 'independent' countries (such as the Latin American countries, China, Thailand (then Siam), Iran (then Persia) and Turkey (then the Ottoman Empire)), unequal treaties (see section 2.3.2). Of course, the obvious exception to this was the USA, which maintained a very high tariff barrier even during this period. However, given that the USA was still a relatively small part of the world economy, it may not be totally unreasonable to say that this is as close to free trade as the world has ever got (or probably ever will).

More importantly, the scope of state intervention before the First World War (and maybe even up to the Second World War) was quite limited by modern standards. For example, before the 1930s, both the hegemony of the doctrine of balanced budget and the limited scope for taxation (given, among other things, the absence of personal and corporate income taxes in most countries) severely limited the scope for active budgetary policy. The narrow tax base restricted government budgets, so large fiscal outlays for developmental purposes were difficult, even if the government had the intention to make them – railways being an obvious exception in a number of countries. In most countries, fully-fledged central banking did not exist until the early twentieth century, so the scope for monetary policy was also very limited. On the whole, banks were privately-owned and little regulated by the state, so the scope for using 'directed credit programmes', which were so widely and successfully used in countries like Japan, Korea, Taiwan and France during the postwar period, was extremely limited. Measures like the nationalization of industry and indicative investment planning, practices that served many European countries, especially France,

Austria and Norway, well in the early postwar years, were regarded as unthinkable outside wartime before the Second World War. One somewhat paradoxical consequence of all these limitations was that tariff protection was far more important as a policy tool in the nineteenth century than it is in our time.

Table 2.1

Average Tariff Rates on Manufactured Products for Selected Developed Countries in Their Early Stages of Development (weighted average; in percentages of value)[1]

	1820[2]	1875[2]	1913	1925	1931	1950
Austria[3]	R	15–20	18	16	24	18
Belgium[4]	6–8	9–10	9	15	14	11
Denmark	25–35	15–20	14	10	n.a.	3
France	R	12–15	20	21	30	18
Germany[5]	8–12	4–6	13	20	21	26
Italy	n.a.	8–10	18	22	46	25
Japan[6]	R	5	30	n.a.	n.a.	n.a.
Netherlands[4]	6–8	3–5	4	6	n.a.	11
Russia	R	15–20	84	R	R	R
Spain	R	15–20	41	41	63	n.a.
Sweden	R	3–5	20	16	21	9
Switzerland	8–12	4–6	9	14	19	n.a.
United Kingdom	45–55	0	0	5	n.a.	23
United States	35–45	40–50	44	37	48	14

Source: Bairoch 1993, p. 40, table 3.3.

Notes:

R = Numerous and important restrictions on manufactured imports existed and therefore average tariff rates are not meaningful.

1. World Bank (1991, p. 97, Box table 5.2) provides a similar table, partly drawing on Bairoch's own studies that form the basis of the above table. However, the World Bank figures, although in most cases very similar to Bairoch's figures, are *unweighted* averages, which are obviously less preferable to the *weighted* average figures that Bairoch provides.
2. These are very approximate rates, and give range of average rates, not extremes.
3. Austria–Hungary before 1925.
4. In 1820, Belgium was united with the Netherlands.
5. The 1820 figure is for Prussia only.
6. Before 1911, Japan was obliged to keep low tariff rates (up to 5%) through a series of 'unequal treaties' with the European countries and the USA. The World Bank table cited in note 1 above gives Japan's *unweighted* average tariff rate for *all goods* (not just manufactured goods) for the years 1925, 1930, 1950 as 13%, 19%, 4%.

Despite these limitations, as I have pointed out in Chapter 1 and will show in more detail in the rest of this chapter, virtually all NDCs actively used interventionist industrial, trade and technology (ITT) policies that are aimed at promoting infant industries during their catch-up periods.[10] As we shall see later, there were some apparent exceptions to this, such as Switzerland and the Netherlands, but these were countries that were either at or very near the technological frontier and thus did not, by definition, need much infant industry promotion. Some countries used activist ITT policies even after the catch-up was successfully achieved (Britain in the early nineteenth century, the USA in the early twentieth century). Tariff protection was obviously a very important policy tool in the ITT policy package used by the NDCs, but, as we shall show later, it was by no means the only one used, or even necessarily the most important.

On the trade front, subsidies and duty drawbacks on inputs for exported goods were frequently used to promote exports. Governments both provided industrial subsidies and used various public investment programmes, especially in infrastructure but also in manufacturing. They supported foreign technology acquisition, sometimes by legal means such as financing study tours and apprenticeships, and sometimes through illegal measures, which included support for industrial espionage, smuggling of contraband machinery and refusal to acknowledge foreign patents. Development of domestic technological capabilities was encouraged through financial support for research and development, education and training. Measures were also taken to raise awareness of advanced technologies (for example, the establishment of model factories, organisation of exhibitions, granting of free imported machinery to private sector firms). In addition, some governments created institutional mechanisms that facilitated public–private cooperation (for example, public–private joint ventures and industry associations with close links with the government). It is important to note that many of these policies are greatly frowned upon these days, even when they have not been made explicitly illegal through bilateral and multilateral agreements.

When they reached the technological frontier, the NDCs used a range of policies in order to help themselves pull away from their existing and potential competitors. Britain, given the duration for which it held the position of 'frontier economy', is most visible in this respect, but other countries also used similar measures when they could. Britain used measures to control transfer of technology to its potential competitors (for example, controls on skilled worker migration or machinery export), and put pressure on the less developed countries to open up their markets, by force if necessary. However, the catch-up economies that were not formal or informal colonies did not simply sit down and accept these restrictive measures. They employed a wide variety of measures to overcome the obstacles created by these restrictions, even resorting to 'illegal' means, such as the poaching of workers and smuggling of machinery.[11]

2.2. The Catch-up Strategies

In this section, I examine the experiences of a range of NDCs – Britain, the USA, Germany, France, Sweden, Belgium, the Netherlands, Switzerland, Japan, Korea and Taiwan – and consider what kinds of industrial, trade and technology (ITT) policies they used when they themselves were developing countries. I show that in most of these countries, the policies that were used are almost the opposite of what the present orthodoxy says they employed 'and currently recommends that the currently developing countries should also use'.

2.2.1. Britain

As the intellectual fountain of the modern *laissez-faire* doctrines, and as the only country that can claim to have practised a total free trade at one stage in its history, Britain is widely regarded as having developed without significant state intervention. However, this could not be further from the truth.

Britain entered its post-feudal age (thirteenth and fourteenth centuries) as a relatively backward economy. Before 1600, it was an importer of technology from the Continent.[12] It relied on exports of raw wool and, to a lesser extent, of low-value-added wool cloth (what was then known as 'short cloth') to the then more advanced Low Countries, especially the towns of Bruges, Ghent and Ypres in Flanders, now part of Belgium.[13] The British monarchs of this time taxed these products mainly for revenue reasons, but since cloth was taxed more lightly than raw wool, this encouraged import substitution in wool cloth and a certain amount of export success.[14] Edward III (1327–77) is believed to have been the first king who deliberately tried to develop local wool cloth manufacturing. He wore only English cloth to set an example to the rest of the country,[15] brought in Flemish weavers, centralized trade in raw wool and banned the import of woollen cloth.[16]

The Tudor monarchs gave further impetus to the development of this industry with what can only be described as a deliberate infant industry promotion policy. The celebrated eighteenth-century merchant, politician and novelist, Daniel Defoe, describes this policy in his now-almost-forgotten book, *A Plan of the English Commerce* (1728).[17] In it, he describes in some detail how the Tudor monarchs, especially Henry VII (1485–1509) and Elizabeth I (1558–1603), transformed England from a country relying heavily on raw wool export to the Low Countries into the most formidable wool-manufacturing nation in the world.[18]

According to Defoe, Henry VII had, prior to his coronation in 1485, 'been a kind of a Refugee in the Court of his Aunt the Dutchess of *Burgundy* [italics original]'.[19] There, he was deeply impressed by the prosperity in the Low Countries based on wool manufacturing, and from 1489 onwards he put in place schemes to promote British wool manufacturing. The measures used included sending royal missions to identify locations suited to wool manufacturing,[20] poaching skilled workers from the Low Countries,[21] increasing duties on, and even temporarily banning the export of, raw wool. Ramsay also documents the legislation in 1489, 1512, 1513 and 1536, which banned the exports of unfinished cloths, save for coarse pieces below a certain market value. This, he observes, reflected the then 'influential view that if it was preferable to export wool in the form of cloth rather than in the raw state then it was likewise better to ship cloth fully dressed and dyed than in a semi-manufactured state, "unbarbed and unshorn" '.[22]

As Defoe emphasizes, Henry VII realized that, given Britain's technology gap with the Low Countries, this transformation was going to take a long time, and therefore he took a gradualist approach.[23] Therefore, he raised export duties on raw wool only when the industry was better established. As soon as it became clear that Britain simply did not have the capacity to process all the raw wool it produced, he withdrew the ban on raw wool export he had imposed.[24] According to Defoe, it was not until the time of Elizabeth I (1587), nearly a hundred years after Henry VII started his import substitution policy (1489), that Britain was confident enough about its wool manufacturing industry's international competitiveness to ban raw wool export completely.[25] This eventually drove the manufacturers in the Low Countries to ruin.

According to Defoe's analysis, other factors besides this import substitution policy helped the achievement of British victory in the wool industry under Elizabeth I. Some of these factors were fortuitous, such as the migration of Protestant Flemish textile workers following the war of independence from Spain in 1567. However, other elements were deliberately created by the state. In order to open new markets, Elizabeth I dispatched trade envoys to the Pope and the Emperors of Russia, Mogul, and Persia. Britain's massive investment in building its naval supremacy allowed it to break into new markets and often to colonise them and keep them as captive markets.[26]

It is difficult to establish the relative importance of the above-mentioned factors in explaining the British success in wool manufacturing. However, it does seem clear that, without what can only be described as the sixteenth-century equivalent of modern infant industry promotion strategy put in place by Henry VII and further pursued by his successors, it would have been very difficult, if not necessarily impossible, for Britain to achieve this initial success in industrialization: without this key industry, which accounted for at least half of Britain's export revenue during the eighteenth century, its Industrial Revolution might have been very difficult, to say the least.[27]

The 1721 reform of the mercantile law introduced by Robert Walpole, the first British Prime Minister, during the reign of George I (1714–27) signified a dramatic shift in the focus of British industrial and trade policies.

Prior to this, the British government's policies were in general aimed at capturing trade (most importantly through colonialization and the Navigation Acts, which required that trade with Britain had to be conducted in British ships[28]) and at generating government revenue. The promotion of wool manufacturing, as discussed above, was the most important exception to this, but even this was partly motivated by the desire to generate more government revenue. In contrast, the policies introduced after 1721 were deliberately aimed at promoting manufacturing industries. Introducing the new law, Walpole stated, through the king's address to Parliament: 'it is evident that nothing so much contributes to promote the public well-being as the exportation of manufactured goods and the importation of foreign raw material'.[29]

The 1721 legislation, and its subsequent supplementary policy changes, included the following measures.[30] First of all, import duties on raw materials used for manufactures were lowered, or even dropped altogether.[31] Second, duty drawbacks on imported raw materials for exported manufactures – a policy that had been well established in the country since the days of William and Mary – were increased.[32] For example, the duty on beaver skins was reduced and in case of export a drawback of half the duty paid was allowed.[33] Third, export duties on most manufactures were abolished.[34] Fourth, duties on imported foreign manufactured goods were significantly raised. Fifth, export subsidies ('bounties') were extended to new items like silk products (1722) and gunpowder (1731), while the existing export subsidies to sailcloth and refined sugar were increased (in 1731 and 1733 respectively).[35] Sixth, regulation was introduced to control the quality of manufactured products, especially textile products, so that unscrupulous manufacturers could not damage the reputation of British products in foreign markets.[36]

Brisco sums up the principle behind this new legislation as follows: '[manufacturers] had to be protected at home from competition with foreign finished products; free exportation of finished articles had to be secured; and where possible, encouragement had to be given by bounty and allowance'.[37] What is very interesting to note here is that the policies introduced by the 1721 reform, as well as the principles behind them, were uncannily similar to those used by countries like Japan, Korea and Taiwan during the postwar period, as we shall see below (section 2.2.7).

With the Industrial Revolution in the second half of the eighteenth century, Britain started widening its technological lead over other countries. However, even then it continued its policy of industrial promotion until the mid-nineteenth century, by which time its technological supremacy was overwhelming.[38]

The first and most important component of this was clearly tariff protection. As we saw from table 2.1, Britain had very high tariffs on manufacturing products as late as the 1820s, some two generations after the start of its Industrial Revolution, and when it was significantly ahead of its competitor nations in technological terms. Measures other than tariff protection were also deployed.

First of all, Britain banned the imports of superior products from some of its colonies if they happened to threaten British industries. In 1699, the Wool Act prohibited exports of woollen products from the colonies, killing off the then superior Irish wool industry (see section 2.3). In 1700, a ban was imposed on the imports of superior Indian cotton products ('calicoes'), debilitating what was then arguably the world's most efficient cotton manufacturing sector. The Indian cotton industry was subsequently destroyed by the ending of the East India Company's monopoly in international trade in 1813, when Britain had become a more efficient producer than India (see section 2.3). By 1873, two generations after the event, it was already estimated that 40–45% of all British cotton textile exports went to India.[39]

By the end of the Napoleonic Wars in 1815, however, there were increasing pressures for free trade in Britain from the increasingly confident manufacturers. By this time, most British manufacturers were firmly established as the most efficient in the world in most industries, except in a few limited areas where countries like Belgium and Switzerland possessed technological leads over Britain (see section 2.2.6). Although a new Corn Law passed in 1815 (Britain had had numerous Corn Laws dating back to 1463) meant an increase in agricultural protection, the pressure for freer trade was building up.[40]

Although there was a round of tariff reduction in 1833, the big change came in 1846, when the Corn Law was repealed and tariffs on many manufacturing goods abolished.[41] The repeal of the Corn Law is these days commonly regarded as the ultimate victory of the Classical Liberal economic doctrine over wrong-headed mercantilism. Although we should not underestimate the role of economic theory in this policy shift, many historians more familiar with the period point out that it should probably be understood as an act of 'free trade imperialism'[42] intended to 'halt the move to industrialisation on the Continent by enlarging the market for agricultural produce and primary materials'.[43]

Indeed, many key leaders of the campaign to repeal the Corn Law, such as the politician Robert Cobden and John Bowring of the Board of Trade, saw their campaign in precisely such terms.[44] Cobden's view on this is clearly revealed in the following passage:

> The factory system would, in all probability, not have taken place in America and Germany. It most certainly could not have flourished, as it has done, both in these states, and in France, Belgium, and Switzerland, through the fostering bounties which the high-priced food of the British artisan has offered to the cheaper fed manufacturer of those countries'.[45]

Symbolic though the repeal of Corn Law may have been, the real shift to free trade only happened in the 1850s. It was only after Gladstone's budgets of the 1850s, and especially that of 1860, in conjunction with the Anglo-French free trade treaty (the so-called Cobden–Chevalier Treaty) signed that year, that most tariffs were eliminated. The following passage succinctly describes the magnitude of trade liberalization that happened in Britain during the 1850s. 'In 1848, Britain had 1,146 dutiable articles; by 1860 she had forty-eight, all but twelve being revenue duties on luxuries or semi-luxuries. Once the most complex in Europe, the British tariff could now be printed "on half a page of Whitaker's Almanack" '.[46]

It is important to note here that Britain's technological lead that enabled this shift to a free trade regime had been achieved 'behind high and long-lasting tariff barriers'.[47] It is also important to note that the overall liberalization of the British economy that occurred during the mid-nineteenth century, of which trade liberalization was just a part, was a highly controlled affair overseen by the state, and not achieved through a *laissez-faire* approach.[48] It should also be pointed out that Britain 'adopted Free Trade painfully slowly: eighty-four years from *The Wealth of Nations* to Gladstone's 1860 budget; thirty-one from Waterloo to the ritual victory of 1846'.[49]

Moreover, the free-trade regime did not last long. By the 1880s, some hard-pressed British manufacturers were asking for protection. By the early twentieth century, reintroduction of protectionism was one of the hottest issues in British politics, as the country was rapidly losing its manufacturing advantage to the USA and Germany: testimony to this was the influence of the Tariff Reform League, formed in 1903 under the leadership of the charismatic politician Joseph Chamberlain.[50] The era of free trade ended when Britain finally acknowledged that it had lost its manufacturing eminence and re-introduced tariffs on a large scale in 1932.[51]

2.2.2. USA

As List pointed out (see Chapter 1), Britain was the first country successfully to launch an infant industry promotion strategy. However, its most ardent user was probably the USA – the eminent economic historian Paul Bairoch once called it 'the mother country and bastion of modern protectionism'.[52]

This fact is rarely acknowledged in the modern literature, however, especially that coming out of the USA, and even many otherwise knowledgeable people do not seem to be aware of it. No less an economic historian than Clive Trebilcock, an authority on European Industrial Revolution, when commenting on the introduction of 1879 tariffs in Germany, stated that tariffs were going up all over the world, including 'even free-trade America'.[53]

Even when the existence of high tariffs is acknowledged, their importance is severely downplayed. For example, in what was until recently the standard overview of US economic history, North mentions tariffs once, only to dismiss them as an insignificant factor in explaining US industrial development. He argues, without bothering to establish the case and by citing only one highly-biased secondary source (the classic study by F Taussig, 1892), 'while tariffs became increasingly protective in the years after the Civil War, it is doubtful if they were very influential in affecting seriously the spread of manufacturing'.[54]

However, a more careful and unbiased reading of the history reveals that the importance of infant industry protection in US development cannot be overemphasized. From the early days of colonization in what later became the USA, protection of domestic industry was a controversial policy issue. To begin with, Britain did not want to industrialize the colonies and duly implemented policies to that effect (see section 2.3. for further details). Around the time of independence, Southern agrarian interests opposed any protection, while Northern manufacturing interests – represented by, among others, Alexander Hamilton, the first Secretary of the Treasury of the USA (1789–95) – wanted it.[55]

Indeed, many point out that it was Alexander Hamilton, in his *Reports of the Secretary of the Treasury on the Subject of Manufactures* (1791), and not Friedrich List as is often thought, who first systematically set out the infant industry argument.[56] In fact, as Henderson and Reinert point out, List started out as a free trade advocate and only converted to the infant industry argument following his period of exile in the USA (1825–30). While he was there, he was exposed to the works of Alexander Hamilton and the then leading US economist and strong advocate of infant industry protection, Daniel Raymond.[57]

In his *Reports*, Hamilton argued that competition from abroad and 'forces of habit' would mean that new industries that could soon become internationally competitive ('infant industries')[58] would not be started in the USA, unless their initial losses were guaranteed by government aid. This aid, he said, could take the form of import duties or, in rare cases, prohibition of import.[59] It is interesting to note that there is a close resemblance between this view and that espoused by Walpole (see section 2.2.1) – a point that was not lost on the contemporary Americans, especially Hamilton's political opponents.[60] In turn, it should also be noted that both the Walpolean and the Hamiltonian views are remarkably similar to the view that lies behind East Asia's postwar industrial policy (see section 2.2.7.).

Initially, the USA did not have a federal-level tariff system, and an attempt to grant the Congress tariff power in 1781 failed.[61] When it acquired the power to tax, the Congress passed a liberal tariff act (1789), imposing a five per cent flat rate tariff on all imports, with some exceptions, such as hemp, glass, and nails. Many tariffs were increased in 1792, although they still fell far short of Hamilton's recommendations, which called for an extensive system of infant industry protection and subsidies. After that, until the war with Britain in 1812, the average tariff level remained around 12.5 per cent, but in order to meet the increased wartime expenses, all tariffs were doubled in 1812.[62]

A significant shift in policy occurred in 1816, when, as List noted (Chapter 1), a new law was introduced to keep the tariff level close to that from wartime as a result of the considerable political influence of the infant industries that had grown up under the 'natural' protection accorded by the war with Britain. This was done despite the fact that the revenue was no longer needed – especially protected were cotton, woollen, and iron goods.[63] In the 1816 tariff law, almost all manufactured goods were subject to tariffs of around 35 per cent.[64] Table 2.1 shows that the average tariff level for manufacturing products in the USA in 1820 was around 40 per cent. Initially, this measure was welcomed by everyone, including the Southern states, which hoped that it would help industries to grow in their territories. However, the Southern states soon turned against it because of their interests in importing superior quality British manufactures and because of the failure of the industries to emerge in their own territories.[65]

The Southern agrarian interests, with the help of the New England (and especially New York) shippers, were able to defeat bills calling for higher tariffs in 1820, 1821 and 1823.[66] However, in 1824, a new, still higher, tariff was enacted. In 1828 the so-called Tariff of Abominations further divided the country. This was because this time the northern and western agricultural interests were adding high tariffs on the raw materials or low value-added manufactures that they produced (e.g., wool, hemp, flax, fur and liquor), thus creating tension with the New England manufacturing states.[67]

Yet another tariff law was passed in 1832. This offered a 40 per cent tariff rate on average for manufactured goods – a much lower cut than the Southerners had wanted – and particularly high protection was accorded to iron and textile goods (e.g., 40–45 per cent on woollen manufactured goods and 50 per cent for clothing). This led to the so-called Nullification Crisis, started by South Carolina's refusal to accept the law. A compromise bill was passed in 1833, which offered few immediate reductions but made a provision for gradual reduction over the next ten years, down to about 25 per cent for manufactured goods and 20 per cent for all goods. However, as soon as this ten-year reduction ended in 1842, a new tariff act was passed, raising duties back up to about the 1832 levels.[68]

There was a reduction in protection in the 1846 tariff law, although the average *ad valorem* duty on the 51 most important categories of imported goods was still 27 per cent. There was a further reduction in 1857, made possible by the coalition of the Democrats, the cloth manufacturers who wanted raw wool placed on the 'free list', and railroad interests who wanted tariff-free iron from abroad. Bairoch describes the period between 1846 and 1861 as one of 'modest protectionism'.[69] However, this protectionism is only 'modest' by the historical standards of the USA (see table 2.1). It must also be pointed out that, given the high transportation costs of the period, which prevailed at least until the 1870s, US tariffs would have been a greater barrier to international trade than the European ones, even if both had been at the same level.[70]

However, the tension surrounding both the tariff and slave issues persisted between North and South, and finally culminated in the Civil War (1861–5). The Civil War is commonly thought to have been fought solely over the issue of slavery, but in fact tariffs were another important issue. Garraty and Carnes state that '[a] war against slavery would not have been supported by a majority of Northerners. Slavery was the root case of secession but not of the North's determination to resist secession, which resulted from the people's commitment to the union'.[71] Given that the South had seen tariffs as the major existing liability of the union while the abolition of slavery was still only a theoretical possibility, the importance of the tariff issue in causing the secession cannot be over-emphasized.

Lincoln's victory in the presidential election of 1860 would have been very difficult, if not impossible, had the leading protectionist states of Pennsylvania and New Jersey not switched their allegiance to the Republican Party thanks to its election pledge to maintain increased protection.[72] The pledge (the 'twelfth plank' of the platform) was deliberately worded ambiguously in such a way as to assuage the free-trade element in the Party.[73] At the same time, it was still acceptable to the protectionist states, given that Lincoln was a 'true blue protectionist' and thus seen as someone who would live up to the spirit of the pledge, once elected.[74]

Early in his political career Lincoln had been a leading member of the hard-line protectionist Whig party and an enthusiastic follower of the charismatic politician, Henry Clay. Clay advocated the 'American

System', which consisted of infant industry protection ('Protection for Home Industries') and infrastructural development ('Internal Improvements'), in explicit opposition to the 'British System' of free trade, and Lincoln fully shared his view.[75] Although during the campaign Lincoln was compelled to keep quiet on most of the controversial issues, including tariffs, in order to hold a diverse and young party together[76], he unwaveringly gave assurance of his protectionist belief when it was deemed necessary.[77]

Although he was consistently anti-slavery, Lincoln had never before advocated forceful abolition of slavery; he considered blacks racially inferior, and was against black suffrage. Given this, there was probably less to fear for the South on the slavery front than on the tariff front upon his election. Indeed, even in the early days of the Civil War, Lincoln made it clear that he was quite willing to allow slavery in the Southern states in order to keep the Union together. He enacted slave emancipation in the autumn of 1862 as a strategic move to win the war rather than out of moral conviction.[78]

In 1862, a new tariff act was introduced. It was disguised as 'compensation' for the increased excise tax and the emergency income tax during the Civil War, in order that the previous margin of protection could be maintained. This raised the rates to 'their highest level in thirty years – much higher, in many cases, than the new excise taxes warranted'.[79] In 1864, tariffs were raised still further, to their highest ever rates, to meet the demands of war expenditure; they remained at those levels after the war, although other internal taxes were repealed.[80] In this way, the victory of the North in the Civil War ensured that the USA remained the most ardent practitioner of infant industry protection until the First World War, and even until the Second World War – with the notable exception of Russia in the early twentieth century (see Table 2.1).[81]

In 1913, following the previous Democratic electoral victory, the Underwood Tariff bill was passed, leading to 'a large increase in the categories of goods allowed free entry and to a substantial drop in average import duties';[82] this reduced the average tariff on manufactured goods from 44 per cent to 25 per cent. However, the onset of the First World War made this bill ineffective and a new emergency tariff legislation was put in place by 1922, following the Republican return to power in 1921. In the 1922 law, although the tariffs did not return to their high 1861–1913 levels, the percentage effectively paid on manufactured imports rose by 30 per cent.[83]

Following the start of the Great Depression there came the 1930 Smoot-Hawley tariff – 'the most visible and dramatic act of anti-trade folly', according to Bhagwati.[84] However, this characterization is very misleading. While the Smoot-Hawley tariff provoked an international tariff war, thanks to its bad timing – especially given the new status of the USA as the world's largest creditor nation following the First World War – it did not constitute a radical departure from the country's traditional trade policy stance.[85]

In fact, the Smoot-Hawley tariff only marginally increased the degree of protectionism in the US economy. As we can see from table 2.1, the average tariff rate for manufactured goods that resulted from this bill was 48 per cent, which still falls within the range of the average rates that had prevailed in the USA since the Civil War, albeit in the upper region of this range. It is only in relation to the brief 'Liberal' interlude of 1913–29 that the 1930 tariff bill can be interpreted as increasing protectionism, although even then it was not by very much. Table 2.1 shows that the average rate of tariff on manufactures in 1925 was 37 per cent and rose to 48 per cent in 1931.

It was only after the Second World War that the USA – with its industrial supremacy unchallenged – finally liberalized its trade and started championing the cause of free trade. However, it should be noted that the USA never practised free trade to the same degree as Britain did during its free-trade period (1860 to 1932). It never had a zero-tariff regime like that of the UK, and it was much more aggressive in using 'hidden' protectionist measures. These included: VERs (voluntary export restraints); quotas on textile and clothing (through the Multi-Fibre Agreement); protection and subsidies for agriculture (compare this with the repeal of the Corn Laws in Britain); and unilateral trade sanctions (especially through the use of anti-dumping duties).[86]

In contrast to the attitude of a generation ago, represented by the above-mentioned work of North, there is now a growing recognition of the importance of protectionism among US economic historians, who used to be extremely wary of saying anything positive about it. Today, there seems at least to be a consensus that tariff protection was critical in the development of certain key industries, such as the textile industry in the early nineteenth century and the iron and steel industries in the second half of the nineteenth century.[87] Although some commentators doubt whether the overall national welfare effect of protectionism was positive, the US growth records during the protectionist period make this scepticism look overly cautious, if not downright biased.

Bairoch points out that, throughout the nineteenth century and up to the 1920s, the USA was the fastest growing economy in the world, despite being the most protectionist during almost all of this period.[88] There is also no evidence that the only significant reduction of protectionism in the US economy, between 1846 and 1861, had any noticeable positive impact on the country's development. Most interestingly, the two best 20-year GDP per capita growth performances during the 1830–1910 period were 1870–1890 (2.1 per cent) and 1890–1910 (two per cent) – both periods of particularly high protectionism.[89] It is hard to believe that this association between the degree of protectionism and overall growth is purely coincidental. Indeed, O'Rourke shows some statistical evidence from ten NDCs, including the USA, during the 'liberal golden age' of 1875–1914, to the effect that protection (measured by average tariff rates) was positively related to growth.[90]

Of course, as many people point out, tariff protection for some industries certainly outlived its usefulness. For example, despite the continuing debate on this issue,[91] it is widely agreed that by the 1830s, American cotton textile producers would not have needed protection, particularly in certain low-value-added segments of the market.[92] It is also very likely that even some of the necessary tariffs may have been set at excessively high levels due to interest-group pressures and the complicated horse-trading that has characterised the country's policy making. Despite these qualifications it seems difficult to deny that, without infant industry protection, the US economy would not have industrialized and developed as fast as it did in its catching-up period.

Important as it may have been, tariff protection was not the only policy deployed by the US government in order to promote the country's economic development during its catch-up phase. From the Morrill Act of 1862, and probably from as early as the 1830s, the government supported an extensive range of agricultural research. Measures used included the granting of government land to agricultural colleges and the establishment of government research institutes, such as the Bureau of Animal Industry and the Bureau of Agricultural Chemistry. In the second half of the nineteenth century, it expanded public educational investments – in 1840, less than half of the total investment in education was public, whereas by 1900 this figure had risen to almost 80 per cent – and raised the literacy ratio to 94 per cent by 1900. The role of the US government in promoting the development of transportation infrastructure, especially through the granting of land and subsidies to railway companies, was also critical in shaping the country's developmental path.[93]

It is important to recognize that the role of the US federal government in industrial development has been substantial even in the postwar era, thanks to the large amount of defence-related procurements and R&D spending, which have had enormous spillover effects.[94] The share of the US federal government in total R&D spending, which was only 16 per cent in 1930,[95] remained between one-half and two-thirds during the postwar years.[96] Industries such as computers, aerospace and the internet, where the USA still maintains an international edge despite the decline in its overall technological leadership, would not have existed without defence-related R&D funding by the country's federal government.[97] The critical role of the US government's National Institutes of Health (NIH) in supporting R&D in pharmaceutical and biotechnology industries, thus maintaining the US lead in these industries, should also be mentioned. Even according to the information provided by the US pharmaceutical industry association, only 43 per cent of pharmaceutical R&D is funded by the industry itself, while 29 per cent is funded by the NIH.[98]

During the nineteenth century, the USA was not only the strongest bastion of protectionist policies, but was also their intellectual home. At that time it was widely believed among US intellectuals that 'the new country required a new economics, one grounded in different political institutions and economic conditions than those prevailing in the Old World'.[99] Some of them went so far as to argue that even internationally competitive US industries should have tariff protection because of the possibility of predatory dumping by large European enterprises, who, after decimating the American firms, would revert to monopolistic pricing.[100]

Well into the last quarter of the nineteenth century, most of the more original US economists of the period seem to have been strong advocates of infant industry protection. The well-known supporters of infant industry promotion, Daniel Raymond (who influenced Friedrich List) and Mathew Carey were the two leading economists of the early nineteenth century, while American economics during the mid-to late nineteenth century was dominated by Carey's son Henry. Henry Carey was described as 'the only American economist of importance' by Marx and Engels in the early 1850s[101] and was one of Lincoln's (somewhat frustrated) economic advisors.[102] Unfortunately, most of these economists have now been airbrushed out of the history of US economic thought, but it was they, rather than the American Classical economists (then regarded as second-rate by the British standard), who were the more prominent intellectual figures of the time.

What is especially interesting to note here is that many US intellectuals and politicians during the country's catch-up period clearly understood that the free trade theory advocated by the British Classical Economists was unsuited to their country. Reinert reports that, due to this concern, Thomas Jefferson tried (in vain) to prevent the publication of Ricardo's *Principles* in the USA.[103] Reinert also cites from List's work the comment by a US Congressman, a contemporary of List, who observed that English trade theory 'like most English manufactured goods, is intended for export, not for consumption at home'.[104]

As I mentioned earlier, Henry Clay, the most prominent protectionist politician of the early nineteenth century and Abraham Lincoln's early mentor, named his economic policy platform the 'American System', in explicit opposition to what he called the 'British System' of free trade. Somewhat later, Henry Carey even argued that free trade was part of British imperialist system that consigned the USA to a role of primary product exporter.[105] It is also reported that during the 1860 election campaign, in which Carey played a key intellectual role, the Republicans in some protectionist states referred disparagingly to the Democrats as a 'Southern-*British*-Antitariff-Disunion party [italics added]'.[106]

2.2.3. Germany

Germany is now commonly known as the home of infant industry protection, both intellectually and in terms of policies. However, historically speaking, tariff protection actually played a far less important role in the economic development of Germany than in that of the UK or the USA.

The tariff protection for industry in Prussia before the 1834 German customs union under its leadership (*Zollverein*) and that subsequently accorded to German industry in general remained mild. Trebilcock, an authority on German industrialization of the period, categorically states that '*Zollverein* tariffs were insufficient to provide effective "infant industry" protection; even the iron manufacturers went without tariff duties until 1844, and lacked successful protection well beyond this'.[107] The Prussian state constantly resisted political pressures for higher tariffs by other member states of *Zollverein*. Although there were increases in tariffs in 1844 (on iron) and 1846 (on cotton yarn), these were relatively small. After that, the *Zollverein* tariff showed a general downward trend until the late 1870s, with a bilateral free trade agreement with France in 1862 and a reduction in steel duties in 1870.[108]

In 1879, however, Otto von Bismarck, the German Chancellor, introduced a great tariff increase to cement the political alliance between the *Junkers* (landlords) and the heavy industrialists – the so-called 'marriage of iron and rye'.[109] However, even after this, substantial additional protection was accorded only to agriculture and the key heavy industries, especially the iron & steel industry, and industrial protection in general remained low.[110] As can be seen from table 2.1, the level of protection in German manufacturing was one of the *lowest* among comparable countries throughout the nineteenth century and the first half of the twentieth century.

The relatively low tariff protection does not mean that the German state took a *laissez-faire* approach to economic development. Under Frederick William I (1713–40) and Frederick the Great (1740–86), the Prussian state, which eventually unified Germany, pursued a range of policies to promote new industries. The conventional measures such as tariff protection (which was not too significant on its own, as I have pointed out above), monopoly grants and cheap supplies from royal factories were of course used, but more important was the direct involvement of the state in key industries.[111]

When Frederick the Great came to power, Prussia was essentially a raw-material exporter, with woollen and linen clothes being the only manufactured export items. Continuing his father's mercantilist policies, he promoted a large number of industries – especially textiles (linen above all), metals, armaments, porcelain, silk, and sugar refining – by providing, among other things, monopoly rights, trade protection, export subsidies, capital investments, and skilled workers from abroad.[112] Frederick also retained a number of business houses to function as (what would today be called) 'management consultants' in order to pioneer development of new industries, especially the cutlery, sugar-refining, metals and munitions industries. These 'model factories' were in many ways hothouse plants that would not have survived exposure to full market competition; however, they were important in introducing new technologies and generating 'demonstration effects'.[113]

In his ambition to transform the country into a military power, Frederick also annexed the industrial province of Silesia and began to work on its development. In particular, he promoted the steel and linen industries, installing the first blast furnace in Germany in the province and recruiting skilled foreign weavers by giving them each a free loom. The development of Silesia as the 'arsenal of Germany' was further promoted after Frederick's death by a number of dynamic bureaucrat-entrepreneurs.[114]

The most important of these was probably Graf von Reden, who successfully introduced advanced technologies from the more developed countries, especially Britain (from which he drew iron-puddling technology, the coke furnace and steam engine), by means of a combination of state-supported industrial espionage and the poaching of skilled workers during the late eighteenth and early nineteenth centuries. Another significant figure was Peter Beuth, who in 1816 became head of the department of trade and industry in the Ministry of Finance. Beuth set up the famous *Gewerbeinstitut* (Craft Institute) in 1820 to train skilled workers, subsidized foreign trips to gather information on new technologies, collected foreign machinery for copying (giving the original pieces to private sector firms), and provided support for business start-ups, especially in machinery, the steam engine and locomotive industries.[115]

By 1842, Silesia was considered technologically almost on a par with Britain, and was certainly the most developed region on the Continent. The success in Silesia was, as had been intended, confined to a narrow range of military-related industries and did not spill over into other regions easily. However, this is an important example of how in a catch-up economy the state could compensate for the scarcity of entrepreneurial talent.[116]

From the early nineteenth century onward, the Prussian state also pioneered a less direct and more sophisticated form of interventionism than that used in Silesia. One important example is the government financing of road building in the Ruhr.[117] Another important example is educational reform, which involved not only building new schools and universities but also the reorientation of their teaching from theology to science and technology – this at a time when science and technology was not being taught in Oxford or Cambridge. The quality of German higher education at the time is proven by the fact that between 1820 and 1920 an estimated 9,000 Americans went to Germany to study.[118]

There were some growth-retarding effects of Prussian government intervention in the first half of the nineteenth century, such as the opposition to the development of banking.[119] However, on the whole, we cannot but agree with the statement by Milward & Saul that '[t]o successive industrialising countries the attitude taken by early nineteenth-century German governments seemed much more nearly in touch with economic realities than the rather idealised and frequently simplified model of what had happened in Britain or France which economists presented to them'.[120]

After the 1840s, with the growth of the private sector, the involvement of the German state in industrial development became less pronounced. However, this did not mean a withdrawal of the state, but rather a transition from a directive to a guiding role – examples of policies of this time include scholarships to promising innovators, subsidies to competent entrepreneurs, and the organization of exhibitions of new machinery and industrial processes.[121]

During the Second Reich (1870–1914), further development of the private sector and the strengthening of the *Junker* element, which was opposed to further industrial development, in the bureaucracy, led to an erosion of state autonomy and capacity.[122] Trebilcock argues that, in terms of industrial development, the German state's role during this period was largely confined to the administration of tariffs and, informally from the late 1890s and more formally from the 1920s, to cartel supervision (for further details on German cartels, see section 3.2.4.D. of Chapter 3).[123]

Despite the relative decline in state capacity and involvement in industrial development during this period, however, the importance of tariff policy and cartel policy for the development of heavy industries at the time should not be underestimated. Tilly points out that tariffs made cartels more workable in heavy industries, thus enabling the firms to invest and innovate more aggressively.[124] Moreover, during this period, Germany pioneered modern social policy, which was important in maintaining social peace – and thus promoting investment – in a newly-unified country that was politically, religiously and regionally very divided (social welfare institutions are discussed below, Chapter 3, section 3.2.6.A.).

2.2.4. France

As with Germany, there is an enduring myth about French economic policy. This is the view, propagated mainly by British Liberal opinion, that France has always been a state-led economy – a kind of antithesis to *laissez-faire* Britain. This characterization may largely apply to the pre-Revolutionary period and to the post-Second World War period; it does not however apply to the rest of the country's history.

French economic policy in the pre-Revolutionary period – often known as *Colbertism* after Jean-Baptiste Colbert (1619–83), the famous finance minister under Louis XIV – was certainly highly interventionist. For example, given its relative technological backwardness vis-à-vis Britain in the early eighteenth century, the French state tried to recruit skilled workers from Britain on a large scale.[125] In addition, like other European states at the time, the French state in the period leading up to the Revolution encouraged industrial espionage by offering bounties to those who procured target technologies, even appointing an official under the euphemistic title of Inspector-General of Foreign Manufactures, whose main task was to organize industrial espionage (see below, section 2.3.3). It is partly through these government efforts that France closed the technology gap with Britain, becoming successfully industrialized by the time of the Revolution.[126]

The Revolution upset this course significantly. Milward and Saul argue that it brought about a marked shift in French government economic policy, because 'the destruction of absolutism seemed connected in the minds of the revolutionaries with the introduction of a more *laissez-faire* system'.[127] In the immediate post-Revolutionary years, there were some efforts to promote industry, and especially technological, development by various governments, particularly that of Napoleon. This was done through schemes such as the organization of industrial exhibitions, public competitions for the invention of specific machinery and the creation of business associations to facilitate consultation with the government.[128]

After the fall of Napoleon, the *laissez-faire* policy regime became firmly established, and persisted until the Second World War. The limitations of this regime are regarded by many historians as one of the major sources of the country's relative industrial stagnation during the nineteenth century.[129]

This can be best illustrated with reference to trade policy. Challenging the conventional wisdom that pitches free-trade Britain against protectionist France during the nineteenth century, Nye examines detailed empirical evidence and concludes that 'France's trade regime was more liberal than that of Great Britain throughout most of the nineteenth century, even in the period from 1840 to 1860 [the alleged beginning of fully-fledged free trade in Britain]'.[130] Table 2.2, which comes from Nye, shows that when measured by net customs revenue as a percentage of net import values (a standard measure of protectionism, especially among historians), France was always less protectionist than Britain between 1821 and 1875, particularly up until the early 1860s.[131] As we can see from the table, the contrast in the degree of protectionism implemented by the two countries was particularly large in the earlier periods, but was still significant in the decades following Britain's shift to free trade in 1846 with the repeal of the Corn Laws.[132]

Table 2.2
Protectionism in Britain and France, 1821–1913
(measured by net customs revenue as a percentage of net import values)

Years	Britain	France
1821–5	53.1	20.3
1826–30	47.2	22.6
1831–5	40.5	21.5
1836–40	30.9	18.0
1841–5	32.2	17.9
1846–50	25.3	17.2
1851–5	19.5	13.2
1856–60	15.0	10.0
1861–5	11.5	5.9
1866–70	8.9	3.8
1871–5	6.7	5.3
1876–80	6.1	6.6
1881–5	5.9	7.5
1886–90	6.1	8.3
1891–5	5.5	10.6
1896–1900	5.3	10.2
1901–5	7.0	8.8
1906–10	5.9	8.0
1911–13	5.4	8.8

Source: Nye 1991, p. 26, Table 1.

It is interesting to note that the partial exception to this century-and-a-half-long period of liberalism in France, namely, the rule of Napoleon III (1848–70), was the only period of economic dynamism in France during this period. Under Napoleon III, the French state actively encouraged infrastructural developments and established various institutions of research and teaching. It also contributed to the modernization of the country's financial sector by granting limited liability to, investment in and overseeing of modern, large-scale financial institutions like *Crédit Mobilier, Crédit Foncier* (the Land Bank) and *Crédit Lyonnais*.[133]

On the trade policy front, Napoleon III signed the famous Anglo-French trade treaty (the Cobden–Chevalier treaty) of 1860, which reduced French tariffs quite substantially and heralded a period of trade liberalism on the

Continent that lasted until 1879.[134] However, as we can see from Table 2.2, the degree of protectionism in France was already quite low on the eve of the treaty (lower than in Britain at the time), and therefore the reduction in protectionism that resulted from this treaty was relatively minor.

The treaty was allowed to lapse in 1892 and many tariff rates, especially the ones on manufacturing, were subsequently raised. However, this had few positive effects of the kind experienced by countries like Sweden during the same period (see section 2.2.5 below), because there was no coherent industrial upgrading strategy behind this tariff increase. If anything, the new tariff regime was actually opposed to such a scheme – the author of the tariff regime, the politician Jules Méline, was explicitly against large-scale industrialization, because of his belief that France should remain a country of independent farmers and small workshops.[135]

The French government was almost as *laissez-faire* in its attitude towards economic matters as the then very *laissez-faire* British government, especially during the Third Republic. Given its political instability and divisions, France was basically run by the permanent bureaucracy, which was itself dominated by the very conservative and technocratic Ministry of Finance. The government budget was made up largely of expenditure in general administration, law and order, education, and transport – the classic areas of involvement of the 'minimal state'. The regulatory role of the state also remained minimal.[136]

The Ministry of Commerce and Industry, the potential centre of industrial policy, was not created in its modern form until 1886; even then it controlled the smallest budget of any ministry. It concentrated largely on promoting exports and setting tariffs, and its industrial promotion activities 'other than a rare subsidy, consisted largely of organising exhibitions, looking after the Chambers of Commerce, gathering economic statistics, and distributing decorations to businessmen'.[137] Even in these limited areas it was not very effective. Moreover, tariffs during this period were largely protective of existing industrial structures (especially agriculture) and were not of the proactive kind that was aimed at industrial upgrading.[138]

It was only after the Second World War that the French elite was galvanized into reorganizing their state machinery in order to address the problem of the country's relative industrial backwardness. During this time, especially until the late 1960s, the French state used indicative planning, state-owned enterprises and what is these days – somewhat misleadingly – termed 'East-Asian-style' industrial policy in order to catch up with the more advanced countries. As a result, France witnessed a very successful structural transformation of its economy, and finally overtook Britain in terms of both output and (in most areas) technology.[139]

2.2.5. Sweden

Sweden, despite its reputation as *the* 'small open economy' during the post-war period, did not enter its modern age with a free trade regime. After the end of the Napoleonic wars, its government enacted a strongly protective tariff law (1816), banning the import and export of some items. As a result of the high tariffs, an outright ban on imported finished cotton goods, and the deliberately low tariffs on raw cotton, cotton cloth production was greatly increased.[140] Once again, it is interesting to note the similarity between this tariff regime and that used by Britain in the eighteenth century (see section 2.2.1), as well as those used by countries like Korea and Taiwan in the postwar period (see section 2.2.7).

However, from about 1830 onward, protection was progressively lowered.[141] A very low tariff regime was maintained until the end of the nineteenth century, especially after the 1857 abolition of tariffs on foodstuffs, raw materials, and machines.[142] As table 2.1 shows, around 1875 Sweden had one of the lowest tariff rates of any of the major economies listed.

This free-trade phase, however, was short-lived. From around 1880 Sweden started using tariffs as a means of protecting the agricultural sector from the newly-emerging American competition. After 1892 (until when it had been bound by many commercial treaties) it also provided tariff protection and subsidies to the industrial sector, especially the newly-emerging engineering sector.[143] As we can see from table 2.1, by 1913 its average tariff rate on manufactured products was among the highest in Europe. Indeed, according to one study conducted in the 1930s, Sweden ranked second after Russia among the 14 European countries studied, in terms of its degree of manufacturing protection.[144]

As a result of this switch to protectionism, the Swedish economy performed extremely well in the following decades. According to one calculation Sweden was, after Finland, the second fastest-growing (in terms of GDP per work-hour) of the 16 major industrial economies between 1890 and 1900, and the fastest-growing between 1900 and 1913.[145]

The tariff protection of the late nineteenth century was particularly successful because it was combined with industrial subsidies as well as supports for R&D aimed at encouraging the adoption of new technologies. Economic historians generally agree that the promotional efforts of that time provided an important impetus to the development of certain infant industries, although one negative side effect was to create the proliferation of relatively inefficient small firms.[146]

Tariff protection and subsidies were not the only tools that Sweden used to promote industrial development. More interestingly, during the late nineteenth century, Sweden developed a tradition of close public–private cooperation to an extent that is unparalleled in other countries during this period, including even Germany with its long tradition of public–private partnership (see section 2.2.3).

This cooperative relationship first developed out of state involvement in the agricultural irrigation and drainage schemes. This same pattern was then applied to the development of railways from the 1850s. In contravention of the then dominant model of private-sector-led development of railways (notably in Britain), the government built the trunk lines (completed by 1870) and allowed the private sector to construct branch lines. The construction and operation of the branch lines were subject to government approval and, after 1882, price control. In 1913, the state-owned railway company accounted for 33 per cent of the railway mileage and 60 per cent of goods transported.[147]

Similar methods of public–private cooperation were applied to the development of other infrastructures – telegraph and telephone in the 1880s and hydroelectric energy in the 1890s. It is also often argued that this long-term technical cooperation with state-owned enterprises in the infrastructural industries was instrumental in making companies like Ericsson (telephones) and ASEA (now part of the Swedish–Swiss firm ABB, which manufactures railway equipment and electrical engineering) into world-class firms.[148]

Public–private collaboration also existed outside the infrastructural sector. In 1747, a semi-autonomous Iron Office was created. Its directors were elected by the Association of Ironmasters (the employers' association), and it maintained a price cartel, disbursed subsidized loans, provided technological and geological information, gave out travel stipends for the sourcing of technology, and promoted metallurgical research. The industry was liberalized in the mid-nineteenth century, starting with the liberalization of trade in pig iron within the country (1835) and achieving the removal of most restrictions by 1858. Even after this, however, the employers' association continued to collaborate with the government in fostering better technical standards and higher skills. It is interesting that all of these initiatives resemble the patterns of public–private collaboration for which the East Asian economies later became famous.[149]

The Swedish state made great efforts to facilitate the acquisition of advanced foreign technology (including through industrial espionage, for a discussion of which see section 2.3.3). However, its emphasis on the accumulation of what the modern literature calls 'technological capabilities' was more notable still.[150] In order to encourage technology acquisition, the Swedish government provided stipends and travel grants for studies and research. A Ministry of Education was established in 1809, and primary education had already been made compulsory by the 1840s. The People's High Schools were established in the 1860s, and a six-year period of compulsory education was introduced in 1878. At higher levels, the Swedish state helped the establishment of technological research institutes, the most famous being the Chalmers Institute of Technology in Gothenburg, and provided industry – particularly metallurgy and wood-related industries – with direct research funding.[151]

Swedish economic policy underwent a significant change following the electoral victory of the Socialist Party in 1932 (which since that date has been out of office for less than ten years) and the signing of the 'historical pact' between the unions and the employers' association in 1936 (the *Saltsjöbaden* agreement). The policy regime that emerged after the 1936 pact initially focused on the construction of a system in which the employers would finance a generous welfare state and high investment in return for wage moderation from the union.[152]

After the Second World War, use was made of the regime's potential for promoting industrial upgrading. In the 1950s and 1960s, the centralized trade union, LO (*Landsorganisationen i Sverige*) adopted the so-called Rehn-Meidner Plan.[153] This introduced the so-called 'solidaristic' wage policy, which explicitly aimed to equalize wages across industries for the same types of workers. It was expected that this would generate pressure on the capitalists in low-wage sectors to upgrade their capital stock or shed labour, while allowing the capitalists in high-wage sectors to retain extra profit and expand faster than would otherwise have been possible. This was complemented by the active-labour-market policy, which provided retraining and relocation support to the workers displaced in this process of industrial upgrading. It is widely accepted that this strategy contributed to Sweden's successful industrial upgrading in the early postwar years.[154]

Sweden's postwar industrial upgrading strategy based on the combination of solidaristic wage bargaining and active-labour-market policy differs quite considerably from the strategies adopted by other countries discussed here. Despite their differences, both types of strategy are in fact based on similar understandings of how real world economies work. They share the belief that a shift to high value-added activities is crucial for a nation's prosperity and that, if left to market forces, this shift may not happen at a rate which is socially desirable.

2.2.6. Other Small European Economies

A. Belgium

We have already talked about the dominance of the fifteenth-century wool industry by the Low Countries. The industry, concentrated in what later became Belgium, subsequently went into a relative decline, not least because of the competition from protected British producers. However, Belgium maintained its industrial strengths and was the second nation – after Britain – to start an Industrial Revolution.

By the early nineteenth century Belgium was one of the most industrialized parts of Continental Europe, although it was significantly disadvantaged by its relatively small size and political weakness vis-à-vis France and Germany. At the time it was the world's technological leader in certain industries, particularly wool manufacturing. Although some of its technological edge had been lost to its competitors by the middle of the nineteenth century, it remained one of the most industrialized and richest countries in the world, specialising in industries like textiles, steel, non-ferrous metals, and chemicals.[155]

Not least because of this technological superiority, Belgium remained one of the less protected economies throughout most of the nineteenth and early twentieth centuries (table 2.1). Hens and Solar argue that the country remained an 'ardent free trader', particularly between the 1860s and the First World War.[156]

However, before this period, Belgium was considerably more protectionist than the Netherlands or Switzerland (see below). During the first three-quarters of the eighteenth century, the Austrian government, which then ruled what was later to become Belgium, protected it strongly from British and Dutch competition and invested in industrial infrastructure.[157] During the early nineteenth century it was subject to active ITT policies as part of the United Kingdom of the Netherlands (1815–30) under William I (see below). Moreover, until the 1850s, some industries were quite heavily protected – tariffs reached 30–60 per cent for cotton, woollen and linen yarn, and 85 per cent on iron. Its Corn Law was only abolished in 1850.[158]

B. The Netherlands

During the seventeenth century the Netherlands was the world's dominant naval and commercial power; during this period, its 'Golden Century', the Dutch East India Company outshone even the British East India Company. However, its naval and commercial strength showed a marked decline in the eighteenth century, the so-called 'Periwig Period' (*Pruikentijd*), with its defeat in the 1780 Fourth Anglo–Dutch War symbolically marking the end of its international supremacy.[159]

It is not easy to explain why the Netherlands failed to translate its naval and commercial strengths into industrial and overall economic domination. Part of the reason must have been that it was simply the natural thing to do – when you have a world-class commercial basis like, say, Hong Kong today, why bother about industry? However, the British government exploited similar strengths to the full in developing its industries (for example, it passed various Navigation Acts that made it compulsory to ship goods in and out of Britain on British vessels). So why did the Netherlands not do the same? That they did not is especially puzzling, given that the Dutch state had not been shy of using aggressive 'mercantilist' regulations on navigation, fishing, and international trade when it was trying to establish its commercial supremacy in the sixteenth and early seventeenth centuries.[160]

Many explanations for this have been offered: high wages due to heavy consumption taxes; lack of coal and iron deposits; the decline of entrepreneurship and the rise of a rentier mentality; and conspicuous consumption, to name just a few. Some historians have also suggested that Belgium's industrial strength was always an obstacle to neighbouring Netherlands' industrial development.[161] Most interestingly, List suggests that the Netherlands' relative decline was due to its failure to construct the set of public policies and institutions necessary for industrial development; Wright meanwhile proposes that low tariffs hampered the development of Dutch industries.[162]

Whatever the exact cause was, the Netherlands failed to industrialize to the same extent as its competitor countries, Britain, Germany and

Belgium. Nevertheless, thanks to the strengths of its commercial network, it remained one of the richest countries in the world until the early twentieth century.[163]

One exception to the policy paralysis that seemed to have gripped the Netherlands between the late seventeenth and early twentieth centuries was the effort made by King William I (1815–40). William I established many agencies providing subsidized industrial financing, the most important of which was the Netherlands Trading Company (*Nederlandsche Handels-Maatschappij*) set up in 1824. The Company supported Dutch industries by means of targeted procurement policies (especially in sugar refining, shipbuilding and textiles), using the profits from its monopoly trade with the colony of Java, which from 1831 onward was forced to produce cash crops such as coffee, sugar and indigo.[164] William I also founded the Fund for the National Industry (1821), the Amortisation Syndicate (1822), and the General Society for Furthering the National Industry (1822). During the 1830s, strong state support was also provided for the development of modern cotton textile industry, especially in the Twente region.[165]

However, from the late 1840s, the country reverted to a *laissez-faire* regime, which lasted until the First World War, and to an extent until the Second World War. First of all, as we can see in table 2.1, the Netherlands remained the least protected economy among the NDCs, except for Britain in the late nineteenth century and Japan before the restoration of tariff autonomy. Second, in 1869 the country abolished patent law (which was first introduced in 1817) on the grounds that it created an artificial monopoly. This move was partly inspired by the anti-patent movement that was sweeping Europe at the time, which in fact had a strong association with the free trade movement (see section 3.2.3.B for further details). Despite international pressures, the country refused to reintroduce the patent law until 1912 (more on this later).[166] Third, the Dutch government deliberately created a private sector company in order to compete with two existing private sector companies in managing the national railway, which it organized and financed.[167] This practice was hardly heard of at the time, and although it is strictly speaking not a *laissez-faire* policy, it is nevertheless a precursor of modern pro-competitive activist industrial policy.

During this extreme *laissez-faire* period, the Dutch economy remained on the whole rather sluggish, and its industrialization relatively shallow. According to the authoritative estimate by Maddison, measured in 1990 dollars, the Netherlands was still the second richest country in the world in 1820 after the UK, even after a century of relative decline ($1,756 vs. $1,561). A century later (1913), however, it had been overtaken by no fewer than six countries – Australia, New Zealand, the USA, Canada, Switzerland and Belgium – and almost by Germany. Germany's per capita income was only about 60 per cent that of the Netherlands in 1820 ($1,561 as opposed to $1,112), but by 1913 was only a shade below it ($3,950 vs. $3,833–for detailed income figures, see table 3.7 in Chapter 3).[168]

It was largely for this reason that the end of the Second World War saw the introduction of more interventionist policies. An active industrial policy was practised, especially in the years up to 1963. This included measures like financial supports for two large firms (one in steel, the other in soda), subsidies to industrialize backward areas, the encouragement of technical education, promoting the development of the aluminium industry through subsidized gas, and the development of key infrastructures.[169]

C. Switzerland

Switzerland was one of Europe's earliest industrializers. Biucchi argues that Switzerland's Industrial Revolution started barely 20 years later than Britain's did. By 1850 Switzerland, like Belgium, was one of the most industrialized economies in the world, although the heterogenous and decentralized nature of the country meant that the degree of industrialization remained uneven across different cantons.[170]

The cotton industry in particular experienced incredible development during the 1820s and 1830s. According to Milward and Saul, '[b]etween one-third and one-half of the cotton yarn woven in Switzerland in 1822 was imported from Britain. Yet by 1835 imports of British yarn had almost ceased'.[171] Switzerland was a world technological leader in a number of important industries, especially in the cotton textile industry, where in many areas it was deemed technologically more advanced than Britain.[172]

Given this very small technological gap (if any) with the leader country, infant industry protection was not very necessary for Switzerland. Also, given its small size, protection would have been more costly for Switzerland than for bigger countries. Moreover, given the country's highly decentralized political structure and very small size, there was little room for centralized infant industry protection.[173]

Biucchi argues that free trade was the most important aspect of Swiss economic policy as early as the sixteenth century. He admits, however, that the 'natural' protection from British competition accorded by Napoleon's intervention provided the Swiss textile industry with a critical breathing space, particularly in view of the technological gap that was emerging as a result of British success in mechanization in the textile industry at the time.[174] Moreover, Switzerland's *laissez-faire* policy did not necessarily mean that its government had no sense of strategy in its policy-making. Its refusal to introduce a patent law until 1907, despite strong international pressure, is such an example. This antipatent policy is argued to have contributed to the development of a number of industries. Especially affected by this were the chemical and pharmaceutical industries, which actively stole technologies from Germany, and the food industry, in which the absence of patents actually encouraged direct foreign investment (more on this in sections 2.3.3 and 3.2.3.B).[175]

2.2.7. Japan and the East Asian NICs

Japan came onto the industrial scene rather late. It was forced open by the Americans in 1854 (the infamous 'Black Ship' incident). Though they had had some glimpses of the European world before this through their contact with Portuguese and Dutch traders, the Japanese were, on gaining wider exposure to the West, shocked by the relative backwardness of their country. Soon afterwards, the feudal political order collapsed and, after the so-called Meiji Restoration of 1868, a modernizing regime was established. Since then the role of the Japanese state has been crucial to the country's development.

In the earlier days of its development, Japan was not able to use trade protection, as the series of 'unequal treaties' that it was forced to sign in 1858 barred it from having tariff rates over five per cent. For example, as we can see in table 2.1, the average rate of tariff on manufactured products in Japan in 1875 was five per cent at a time when the USA, despite having a much smaller technological gap with Britain, boasted an average industrial tariff rate up to 50 per cent. The Japanese government therefore had to use other means to encourage industrialization until it recovered tariff autonomy, which did not happen until 1911.

To begin with, in a manner similar to that of the Prussian state in the early nineteenth century in the absence of private sector entrepreneurial initiatives (see section 2.2.3 above), the Japanese state established state-owned model factories (or 'pilot plants') in a number of industries – notably in shipbuilding, mining, textiles (cotton, wool and silk), and military industries.[176] Although most of these were soon sold off to the private sector at discounted prices, this did not mean the end of state involvement in the industry. In the 1870s and 1880s, for instance, most state shipyards were privatized, but were still given large subsidies even after privatization. Together with the related merchant marine industry, the shipbuilding industry claimed between 50 and 90 per cent of all state subsidies before 1924. The first modern steel mill (the State Yawata Iron Works) was also established by the government in 1901.[177]

State involvement in large-scale projects, however, did not stop with model factories but extended to infrastructural development. The Meiji state built the country's first rail line in 1881. It had to provide massive concessions to private investors to interest them in railways[178] and throughout the 1880s and the 1890s subsidized the private sector rail companies; indeed, in the 1880s 36 per cent of all state subsidies went to railways. In 1906, the major trunk lines were nationalized. The Japanese government also started building telegraph infrastructure in 1869, and by 1880 all major cities were linked in this way.[179]

How do we evaluate the role of state-owned enterprises in industry and infrastructure in early modern Japan? Many commentators are not very positive about them, given that they were mostly unprofitable.[180] However, other scholars see more positive aspects. For example, in his classic study, Thomas Smith sums up his verdict on the role of Japanese state-owned enterprises in the early Meiji period in the following way:

> What did government enterprise accomplish between 1686 and 1880? Quantitatively, not much: a score or so of modern factories, a few mines, a telegraph system, less than a hundred miles of railway. On the other hand, new and difficult ground had been broken: managers and engineers had been developed, a small but growing industrial labour force trained, new markets found; perhaps most important, going enterprises had been developed to serve as a base for further industrial growth.[181]

In addition, the Japanese government implemented policies intended to facilitate the transfer of advanced foreign technologies and institutions. For example, it hired many foreign technical advisers; their number peaked at 527 in 1875[182] but fell quickly to 155 by 1885, suggesting a rapid absorption of knowledge on the part of the Japanese. The Ministry of Education was established in 1871; by the turn of the century it claimed a 100 per cent literary ratio.[183]

Moreover, the Meiji state tried to import and adapt from the more advanced countries those institutions that it regarded as necessary for industrial development. It is not easy to ascribe exactly the 'templates' for different Japanese institutions of the time to particular foreign countries, but it is clear that what emerged initially was an institutional patchwork.[184] The criminal law was influenced by the French law, while the commercial and civil laws were largely German, with some British elements. The army was built in the German mould (with some French influence), and the navy in the British. The central bank was modelled on the Belgian one, and the overall banking system on the American. The universities were American, and the schools initially American but quickly changed to the French and German models, and so on.

Needless to say, it took time for these institutions take root. However, the speed with which the Japanese assimilated and adapted them is regarded by historians as remarkable. Various institutional innovations, such as lifetime employment and durable subcontracting networks, which emerged during the postwar period, also deserve attention.

Following the ending of the unequal treaties in 1911, the post-Meiji Japanese state started introducing a range of tariff reforms intended to protect infant industries, to make imported raw materials more affordable and to control luxury consumer goods.[185] Once again, we can see great similarities between these policies and those previously used by other countries during their developmental periods.

As we can see in table 2.1, by 1913 Japan had become one of the more protectionist countries, although it was still less protective of its manufacturing industries than the USA. In 1926, tariffs were raised for some new industries, such as woollen textiles. Despite this, tariff was 'never more than a secondary weapon in the armoury of economic policy',[186] although some key industries were indeed heavily protected (e.g, iron and steel, sugar, copper, dyestuffs, and woollen textiles). Here we can find some parallel between Japan after 1911, on the one hand, and Germany and Sweden in the late nineteenth and early twentieth centuries, on the other hand. All of them used 'focused' tariff protection, whereby the overall tariff regime remained moderately protective but strong protection was accorded to some key industries, rather than the 'blanket' protection used by countries such as the USA, Russia and Spain at the time.

During the 1920s, under strong German influence, Japan began to encourage the rationalization of key industries by sanctioning cartel arrangements and encouraging mergers, which were aimed at restraining 'wasteful competition', achieving scale economies, standardization and the introduction of scientific management.[187] These efforts were intensified, and government control over cartels was strengthened, in the 1930s in response to the world economic crisis following the Great Depression and the war efforts, especially with the enactment of the 1931 Important Industries Control Law. Thus the basic pattern of post-war industrial policy was established.[188] As in many other NDCs, Japan's military build-up during the 1930s is believed to have contributed to the development of heavy industries (although with an ultimately disastrous political outcome) by stimulating demand and creating technological spillover.[189]

Despite all these developmental efforts, during the first half of the twentieth century, Japan was not on the whole the economic superstar that it became after the Second World War. According to the authoritative study by Maddison, Japan's per capita income growth rate was only one per cent per annum between 1900 and 1950. This was somewhat below the average for the 16 largest now-OECD economies that he studied, which was 1.3 per cent per annum,[190] although it must be noted that part of this rather poor performance was due to the dramatic collapse in output following Japan's defeat in the Second World War.[191]

After the Second World War, however, Japan's growth record was unrivalled, particularly until the 1970s. Between 1950 and 1973, per capita GDP in Japan grew at a staggering 8 per cent per annum, more than double the 3.8 per cent average achieved by the 16 NDCs mentioned above (the 3.8 per cent average includes Japan). The next best performers among the NDCs were Germany and Austria (both at 4.9 per cent), and Italy (4.8 per cent); even the East Asian 'miracle' developing countries like Taiwan (6.2 per cent) or Korea (5.2 per cent) came nowhere near Japan, despite the bigger 'convergence' effect that they could expect given their greater backwardness.[192]

There has long been an ideologically-charged debate about the causes of the economic 'miracle' in postwar Japan and East Asian NICs over the last two to three decades. Despite some lingering disagreements, there is now a broad consensus that the spectacular growth of these countries, with the exception of Hong Kong, is fundamentally due to activist industrial, trade and technology (ITT) policies by the state.[193]

Surveying the postwar experiences of the East Asian countries, we are once again struck by the similarities between their ITT policies and those used by other NDCs before them, starting from eighteenth-century Britain, through to nineteenth-century USA, and late nineteenth and early twentieth-century Germany and Sweden. However, it is also important to note that the East Asian countries have not exactly copied the policies that the more advanced countries had used earlier. The ITT policies that they, and some other NDCs like France, used during the postwar period were far more sophisticated and fine-tuned than their historical equivalents. The East Asian countries used more substantial and better-designed export subsidies (both direct and indirect) and in fact imposed very few export taxes in comparison to the earlier cases.[194] As I have repeatedly pointed out, tariff rebates for imported raw materials and machinery for export industries were widely employed – a method that many NDCs, notably Britain, had themselves used to encourage exports.[195]

Coordination of complementary investments, which had previously been done in a rather haphazard way, if ever, was systematized through indicative planning and government investment programmes.[196] Regulations of firm entry, exit, investments and pricing were implemented in order to 'manage competition' in such a way as to reduce 'wasteful competition'.[197] Once again, these regulations in part reflected the late nineteenth and early twentieth-century cartel policies, but displayed far more awareness than their historic counterparts of the dangers of monopolistic abuse, and more sensitivity to its impact on export market performance. There were also subsidies and restrictions on competition intended to help technology upgrading and a smooth winding down of declining industries.[198]

The East Asian governments also integrated human-capital-related and learning-related policies into their industrial policy framework far more tightly than their predecessors had done, through 'manpower planning'.[199] Technology licencing and foreign direct investments were regulated in an attempt to maximize technology spillover in a more systematic way.[200] There were serious attempts to upgrade the country's skill base and technological capabilities through subsidies to (and public provision of) education, training and R&D.[201]

With the recent crisis in Korea and the prolonged recession in Japan, it has become popular to argue that activist ITT policies have been proved to be mistaken. While this is not the place to enter this debate, a few points may be made.[202] First of all, whether or not we believe that the recent troubles in Japan and Korea are due to activist ITT policies, we cannot deny that these policies were behind their 'miracle'. Second, Taiwan, despite having used activist ITT policies, did not experience any financial or macroeconomic crisis. Third, all informed observers of Japan, regardless of their views, agree that the country's current recession cannot be attributed to government industrial policy – it has more to do with factors like structural savings surplus, ill-timed financial liberalization (which led to the bubble economy) and macroeconomic mismanagement. Fourth, in the case of Korea, industrial policy had been largely dismantled by the mid-1990s, when the debt build-up that led to the recent crisis started, so it cannot be blamed for the crisis. Indeed, it could be argued that, if anything, the demise of industrial policy contributed to the making of the crisis by making 'duplicative investments' easier.[203]

2.3. The Pulling-Ahead Strategy by the Leader and the Responses of the Catching-up Countries – Britain and its Followers

Once a country gets ahead of other countries, it has a natural incentive to use its economic and political powers to pull ahead even further. Britain's policies, especially those of the eighteenth and nineteenth centuries, are the best examples of this. What is disconcerting is that these policies have so many parallels with those pursued in our time by developed countries in relation to their developing counterparts.

2.3.1. The Colonies

Britain instituted a strong set of policies intended to prevent the development of manufacturing in the colonies, especially America. List reports that in 1770, William Pitt the Elder (then the Earl of Chatham), 'made uneasy by the first manufacturing attempts of the New Englanders, declared that the colonies should not be permitted to manufacture so much as a horseshoe nail'.[204] Brisco's characterization of the colonial policy under Walpole describes the gist of this strategy:

> By commercial and industrial regulations attempts were made to restrict the colonies to the production of raw materials which

> England was to work up, to discourage any manufactures that would any way compete with the mother country, and to confine their markets to the English trader and manufacturer.[205]

The policies deployed by Britain included the following. First, policies were deployed to encourage primary production in the colonies. For example, in the 1720s, Walpole provided export subsidies ('bounties') to and abolished British import duties on raw materials produced in the American colonies (such as hemp, wood and timber). This was done in the belief that encouraging the production of raw material would 'divert them from carrying on manufactures which interfered with those of England'.[206] Note that this is exactly the same logic that Cobden used in justifying the repeal of the Corn Law, which he thought was unwittingly helping continental Europe and the USA to industrialize by making their agricultural exports more difficult (see section 2.2.1 above).

Second, some manufacturing activities were outlawed. For example, the construction of new rolling and slitting steel mills in America was outlawed, which forced the Americans to specialize in the low-value-added pig and bar iron, rather than high-value-added steel products.[207] Some historians argue that this kind of policy did not actually damage the US economy significantly at the time, as the country did not have comparative advantage in manufacturing.[208] It seems reasonable to argue, however, that such policy would have become a major obstacle, if not an insurmountable barrier, to US industrial development if the country had remained a British colony beyond the early (mainly agrarian and commercial) stages of development.[209]

Third, exports from the colonies that competed with British products were banned. We have already mentioned that the cotton textile industry of India was dealt a heavy blow in the eighteenth century by the British ban on cotton textile imports from India ('calicoes'), even when the latter's products were superior to the British ones (see section 2.2.1 above).[210] Another example of this came in 1699, when Britain banned the export of woollen cloth from its colonies to other countries (the Wool Act), essentially destroying the Irish woollen industry. This Act also stifled the emergence of the woollen manufacturing industry in the American colonies.[211] In yet another example, a law was introduced in 1732, which mainly targeted the beaver-skin hat industry that had grown up in America; this law banned the exports of hats from colonies either to foreign countries or to other colonies.[212]

Fourth, the use of tariffs by colonial authorities was banned or, if they were considered necessary for revenue reasons, countered in a number of ways. When in 1859 the British colonial government in India imposed small import duties on textile goods (between three and ten per cent) for purely fiscal reasons, the local producers were taxed to the same extent in order to provide a 'level playing field'.[213] Even with this 'compensation', the British cotton manufacturers put constant pressure on the government for the repeal of the duties, which they finally obtained in 1882.[214] In the 1890s, when the colonial government in India once again tried to impose tariffs on cotton products – this time in order to protect the Indian cotton industry, rather than for revenue reasons – the cotton textile pressure groups thwarted the attempt. Until 1917, there was no tariff on cotton goods imports into India.[215]

2.3.2. Semi-Independent Countries

Outside the formal colonies, the British (and other NDCs') attempts to impede the development of manufacturing in less developed countries mainly took the form of imposing free trade through so-called 'unequal treaties' during the nineteenth century. These treaties normally involved the imposition of tariff ceilings, typically at the five per cent flat rate, and the deprivation of tariff autonomy.[216]

It is extremely disconcerting to note that the binding of tariffs at a low, uniform rate (although not necessarily below five per cent) is exactly what modern-day free-trade economists recommend to developing countries. The classic work by Little et al. argues that the appropriate level of protection is at most 20 per cent for the poorest countries and virtually zero for the more advanced developing countries. World Bank argues that '[e]vidence suggests the merits of phasing out quantitative restrictions rapidly, and reducing tariffs to reasonably *low and uniform* levels, such as a range of 15–25 percent [emphasis added]'.[217]

Britain first used unequal treaties in Latin America, starting with Brazil in 1810, as the countries in the continent acquired political independence. Starting with the Nanking Treaty (1842), which followed the Opium War (1839–42), China was forced to sign a series of unequal treaties over the next couple of decades. These eventually resulted in a complete loss of tariff autonomy and, symbolically, a Briton being the head of customs for 55 years, from 1863 to 1908. From 1824 onwards, Siam (now Thailand) signed various unequal treaties, ending with the most comprehensive one in 1855. Persia signed unequal treaties in 1836 and 1857, as did the Ottoman Empire in 1838 and 1861.[218]

Even Japan lost its tariff autonomy following the unequal treaties signed after its opening up in 1854 (see section 2.2.7 above). It was eventually able to end the unequal treaties, but that did not happen until 1911.[219] In this context, it is also interesting to note that when Japan forcefully opened up Korea in 1876 it exactly imitated the Western countries, forcing Korea to sign an unequal treaty that deprived the latter of its tariff autonomy – despite the fact that Japan itself still did not have tariff autonomy itself.

The larger Latin American countries were able to regain tariff autonomy from the 1880s, before Japan did. Many others regained it only after the First World War, but Turkey had to wait for tariff autonomy until 1923 (despite the unequal treaty having been signed as early as 1838!) and China until 1929.[220] Amsden shows how industrialization in these countries was only able to begin in earnest when they regained their tariff (and other policy) autonomy.[221]

2.3.3. Competitor Nations

In relation to other competitor nations of Europe (and later the USA), Britain could not use the blatant measures mentioned above in order to pull away. Rather, it concentrated mainly on preventing the outflow of its superior technologies, although such measures were not always effective.[222]

Until the mid-nineteenth century, when the machinery came to embody key technologies, the most important means of technological transfer was the movement of skilled workers, in whom most technological knowledge was then embodied. As a result, the less advanced countries tried to recruit skilled workers from the more advanced countries, especially from Britain, and also to bring back nationals who were employed in establishments in these countries. This was often done through a concerted effort orchestrated and endorsed by their governments – while the governments of the more advanced countries tried their best to prevent such migration.

As mentioned above (section 2.2.4), it was thanks to France's, and other European countries', attempts to recruit skilled workers on a large scale that in 1719 Britain was finally galvanized into introducing a ban on the emigration of skilled workers, particularly on 'suborning', or attempting to recruit such workers for jobs abroad. According to this law, suborning was punishable through fine or even imprisonment.

Emigrant workers who did not return home within six months of being warned to do so by an accredited British official (usually a diplomat stationed abroad) would in effect lose their right to lands and goods in Britain and have their citizenship withdrawn. The law specifically mentioned industries such as wool, steel, iron, brass and other metals, as well as watchmaking; in practice, however, it covered all industries.[223] The ban on the emigration of skilled labour and suborning lasted until 1825.[224]

Subsequently, as increasing amounts of technologies became embodied in machines, machine exports came under government control. In 1750, Britain introduced a new act banning the export of 'tools and utensils' in wool and silk industries, while strengthening the punishments for suborning skilled workers. This ban was widened and strengthened through subsequent legislations. In 1774, another act was introduced to control machine exports in the cotton and linen industries. In 1781, the 1774 Act was revised and the wording 'tools and utensils' changed to 'any machine, engine, tool, press, paper, utensil or implement whatsoever', reflecting the increasing mechanization of the industries. In 1785, the Tools Act was introduced in order to ban exports of many different types of machinery, which also included a ban on suborning. This ban was loosened in 1828 under the President of the Board of Trade William Huskisson, a prominent free-trader, and finally abolished in 1842.[225]

Up until the seventeenth century, when it was one of world's technological leaders, the Netherlands took an extremely open attitude towards foreigners' access to its technologies. However, with its technological edge constantly being eroded, its attitude, both at the firm and government levels, changed, and in 1751 the government finally introduced a law prohibiting the export of machinery and the emigration of skilled workers. Unfortunately, the law was much less successful than Britain's, and the outflow of skilled workers and machinery continued.[226]

In the face of these measures to prevent technology outflows by the advanced countries, the less developed ones deployed all sorts of 'illegitimate' means to gain access to advanced technologies. The entrepreneurs and the technicians of these countries, often with explicit state consent or even active encouragement by their governments (including offers of bounty for securing specific technologies), were routinely engaged in industrial espionage.[227] Landes, Harris and Bruland, among others, document an extensive range of industrial espionage directed at

Britain by countries such as France, Russia, Sweden, Norway, Denmark, the Netherlands, and Belgium.[228] Many states also organized and/or backed the recruitment of workers from Britain and other more advanced countries. France's attempt under John Law (see section 2.2.4) and Prussia's attempt under Frederick the Great (see section 2.2.3) are just some of the better known examples.

Despite all these efforts, legitimate and illegitimate, technological catching-up was not easy. As the recent literature on technology transfer shows, technology contains a lot of tacit knowledge that cannot easily be transferred. This problem could not even be solved by the importation of skilled workers, even in the days when they embodied most of the key technologies. These people faced language and cultural barriers, and more importantly did not have access to the same technological infrastructure as they had at home. Landes documents how it took decades for the Continental European countries to assimilate British technologies, even working as they did by importing some skilled workers and perhaps a key machine.[229]

Therefore, as is the case with modern-day developing countries, these technology transfers were most effective when backed by the policies intended to enhance what the modern economics of technology calls 'technological capabilities'.[230] As I have mentioned in various places in the preceding section, many governments set up institutions of teaching (e.g., technical schools) and of research (e.g., various non-teaching academies of sciences). I have also pointed out that they took measures to raise awareness of advanced technologies by setting up museums, organizing international expositions, bestowing new machinery on private firms and establishing 'model factories' that used advanced technologies. Government financial incentives for firms to use more advanced technology, especially through rebates and exemptions of duties on imports of industrial equipment, were also widely used.[231] It is interesting to note that tariff rebate or exemption on certain imported capital goods (which, interestingly, coexisted with restrictions on the importation of certain other capital goods) was until recently one of the key tools of the East Asian industrial policy.

By the middle of the nineteenth century, the key technologies had become so complex that the importing of skilled workers and machinery was not enough to achieve command over a technology. Reflecting this, the British bans on skilled worker emigration and machinery exports had by that point been abolished. From then on, an active transfer by the owner of technological knowledge through the licensing of patents emerged as a key channel of technology transfer in a number of industries. This made the policies and institutions regarding the protection of intellectual property rights (henceforth IPR) a lot more important than they had previously been. This eventually culminated in the emergence of the international IPR regime, following the 1883 Paris Convention on patents and the Berne Convention of 1886 on copyrights, under pressure from the technologically more advanced countries, especially the USA and France.

Between 1790 and 1850, most NDCs established their patent laws (see section 3.2.3.B of chapter 3 for details). However, all these earlier patent laws were highly deficient, judged by the modern standards demanded even from the developing countries after the TRIPS (trade-related intellectual property rights) agreement in the WTO.[232]

Particularly with regard to our main interest in this chapter, it must be pointed out that these laws accorded only very inadequate protection to the IPR of foreign citizens.[233] In most countries, including Britain (before the 1852 reform), the Netherlands, Austria and France, the patenting of imported inventions by their nationals was often explicitly allowed. In the USA, before the 1836 overhaul of patent law, patents were granted without any proof of originality, thus enabling the patenting of imported technologies. As we have already mentioned, Switzerland did not have a patent system until 1907, and although the Netherlands introduced a patent law in 1817, it was abolished in 1869 and was not reintroduced until 1912.

What is notable is that, despite the emergence of an international IPR regime in the last years of the nineteenth century, even the most advanced countries were still routinely violating the IPR of other countries' citizens well into the twentieth century. As mentioned above, Switzerland and the Netherlands did not have a patent law until 1907 and 1912 respectively. Even the USA, already a strong advocate of patentee rights, did not acknowledge foreigners' copyrights until 1891.[234] As late as the last decades of the nineteenth century, when Germany was about to overtake Britain technologically, there was great concern in Britain over the widespread German violation of its trademarks.[235] At the same time, the Germans were complaining about the absence of a patent law in Switzerland and the consequent theft of German intellectual property by Swiss firms, notably in the chemical industry.

Although Britain did not have a trademark law until 1862, Kindleberger notes that 'as early as the 1830s a number of British manufacturers were continuously engaged in litigation to protect trademarks'.[236] In 1862, it introduced a trademark law (the Merchandise Mark Act), which banned 'commercial thievery', such as the forging of trademarks and the labelling of false quantities. In the 1887 revision of the act, mindful of foreign, particularly German, infringement of the British trademark law, the British Parliament specifically added the place or the country of manufacture as part of the necessary 'trade description'. This revised act banned not only patently false descriptions but also misleading descriptions – such as the then widespread German practice of selling counterfeit Sheffield cutlery with fake logos. According to this act, 'it [was] a penal offence to sell an article made abroad which has upon it any word or mark leading the purchaser to believe that it is made in England, in the absence of other words denoting the real place of origin'.[237] According to Kindleberger, the law also made specific provision requiring that 'foreign goods marked with the name of an English dealer carry indication or place name of their foreign origin as well'.[238]

However, the German firms employed a range of measures to get around this act. For example, they placed the country of origin's stamp on the packaging instead of the individual articles, so that once the packaging was removed customers could not tell the country of origin of the product (a technique said to have been common amongst the imports of watches and files). Alternatively, they would send some articles over in pieces and have them assembled in England (a method apparently common for pianos and bicycles), or would place the stamp for the country of origin where it was practically invisible. Williams documents: 'One German firm, which exports to England large numbers of sewing-machines, conspicuously labeled "Singers" and "North-British Sewing Machines", places the Made in Germany stamp in small letters underneath the treadle. Half a dozen seamstresses might combine their strength to turn the machine bottom-upwards, and read the legend: otherwise it would go unread'.[239]

2.4. Policies for Industrial Development: Some Historical Myths and Lessons

In this chapter, I have examined the history of industrial, trade and technological (ITT) policies in a number of NDCs when they were developing countries – Britain, the USA, Germany, France, Sweden, Belgium, the Netherlands, Switzerland, Japan, Korea, and Taiwan. The picture that emerges from this historical review is fundamentally at odds with the picture held by Neo-Liberal commentators, and indeed by many of their critics.

In this final section of the chapter, I first summarize my review of the role of ITT policies in the development of a number of key individual NDCs (section 2.4.1). I then draw an overall picture from these country profiles and conclude that, while virtually all countries used infant industry promotion measures, there was considerable diversity across countries in terms of the exact policy mix (section 2.4.2). I then compare the ITT policies of the NDCs in earlier times with those of today's developing countries and argue that, once we consider the productivity gap they need to overcome, today's developing countries are actually far less protectionist than the NDCs themselves were in the past (section 2.4.3).

2.4.1. Some historical myths and facts about policies in earlier times

A. Almost every successful country used infant industry protection and other activist ITT policies when they were 'catching-up' economies

My discussion in this chapter reveals that almost all NDCs had adopted some form of infant industry promotion strategy when they were in catching-up positions. In many countries, tariff protection was a key component of this strategy, but was neither the only nor even necessarily the most important component in the strategy. Interestingly, it was the UK and the USA, the supposed homes of free trade policy, which used tariff protection most aggressively (see sections B and C below).

The apparent exceptions to this historical pattern among the countries I have reviewed are Switzerland, the Netherlands and to a lesser extent Belgium, although even in these cases some qualifications need to be made. Switzerland benefited from the 'natural' protection accorded by the Napoleonic Wars at a critical juncture in its industrial development. The government of the Netherlands on the one hand used aggressive policies to establish its naval and commercial supremacy in the sixteenth and seventeenth centuries, and on the other set up industrial financing agencies and promoted cotton textiles industry in the 1830s. Belgium may have had a low average tariff rate in the nineteenth century, but the Austrian government that ruled it during most of the eighteenth century was a lot more protectionist, and certain sectors were heavily protected until the mid-nineteenth century. Having said all this, it is still reasonable to describe these three economies, or at the very least Switzerland and the Netherlands, as having developed under broadly liberal ITT policies.

It may be argued that these two economies refrained from adopting protectionist trade policies because of their small size and hence the relatively large costs of protection. However, this is not a persuasive explanation. For one thing Sweden, another small country, used infant industry protection successfully between the late nineteenth and early twentieth centuries, when it was trying to catch up with the more developed countries in a number of heavy industries. A more plausible reason for the absence of infant industry protection in our trio of small European countries is that, unlike Sweden, they were already highly technologically advanced by the early nineteenth century. They stood very close to the world's technological frontier throughout the period of European Industrial Revolution, which meant that they simply did not need much infant industry protection (see section 2.2.6 for details).

Of course, against all these arguments, it may be said that the NDCs were able to industrialize independently of, or even despite, activist ITT policies. Many historical events are 'over-determined', in the sense that there is more than one plausible explanatory factor behind them; it is inherently difficult to prove that activist ITT policies, or for that matter any other factor in particular, was the key to the success of these countries.[240] However, it seems to be a remarkable coincidence that so many countries that have used such policies, from eighteenth-century Britain to twentieth-century Korea, have been industrial successes, especially when such policies are supposed to be very harmful according to the orthodox argument.

B. The myth of Britain as a free-trade, laissez-faire economy

Contrary to popular myth, Britain had been an aggressive user, and in certain areas a pioneer, of activist ITT policies intended to promote infant industries until it established its industrial hegemony so clearly in the mid-nineteenth century and adopted free trade.

Such policies, although limited in scope, date back to the fourteenth century (Edward III) and the fifteenth century (Henry VII) in relation to the wool trade, the leading industry of the time. Between Walpole's trade policy reform of 1721 and the repeal of the Corn Laws in 1846, Britain had implemented the kinds of ITT policies that became famous for their use in the East Asian 'industrial policy states' of Japan, Korea and Taiwan after the Second World War. Many policies that we frequently think of as East Asian inventions – such as export subsidies and import tariff rebates on inputs used for exporting – were widely used in Britain during this period. In addition, it should be noted that even Britain's free trade policy was motivated in part by its desire to promote its industries. Many of the strongest campaigners for free trade, including their leader Richard Cobden, believed that free imports of agricultural products by Britain would discourage manufacturing in competitor countries that would not have developed without the presence of the British Corn Laws.

C. The USA as 'the mother country and bastion of modern protectionism'

It was the USA, and not Germany as is commonly believed, which first systematized the logic of infant industry promotion that Britain had used so effectively in order to engineer its industrial ascent. The first systematic arguments for infant industry were developed by American thinkers such as Alexander Hamilton and Daniel Raymond, while Friedrich List, the supposed intellectual father of the infant industry protection argument, first learned about it during his exile in the USA.

The US government put this logic into practice more diligently than any other country for over a century (1816–1945). During this period, the USA had one of the highest average tariff rates on manufacturing imports in the world. Given that the country enjoyed an exceptionally high degree of 'natural' protection due to high transportation costs, at least until the 1870s, it seems reasonable to say that throughout its industrial catching-up the US industries were the most protected in the world. When the maverick American right-wing populist politician Pat Buchanan says that free trade is an 'un-American' thing, he does in a way have a point.

It is certainly true that the US industries did not necessarily need all the tariff protections that were put in place, and that many tariffs eventually outlived their usefulness. However, it is also clear that the US economy would not have got where it is today without strong tariff protection at least in some key infant industries. The role of the US government in infrastructural development and supporting R&D, which continues to this day, also needs to be noted.

D. The myth of France as the dirigiste counterpoint to laissez-faire Britain

The pre-revolutionary French state was actively involved in industrial promotion. However, this 'Colbertist' tradition was largely suppressed due to the libertarian ideologies of the French Revolution and the ensuing political stalemate that over the next century and half produced a series of weak and visionless (if not actively backward-looking) governments.

Thus, despite its public image as an inherently *dirigiste* country, France ran a policy regime in many ways more *laissez-faire* than either Britain or especially the USA throughout most of the nineteenth century and the first half of the twentieth century. For example, between the 1820s and the 1860s, the degree of protectionism actually remained lower in France than in Britain.

The *laissez-faire* period in French history was largely associated with the country's relative industrial and technological stagnation – a fact that indirectly proves the validity of the infant industry argument. It is largely because of the country's industrial success through the decidedly interventionist strategy pursued after the Second World War that it has come to acquire its current image as inherently interventionist.

E. The limited use of trade protection in Germany

Despite its frequent identification as the home of infant industry protection, Germany never really used tariff protection extensively. Until the late nineteenth century, it had one of the most liberal trade regimes in the world, although some key heavy industries did receive substantial tariff protection.

However, this does not mean that the German state was *laissez-faire* in the way that its French counterpart was during most of the nineteenth and the first half of the twentieth centuries. As the early Prussian experience from the eighteenth century onwards best illustrates, infant industries could be – and were – promoted through means other than tariffs, including state investment, public–private cooperation and various subsidies.

Although the subsequent development of the private sector, partly due to the success of such attempts, made direct state intervention unnecessary and unpopular, the state still played an important 'guiding' role. This was particularly the case in relation to some heavy industries in the late nineteenth and early twentieth centuries (which during this time were also given strong tariff protection). This was also the period when the German state pioneered the establishment of social welfare institutions in an attempt to defuse revolutionary agitation and establish social peace (see section 3.2.6.A in chapter 3 for further details).

Therefore, while Germany can hardly be described as the same kind of *laissez-faire* state as France in the nineteenth and early twentieth centuries, state intervention in Germany's main catching-up period was not as extensive as some people think, particularly in relation to tariff protection.

F. Sweden was not always the 'small open economy' that it later came to represent.

Although its does not require as dramatic revision as the cases discussed above, the Swedish experience also contains some myths that need dispelling.

In general, Sweden's tariff protection during its catch-up period was not extensive, despite the country's economic backwardness. However, the Swedish state seems to have used tariff protection strategically – to promote textile industry in the early nineteenth century and to bolster the mechanical and electrical industries later in the nineteenth century. It is interesting to note that its tariff regime for the textile industry in the early nineteenth century was in fact a classic late twentieth-century 'East Asian' (and also an eighteenth-century British) promotional strategy, involving as it did high tariffs on final products and low tariffs on raw material imports.

Another point worth noting is that from an early stage Sweden also developed interesting forms of public–private cooperation in infrastructural development and in some key industries, especially iron. This collaboration is remarkably similar to that which we find in East Asia during the postwar period. The early emphasis it placed on education, skill formation and research is also notable.

G. State activism in early modern Japan was limited due to external constraints

When it first opened up and embarked on its modern industrial development, Japan could not use tariff protection to promote new industries because of the unequal treaties that it was forced to sign, which bound its tariff rate to below five per cent. Other means for industrial promotion had to be found, and so the Japanese state set up model factories in key industries (which were soon privatized for revenue and efficiency reasons), provided subsidies to key industries and invested in infrastructure and education. However, given the importance of tariffs as a tool for industrial promotion at the time (when other policy tools had not yet been invented and/or were considered 'too radical'), its lack of tariff autonomy was a considerable handicap.

It was only in the early twentieth century, with the termination of the unequal treaties in 1911, that Japan was able to establish a more comprehensive industrial development strategy that included tariff protection as a key element. Japan's vastly superior performance during the postwar period, when it came up with an impressive array of 'innovations' in ITT policy tools, also shows how the ability to use a wider range of policy tools can make state intervention more effective.

H. 'Poachers turned gamekeepers': policies shift with development

One important fact that has emerged from my discussion in this chapter is that the NDCs shifted their policy stances according to their relative position in the international competitive struggle. Part of this is deliberate 'ladder-kicking', but it also seems to be due to natural human tendency to reinterpret the past from the point of view of the present.

When they were in catching-up positions, the NDCs protected infant industries, poached skilled workers and smuggled contraband machines from more developed countries, engaged in industrial espionage, and wilfully violated patents and trademarks. However, once they joined the league of the most developed nations, they began to advocate free trade and prevent the outflow of skilled workers and technologies; they also became strong protectors of patents and trademarks. In this way, the poachers appear to have turned gamekeepers with disturbing regularity.

Nineteenth-century Britain upset many countries, in particular Germany and the USA, which regarded Britain's preaching of virtues of free trade as hypocrisy, given that during the eighteenth century Britain used infant industry protection measures more strongly than any other country. The same sentiment might be expressed today, when American trade negotiators preach the virtues of free trade to the developing countries, or when Swiss pharmaceutical firms argue for strong protection of intellectual property rights.

2.4.2. 'Not by tariff alone': diverse models of infant industry promotion

As has been shown above, virtually all successful NDCs used infant industry protection during their catching-up periods. Of course, this does not allow us to conclude that such policies therefore automatically guarantee economic success. We know of too many examples from history and contemporary experience that contradict such a naïve proposition. However, there is a remarkably persistent historical pattern, stretching from eighteenth-century Britain to late twentieth-century Korea, in which successful economic development was achieved through infant industry protection measures. This pattern is simply too strong to be dismissed as a fluke. Therefore, those who believe in the virtues of free trade and *laissez-faire* ITT policies for currently developing countries need to explain why they believe this historical pattern is no longer relevant (more on this in chapter 4).

Important as tariff protection may have been in the development of most NDCs, it was – I repeat – by no means the only, nor even necessarily the most important, policy tool used by these countries in promoting infant industries. There were many other tools, such as export subsidies, tariff rebates on inputs used for exports, conferring of monopoly rights, cartel arrangements, directed credits, investment planning, manpower planning, R&D supports and the promotion of institutions that allow public-private cooperation. Tariffs were not, and are not, the only policy tool available to a state intent on developing new industries or upgrading old ones. In some countries, such as Germany up to the late nineteenth century or Japan before the restoration of its tariff autonomy in 1911, tariff protection was not even the most important tool for infant industry promotion.

Indeed, there was a considerable degree of diversity among the NDCs in terms of their policy mix, depending on their objectives and the conditions they faced. For example, the USA used tariff protection more actively than Germany, but the German state played a much more extensive and direct role in infant industry promotion than its US counterpart. As another example, Sweden relied upon public–private joint activity schemes far more than, say, Britain did.

Thus, despite some remarkably strong historical patterns, there is also considerable diversity in the exact mix of policy tools used for industrial promotion across countries. This, in turn, implies that there is no 'one-size-fits-all' model for industrial development – only broad guiding principles and various examples from which to learn.

2.4.3. Comparison with today's developing countries

Discussions of trade policy by those who are sceptical of activist ITT policies rarely acknowledge the importance of tariff protection in the economic development of the NDCs.[241] Even those few which do so dismiss the relevance of that historical evidence by pointing out that the levels of protection found in the NDCs in earlier times are substantially lower than those that have prevailed in today's developing countries.

Little et al. argue that '[a]part from Russia, the United States, Spain, and Portugal, it does not appear that tariff levels in the first quarter of the twentieth century, when they were certainly higher for most countries than in the nineteenth century, usually afforded degrees of protection that were much higher than the sort of degrees of promotion for industry which we have seen, in the previous chapter, to be possibly justifiable for developing countries today [which they argue to be at most 20 per cent even for the poorest countries and virtually zero for the more advanced developing countries]'.[242] Similarly, the World Bank argues that '[a]lthough industrial countries did benefit from higher natural protection before transport costs declined, the average tariff for twelve industrial countries ranged from 11 to 32 per cent from 1820 to 1980 . . . In contrast, the average tariff on manufactures in developing countries is 34 per cent'.[243]

This argument sounds reasonable enough, especially when we consider the fact that tariff figures are likely to underestimate the degree of infant industry promotion in today's developing countries when compared to those for the NDCs in earlier times. As I pointed out at the beginning of the chapter (section 2.1), limited fiscal capabilities and lack of regulatory power of the state seriously limited the scope for ITT policies other than tariff policy in the NDCs in earlier times. Governments in today's developing countries tend to use a wider range of policy tools for infant industry promotion, although some of these tools (e.g., export subsidies except for the poorest countries) have been 'outlawed' by the WTO.[244]

However, this argument is highly misleading in one important sense. The problem is that the productivity gap between today's developed countries and developing countries is much greater than that which used to exist between the more developed and less developed NDCs in earlier times. This means that today's developing countries need to impose much higher rates of tariff than those used by the NDCs in the past, if they are to provide the same degree of actual protection to their industries as that once accorded to the NDC industries.[245] In other words, given the greater productivity gap they face, today's developing countries need to use much higher tariffs compared to the NDCs in earlier times, just to get the same protective effects.

Before we show this, we must admit that it is not simple to measure international productivity gaps. Per capita income figures are obvious, although rough, proxies, but it is worth debating whether to use incomes measured in current dollars or in purchasing power parity (PPP) terms. Incomes measured in current dollars are arguably better reflections of the productivity gap in the tradeable sector, which is more relevant in determining tariff levels. However, they are subject to the vagaries of exchange-rate fluctuations that may have nothing to do with productivity differentials. PPP income figures are better reflections of a country's overall productivity, but they tend to underestimate, often greatly, the productivity differentials in the tradeable sector. In what follows, I have used PPP income figures, partly because they provide a better measure of an economy's overall productivity and partly because the best available historical estimate of NDC incomes by Maddison uses them.[246]

According to Maddison's estimate, throughout the nineteenth century the ratio of per capita income in PPP terms between the poorest NDCs (say, Japan and Finland) and the richest NDCs (say, the Netherlands and the UK) was about 2 or 4 to 1.[247] Nowhere is this as big as the gap between today's developing and developed countries. Recent data from the World Bank website show that in 1999 the difference in per capita income in PPP terms between the most developed countries (e.g., Switzerland, Japan, the USA) and the least developed ones (e.g., Ethiopia, Malawi, Tanzania) is in the region of 50 or 60 to 1.[248] Middle-level developing countries like Nicaragua ($2,060), India ($2,230) and Zimbabwe ($2,690) have to contend with productivity gaps in the region of 10 or 15 to 1. Even for quite advanced developing countries like Brazil ($6,840) or Columbia ($5,580), the productivity gap with the top industrial countries is about 5 to 1.

When in the late nineteenth century the USA accorded an average tariff protection of over 40 per cent to its industries, its per capita income in PPP terms was already about three quarters that of Britain ($2,599 vs. $3,511 in 1875).[249] And this was when the 'natural protection' accorded by distance, which was especially important for the USA, was considerably higher than today, as even the above quote from World Bank acknowledges.[250] Compared to this, the 71 per cent trade-weighted average tariff rate that India had just prior to the WTO agreement – despite the fact that its per capita income in PPP terms is only about one fifteenth that of the USA – makes the country look like a veritable champion of free trade. Following the WTO agreement, India cut its trade-weighted average tariff to 32 per cent, bringing it down to a level below which the USA's average tariff rate never sank between the end of the Civil War and the Second World War.

To take a less extreme example, in 1875 Denmark had an average tariff rate of around 15–20 per cent, when its per capita income was slightly less than 60 per cent that of Britain ($2,031 vs. $3,511). Following the WTO agreement, Brazil cut its trade-weighted average tariff from 41 per cent to 27 per cent, a level that is not far above the Danish level, but its income in PPP terms is barely 20 per cent that of the USA ($6,840 vs. $31,910).[251]

Given the productivity gap, even the relatively high levels of protection that had prevailed in the developing countries until the 1980s do not seem excessive by the historical standards of the NDCs. When it comes to the substantially lower levels that have come to prevail after two decades of extensive trade liberalization in these countries, it may even be argued that today's developing countries are actually less protectionist than the NDCs used to be.

Chapter 3

Institutions and Economic Development:
'Good Governance' in Historical Perspective

3.1. Introduction

The issue of institutional development, under the slogan of 'good governance', has recently come to occupy the centre stage of development policy debate. During the last decade or so, the international development policy establishment (henceforth IDPE) has come to recognize the limitations of its former emphasis on 'getting the prices right' through 'good policies'. It has now come to accept the importance of the institutional structure that underpins the price system.[1] Particularly following the recent Asian crisis, which has been widely interpreted as a result of deficient institutional structures, the IDPE has begun to move its emphasis to 'getting the institutions right' and attach what Kapur and Webb call 'governance-related conditionalities'.[2]

On the offensive these days are those who believe that every country should adopt a set of 'good institutions' (unfortunately often implicitly equated with US institutions), with some minimal transition provisions (five–ten years) for the poorer countries – various agreements in the WTO being the best example of this. Backing up this claim is a rapidly growing body of literature, especially from the World Bank and its associates, which tries to establish statistical correlation between institutional variables and economic development, with the supposed causality running from the former to the latter.[3]

Exactly which institutions should go into the 'good governance' package differs from one recommendation to another, not least because we still do not fully understand the relationship between particular institutions and economic development. However, this package of 'good institutions' frequently includes democracy; a clean and efficient bureaucracy and judiciary; strong protection of (private) property rights, including intellectual property rights; good corporate governance institutions, especially information disclosure requirements and bankruptcy law; and well-developed financial institutions. Less frequently included but still important are a good public finance system and good social welfare and labour institutions providing 'safety nets' and protecting workers' rights.[4]

Critics argue that, apart from the fact that the international financial institutions (IFIs) do not have an official mandate to intervene in most of these 'governance' issues,[5] the institutions of developed countries can be too demanding for developing countries in terms of their financial and human resource requirements. Some critics also argue that some of these institutions may go against the social norms and cultural values of some of the countries concerned. Many emphasize the difficulty of institutional transplantation and warn against the attempt to impose a common institutional standard on countries with different conditions.

These critics have an important point to make, but in the absence of some idea of which institutions are necessary and/or viable under what conditions, they are in danger of simply justifying whatever institutional status quo exists in developing countries. So what is the alternative?

One obvious approach is to find out directly which of the 'best practice' institutions are suitable for particular developing countries by transplanting them and seeing how they fare. However, as we see from the failures of structural adjustment in many developing countries and of transition in many former Communist economies, this does not usually work and can be very costly.

Another alternative is for the developing countries to wait for spontaneous institutional evolution. It could be argued that the best way to obtain institutions that suit the local conditions is to let them evolve naturally, as indeed happened in the now-developed countries (NDCs) when they themselves were developing. However, such spontaneous evolution may take a long time. Moreover, given the nature of the evolutionary process, there is no guarantee that such an approach will in fact yield the best possible institutions, even when viewed from the perspective of specific national requirements.

These, then, point us to the third – and my preferred – alternative route, which is to learn from history. Just as we looked at the issue of 'good policies' from a historical perspective in the last chapter, we can, and should, draw lessons from the historical, as opposed to the current, state of developed countries in the area of institutional development. In this way, developing countries can learn from the experiences of developed countries without having to pay all the costs involved in developing new institutions (one of the few advantages of being a 'latecomer'). This is significant because, once established, institutions may be more difficult to change than policies. This will also help donors wanting to encourage the adoption of particular institutions by the recipients of their financial support to decide whether or not the particular 'we're-not-ready-yet' arguments put to them by some recipient country governments are reasonable.

As I pointed out in Chapter 1, despite the obvious relevance of the historical approach in understanding the problems of development in our time, surprisingly little work has adopted it. This aberration is even more serious in the area of institutional development.[6] This chapter tries to fill this important gap.

In section 3.2, I examine how various institutions that are currently regarded as essential components of the 'good governance' structure evolved in the NDCs when they were developing countries themselves, mainly between the early nineteenth and early twentieth centuries. I look at six broad areas – democracy (section 3.2.1), bureaucracy and judiciary (section 3.2.2), property rights (section 3.2.3), corporate governance (section 3.2.4), private and public financial institutions (section 3.2.5) and welfare and labour institutions (section 3.2.6).

In section 3.3, I discuss how institutional developments achieved in NDCs in the past compare with those of today's developing countries at similar levels of development. The first subsection (3.3.1) shows NDCs in the process of institutional evolution in earlier times by offering three 'snapshots' (1820, 1875 and 1913). Section 3.3.2 discusses how the process of institutional development in the NDCs was 'long and winding'. Section 3.3.3 compares the level of institutional development in the NDCs in the past with that of today's developing countries, and shows that, at comparable stages of development, the former actually have much higher levels of institutional development than those achieved by today's NDCs.

3.2. The history of institutional development in the developed countries

3.2.1. Democracy

There has been a particularly heated debate on the relationship between democracy and economic development.[7] In the early post-war period, there was a popular argument that developing countries cannot afford 'expensive' democratic institutions. Today, the dominant view in the IDPE is that democracy helps economic development and therefore has to be promoted as a precondition for development.[8] However, still others point out that democracy is more of an outcome of, rather than a precondition for, development, and is therefore not really a variable we can manipulate, whether or not we think it is good for development.

No attempt is made here to settle this difficult and long-standing debate. However, the historical experience of developed countries in this regard tells us an interesting story that should make the reader pause before readily buying into the current orthodoxy that democracy is a precondition for development.

When voting was first introduced in the NDCs, it was confined to a very small minority of property-owning males (usually aged over 30), often with an unequal number of votes apportioned according to a scale based on property, educational achievement or age.

In France between 1815 and 1830, for example, the franchise was granted only to males above 30 who paid at least 300 francs in direct taxes, which meant that only 80,000–100,000 people out of a population of 32 million (that is, 0.25–0.3 per cent of the population) could vote. Between 1830 and 1848, there was some relaxation of franchise requirements, but still only 0.6 per cent of all French people could vote.[9] In England before the 1832 Reform Act, which was the watershed event in the extension of suffrage in the country, it was widely agreed among contemporary observers that landlords could decide 39 out of 40 county elections through their influence on the tenants, bribery and patronage.[10] Even after this act, voting rights were only extended from 14 per cent to 18 per cent of men, partly because many craftsmen and labourers with no or little property were disenfranchised as a result of the act, which established a closer link between property and enfranchisement. In Italy, even after the lowering of the voting age to 21 and the reduction of tax-paying requirements in 1882, only around two million men (equivalent to seven per cent of the population) could vote, due to lower but still extant tax payment and literacy requirements.[11]

It was not until 1848, the year that France introduced universal male suffrage, that even limited forms of democracy began to appear in NDCs. As we see in table 3.1, most NDCs introduced universal male suffrage between the mid-nineteenth century and the first couple of decades of the twentieth century. However, even this process was not without reversals.

Table 3.1
Introduction of Democracy in the NDCs

Country	Universal Male Suffrage	Universal Suffrage
Australia	1903[1]	1962
Austria	1907	1918
Belgium	1919	1948
Canada	1920[2]	1970
Denmark	1849	1915
Finland	1919[3]	1944
France	1848	1946
Germany	1849[2]	1946
Italy	1919[4]	1946
Japan	1925	1952
Netherlands	1917	1919
New Zealand	1889	1907
Norway	1898	1913
Portugal	n.a.	1970
Spain	n.a.	1977 (1931)**
Sweden	1918	1918
Switzerland	1879	1971
UK	1918[5]	1928
USA	1965 (1870)*	1965

Sources: Therborn 1977 and Silbey 1995 for democracy indicators. Additional information from Foner 1998 on the USA and Carr 1980 on Spain. For more details on the introduction of universal suffrage, see table 3.2.

1. With racial qualifications.
2. With property qualifications.
3. Communists excluded.
4. With restrictions.
5. All men and women over 30.
 * Universal male suffrage was introduced in 1870, but reversed between 1890 and 1908 through the disenfranchisement of the blacks in the Southern states. It was only restored in 1965. For further details, see the text.
** Universal suffrage was introduced in 1931 but reversed after General Franco's military coup in 1936. It was only restored in 1977, following Franco's death in 1975. See the text for details.

For example, during the late nineteenth century, when an electoral victory by the Social Democratic Party became a possibility, at least in local elections, Saxony abandoned the universal male suffrage that had earlier been adopted, moving over to the Prussian-style three-class voting system (which Prussia itself used from 1849 to 1918).[12] In this system, each of the three classes (classified according to income) elected the same number of delegates to the parliament, which meant that the top two classes (accounting respectively for 3–5 per cent and 10–15 per cent of the population) could always outvote the poorest class. In 1909,

Saxony moved still further away from democracy by giving voters between one and four votes depending on their income and status. For example, those with a large farm gained three additional votes, while additional ballots were allotted to the well-educated and those over 50 years of age.

In the USA, black males were allowed to vote from 1870 following the Fifteenth Amendment to the Constitution, which forbade states to deny the vote to anyone 'on account of race, colour, or previous condition of servitude'. However, the Southern states subsequently disenfranchised them again from between 1890 (Mississippi) and 1908 (Georgia). Not being able to introduce overtly racist measures, they instead adopted methods such as poll tax and property requirements (which also disenfranchised some poor whites), as well as literacy tests (which were applied to illiterate whites extremely leniently). After this, all but a handful of blacks in the Southern states could vote. For example, in Louisiana, 130,000 black votes were cast in the election of 1896, but in 1900 only 5,000 were cast.[13] Moreover, the threat of violence kept many of the few qualified black voters from registering and, of those who registered, from voting. This state of affairs lasted until the 1965 Voting Rights Act, introduced after the Civil Rights Movement.

In Spain, when the introduction of universal suffrage in 1931 resulted in a series of left or centre-left Republican governments, conservative forces reacted against it with a military coup in 1936, thus suspending democracy until the end of the Franco dictatorship in 1977.[14]

Although universal male suffrage among the majority (white) population was attained in most NDCs by the end of the First World War, these countries could hardly be called democracies even in the purely formal sense of the word, because women and ethnic minorities were disenfranchised. It was not until 1946 that the majority of the 19 NDCs featured in table 3.1 attained universal suffrage.

Australia and New Zealand were the first countries to give women votes (in 1903 and 1907 respectively), although Australia did not enfranchise non-whites until 1962. Norway allowed votes for tax-paying women or women married to tax-paying men in 1907, although universal suffrage was only introduced in 1913.[15] Women were only allowed to vote in the USA in 1920 and in the UK in 1928. In many other countries (for example, Germany, Italy, Finland, France and Belgium), women were not given votes until after the Second World War. In the case of Switzerland, female suffrage was granted almost a hundred years after the introduction of universal male suffrage (1971 as against 1879).

Some countries also had voting restrictions based on political creeds – Finland banned Communists from voting until 1944. In countries with significant non-white minority groups, for example Australia, there were racial restrictions. In the case of the USA, even in the Northern states, black suffrage was continuously limited right up to the Civil War. In 1821, for instance, the state of New York removed the property qualification on white voters but for black voters raised it to $250, 'a sum beyond the reach of nearly all the state's black residents'. By 1860, blacks (males only, of course) could vote on the same basis as whites in only five New England states.[16] Even after the Fifteenth Amendment (1870), various obstacles, both formal (e.g., literacy, 'character' and property requirements) and informal (e.g., threats of violence), kept blacks from the ballot boxes.[17]

Even when the NDCs achieved formal democracy, it was often of very poor quality, as in the case of many modern-day developing countries. We have already mentioned the 'quality' problem relating to selective enfranchisement according to race, gender and property ownership. But that was not all.

First of all, secret balloting was not common until the twentieth century. Norway, which was relatively advanced in terms of democratic institutions,[18] only introduced secret balloting in 1884. In Prussia, employers could exert pressure on their workers to vote in a particular way until the electoral reform of 1919 because balloting was not held in secret. France only introduced the voting envelope and voting booth in 1913 – several decades after the introduction of universal male suffrage.[19]

Second, vote buying and electoral fraud were also very common. For example, bribery, threats and promises of employment to voters were widespread in British elections until the late nineteenth century. The first serious attempt to control electoral corruption was the Corruption Practices Act of 1853–4. This act for the first time defined activities like bribery, 'treating', undue influence and intimidation, while establishing the procedures for election accounts and auditing. However, the measures were ineffective.[20] The Corrupt and Illegal Practices Act introduced in 1883 managed significantly to reduce electoral corruption, but the problem still persisted well into the twentieth century, especially in local elections.[21] In the decades following the introduction of universal male suffrage in the USA, there were numerous cases of public officials being used for party political campaigns (including forced donations to electoral campaign funds), as well as of electoral fraud and vote-buying.[22]

With such expensive elections, it was no big surprise that elected officials were corrupt. In the late nineteenth century, legislative corruption in the USA, especially in state assemblies, got so bad that the future US president Theodore Roosevelt lamented that the New York assemblymen, who engaged in the open selling of votes to lobbying groups, 'had the same idea about Public Life and Civil Service that a vulture has of a dead sheep'.[23]

In this light, the road to democracy in the NDCs was a rocky one. It was only through several decades of political campaigning (e.g., for female or black suffrage) and electoral reforms that these countries acquired even the basic trappings of democracy – universal suffrage and secret ballots – and even then its practice was swamped with electoral fraud, vote-buying and violence.

It is interesting to note that, compared to NDCs in their early stages of development, today's developing countries actually seem to have had a better record in this regard. As we can see from table 3.2, no NDC granted universal suffrage below the level of $2,000 per capita income (in 1990 international dollars), but most of the wide selection of currently developing countries featured in table 3.2 did so well below that level of development.

Of course, many of these countries have experienced reversals in their democratic progresses in just the same way that the NDCs did, especially through military coups. However, it is important to note that, even as they were suspending elections altogether, none of the non-democratic governments in currently developing countries reintroduced selective disenfranchisement based on factors like property ownership, gender and race – factors that had been widely accepted as legitimate criteria for enfranchisement in NDCs in the early days. This shows that the idea, if not necessarily the practice, of universal suffrage is much more widely accepted in today's developing countries than it was in the NDCs when they were at similar stages of development.

3.2.2. The bureaucracy and the Judiciary

A. The bureaucracy

Few people, even those who are generally sceptical of state activism, would disagree that an effective and clean bureaucracy is crucial for

Table 3.2
Income per capita at attainment of universal suffrage

GDP p.c. (in 1990 international dollars)	NDCs Developing (Year universal suffrage was attained; GDP p.c.)	Countries (Year universal suffrage was attained; GDP p.c.)
<$1,000		Bangladesh (1947; $585)[1] Burma (1948; $393)[2] Egypt (1952; $542) Ethiopia (1955; $295) India (1947; $641) Indonesia (1945; $514) Kenya (1963; $713) Pakistan (1947; $631)[1] South Korea (1948; $777) Tanzania (1962; $506) Zaire (1967; $707)
$1,000–$1,999		Bulgaria (1945; $1,073) Ghana (1957; $1,159) Hungary (1945; $1,721) Mexico (1947; $1,882) Nigeria (1979; $1,189) Turkey (1946; $1,129)
$2,000–$2,999	Austria (1918; $2,572) Germany (1946; $2,503) Italy (1946; $2,448) Japan (1952; $2,277)[3] Norway (1913; $2,275) Sweden (1918; $2,533)	Colombia (1957; $2,382) Peru (1956; $2,732) Philippines (1981; $2,526)
$3,000–$3,999	Denmark (1915; $3,635) Finland (1944; $3,578) France (1946; $3,819)	Taiwan (1972; $3,313) Chile (1949; $3,715)
$4,000–$4,999	Belgium (1948; $4,917) Netherlands (1919; $4,022)	Brazil (1977; $4,613)
$5,000–$9,999	Australia (1962; $8,691) New Zealand (1907; $5,367)[4] Portugal (1970; $5,885) UK (1928; $5,115)	Argentina (1947; $5,089) Venezuela (1947; $6,894)
>$10,000	Canada (1970; $11,758)[5] Switzerland (1971; $17,142) USA (1965; $13,316)	

Sources: Therborn (1977); *Elections* (1989); Maddison (1995)
1. GDP p.c. in 1948.
2. GDP p.c. in 1950.
3. Universal suffrage was granted in 1946 under the constitution drawn up by the occupying forces after the Second World War, but it did not come into effect until 1952 with the end of US military rule.
4. When dominion status was achieved.
5. When the Election Act that year granted full franchise.

economic development.[24] There is, however, currently a serious debate on how exactly we should define effectiveness and cleanliness, and on how we should design a bureaucratic incentive system to attain these characteristics.

The dominant view during the last century was that espoused by the German economist–sociologist Max Weber. In his view, the modern bureaucracy is based on meritocratic recruitment; long-term, generalist and closed career paths; and corporate coherence maintained by rule-bound management.[25] More recently, however, 'New Public Management' (NPM) literature has challenged the Weberian orthodoxy. It argues for a bureaucratic reform based on more short-term, specialist and 'open' career paths; keener monetary incentives; and a more 'businesslike' (or arm's-length) management style based on quantifiable and transparent performance.[26]

Although some of the changes advocated by the NPM may be useful in fine-tuning what is basically a Weberian bureaucracy that already exists in the developed countries, the more relevant question for most developing countries is how their bureaucracies might attain even the most basic 'Weberian-ness'.[27] This is also the task with which the NDCs were confronted with in the earlier days of their development.

It is well known that, up to the eighteenth century, open sales of public offices and honours – sometimes with widely-publicized price tags – was a common practice in most NDCs. Prior to the extensive bureaucratic reform in Prussia under Frederick William I (1713–40), although offices were not formally sold, they were very often given to those willing to pay the highest amount for the tax that was customarily imposed on the first year's salary.[28]

Partly because they were openly bought and sold, public offices were formally regarded as private property in many of these countries. In France, for example, it was very difficult to introduce disciplinary measures for bureaucrats until the Third Republic (1873) for this very reason.[29] In Britain, prior to the reform carried out in the early nineteenth century, government ministries were private establishments unaccountable to Parliament, paid their staff by fees rather than salaries, and kept many obsolete offices as sinecures.[30] Associated with the sale of public office was tax farming, which was most widespread in pre-Revolution France but which was also practised in other countries, including Britain and the Netherlands (see section 3.2.5.D for further details).

The 'spoils' system, where public offices were allocated to the loyalists of the ruling party, became a key component in American politics from the emergence of the two-party system in 1828 with the election of President Jackson. This got much worse for a few decades after the Civil War.[31] There was a loud cry for civil service reform throughout the nineteenth century to create a professional and non-partisan bureaucracy, but no progress was made until the Pendleton Act of 1883 (see below for further details on the act).[32] Italy and Spain continued the spoils system throughout the nineteenth century.[33]

In addition to the sale of public office, there was widespread nepotism. Although concrete historical data on this is obviously difficult to come by – and whatever data we do have should be interpreted with caution – Armstrong reports that significant proportions of elite administrators in France and Germany had fathers who were top officials themselves, suggesting a significant degree of nepotism.[34] For instance, among the high-ranking bureaucrats of pre-industrial France (the early nineteenth century), about 23 per cent had fathers who served as elite administrators. At the country's industrial take-off in the mid-nineteenth century, the proportion was still as high as 21 per cent. Corresponding figures for Prussia were 31 per cent and 26 per cent respectively.[35] Feuchtwanger argues that, even after the extensive bureaucratic reform under Frederick William I (see below), 'nepotism was still rife and many offices were virtually hereditary'.[36] In Prussia, competition from educated lower-middle class men was eliminated by changing the entrance requirements, such that by the 1860s, 'a carefully controlled recruitment process produced an administrative elite including the aristocracy and wealthier middle-class elements'.[37]

With the sales of offices, spoils system and nepotism, it is hardly surprising that professionalism was conspicuously lacking in the bureaucracies of most NDCs at least until the late nineteenth century. The Jacksonians in the USA had a contempt for expert knowledge, and were against the professionalization of the bureaucracy on the grounds that the largest possible number of citizens should be able to participate in the act of government. Even after the 1883 Pendleton Act, which set up the Civil Service Commission to administer competitive recruitment to the federal bureaucracy, only about 10 per cent of civil service jobs were subject to competitive recruitment. Italian bureaucrats in the late nineteenth century had 'no legal, or even conventional, guarantees on tenure, dismissals, pension, etc., and no recourse to the court'. Until the early twentieth century, civil service careers in Spain were heavily determined by what was known as *padrinazgo* (godfathership). Even in Belgium, which in the nineteenth century was the second most industrialised country after Britain, the civil service was not fully professionalised until 1933.[38]

It was only through a long-drawn-out process of reform that the bureaucracies in the NDCs were able to be modernized. The pioneer in this regard was Prussia. An extensive bureaucratic reform was implemented by Frederick William I from 1713, the year of his accession to the throne. The key measures included: the centralization of authorities scattered over two dozen separate territorial entities (many of them not even physically contiguous) and overlapping departments; the transformation of the status of the bureaucrats from private servants of the royal family into servants of the state; regular payments in cash (rather than in kind as before) of adequate salaries; and the introduction of a strict supervision system.[39] Thanks to these measures and to the additional measures introduced by his son, Frederick the Great (1740–86), by the early nineteenth century Prussia could be said to have installed the key elements of a modern (Weberian) bureaucracy – an entrance examination, a hierarchical organization, pension systems, a disciplinary procedure and security of tenure. Other German states such as Bavaria, Baden and Hesse also made important progress along this path during the early nineteenth century.[40]

In Britain, sinecures were eliminated through a series of reforms between 1780 and 1834. Bureaucratic remuneration was changed in the first half of the nineteenth century from a fee-based to a salary system. It was also only around this time that the status of government ministries in Britain was changed from private establishments to government ministries in the modern sense. It was only after 1860 that the British Civil Service was substantially modernized.[41] The USA made some important progress with the professionalization of the bureaucracy in the last two decades of the nineteenth century, as the proportion of federal government jobs subject to competitive recruitment rose from 10 per cent in 1883, when the Pendleton Act was introduced, to nearly 50 per cent by 1897.[42]

B. The Judiciary

In the contemporary discourse on 'good governance', there is a strong emphasis on a politically independent judiciary administering 'rule of law'.[43] However, we have to be somewhat careful in embracing this 'independent judiciary' rhetoric.

It could be argued that a judiciary with a very high degree of political independence (for example, the German or Japanese judiciary) is not necessarily desirable, as it lacks democratic accountability. This is why some countries elect some of their judicial officials – the best-known examples being the USA today, and the UK in the nineteenth century.[44] In the UK, the boundary between the judiciary and the legislature is also blurred, since its highest judges sit in the House of Lords; however, few people would argue that this is a major problem.

Given this, we need to understand the quality of the judiciary not simply in terms of its political independence, but in a number of dimensions – the professionalism of the judicial officials, the quality of their judgments (not simply from a narrow 'rule of law' point of view, but also from a broader societal point of view) and the cost of administering the system.

Like their counterparts in modern-day developing countries, the judiciary in many NDCs suffered from excessive political influence and corruption in appointments (or, where applicable, elections) up to, and often beyond, the late nineteenth century. It was also frequently filled exclusively with men from a narrow, privileged social background with little, if any, training in law, with the result that justice was often dispensed in biased and unprofessional ways.

In the UK, even the anti-corruption laws of 1853–4 and 1883 (see above) did not affect the election of coroners, which was subject to widespread corruption and party political manoeuvring. Elections for county coroners were only abolished in 1888, and it was not until 1926 that professional qualifications for county coroners became compulsory.[45]

During the late nineteenth century Germany made impressive progress towards 'rule of law' and by the end of the century had gained a largely independent judiciary. However, there was still a lack of equality before the law, with military and middle-class crimes less diligently brought to court and less severely punished. This problem of 'class justice' dogged other NDCs just as badly at this time – including the UK, the USA and France.[46] In Italy, at least until the late nineteenth century, judges did not usually have a background in law and 'could not protect themselves, let alone anyone else, against political abuses'.[47]

3.2.3. Property rights regimes

In the 'good governance' discourse, the 'quality' of property rights regimes is regarded as crucial, as it is believed to be a key determinant of investment incentives and thus of wealth creation. However, measuring the 'quality' of a property rights regime is not easy, because it has numerous components – contract law, company law, bankruptcy law, inheritance law, tax law and laws regulating land use (e.g., urban zoning laws, environmental standards, and fire safety regulations), to name just a few.

In many empirical studies, this 'aggregation problem' is avoided by asking survey respondents to give a numerical value to the overall quality of the property rights institutions (e.g., 'security of contract and property rights' or 'enforcement of contracts or property rights').[48] However, even this highly inadequate 'solution' to the problem is not available for the historical comparison that we are attempting in this chapter.

Therefore, in contrast to other aspects of institutional development discussed in this chapter that are more 'measurable' (e.g., democracy measured by the existence of universal suffrage, development of financial institutions measured by, among other things, the existence of the central bank), it is impossible to provide a generalized comparison of the quality of property rights regimes through history and across countries.

One aspect of the property rights system that does easily lend itself to this kind of analysis is that of intellectual property rights, which are defined by a small number of clearly identifiable laws (e.g., patent law, and to a lesser extent, copyright law and trademark law). In this section we therefore provide a detailed empirical analysis of the evolution of intellectual property rights regimes in the NDCs. First, however, a few general theoretical comments on the role of property rights in economic development (with some historical references) are in order.

A. Some misconceptions about property rights and economic development

In the orthodox discourse of today, it is widely believed that the stronger the protection of property rights, the better it is for economic development, as such protection encourages the creation of wealth. While it may be reasonable to argue that persistent uncertainty about the security of property rights is harmful for long-term investment and growth, the role of property rights in economic development is far more complex than this type of argument suggests.

Security of property rights cannot be regarded as something good in itself. There are many examples in history in which the preservation of certain property rights has proved harmful for economic development and where the violation of certain existing property rights (and the creation of new ones) was actually beneficial for economic development.

The best known example is probably that of Enclosure in Britain, which violated existing communal property rights by enclosing common land, but contributed to the development of woollen industry by promoting sheep farming on the confiscated land. To turn to other instances, De Soto documents how the recognition of squatter rights in the violation of the rights of existing property owners was crucial in developing the American West. Upham cites the famous Sanderson case in 1868, where the Pennsylvania Supreme Court overrode the existing right of landowners to claim access to clean water in favour of the coal industry, which was one of the state's key industries at the time.[49] Land reform in Japan, Korea and Taiwan after the Second World War violated the existing property rights of the landlords but contributed to the subsequent development of these countries. Many argue that the nationalization of industrial enterprises after the Second World War in countries like Austria and France contributed to their industrial development by transferring certain industrial properties from a conservative and non-dynamic industrial capitalist class to professional public-sector managers with a penchant for modern technology and aggressive investments.

Hence, what matters for economic development is not simply the protection of all existing property rights regardless of their nature, but which property rights are protected under which conditions. If there are groups who are able to utilize certain existing properties better than their current owners, it may be better for the society not to protect existing property rights, but to create new ones that transfer the properties concerned to the former groups. With this general point in mind, let us take a detailed look at intellectual property rights institutions.

B. Intellectual property rights

The first patent system was invented in Venice in 1474, granting ten years' privileges to inventors of new arts and machines. In the sixteenth century, some German states, notably Saxony, used patents, although not entirely systematically. British patent law came into being in 1623 with the Statute of Monopolies, although many researchers[50] argue that it did not really deserve the name of a 'patent law' until its reform in 1852. Patent law was adopted by France in 1791, by the USA in 1793 and by Austria in 1794.

As mentioned in Chapter 2, most of the other NDCs established their patent laws in the first half of the nineteenth century – Russia (1812), Prussia (1815), Belgium and the Netherlands (1817), Spain (1820), Bavaria (1825), Sardinia (1826), the Vatican state (1833), Sweden (1834), Württemberg (1836), Portugal (1837), Saxony (1843). Japan established its first patent law in 1885.[51] These countries initiated other elements of their intellectual property rights regimes, such as copyright laws (first introduced in Britain in 1709) and trademark laws (first introduced in Britain in 1862), in the second half of the nineteenth century.

At this point, it should be noted that all these early intellectual property rights (IPR) regimes were highly 'deficient' by the standards of our time.[52] Patent systems in many countries lacked disclosure requirements, incurred very high costs in filing and processing patent applications, and afforded inadequate protection to the patentees. Most patent laws were very lax in checking the originality of the invention. In the USA for example, before the 1836 overhaul of the patent law, patents were granted without any proof of originality. This not only led to the patenting of imported technologies, but also encouraged racketeers to engage in 'rent-seeking' by patenting devices already in use ('phony patents') and by demanding money from their users under threat of suit for infringement.[53] Few countries allowed patents on chemical and pharmaceutical substances (as opposed to the processes), although this practice has been 'outlawed' by the TRIPS (trade-related intellectual property rights) agreement in the WTO, except for the poorest countries (and even then they are only exempt until 2006).[54]

These laws afforded only very inadequate protection, particularly in relation to the protection of foreign IPR, which is now becoming a major point of contention after the TRIPS agreement (for further details, see the references cited in section 2.3.3). As pointed out above, most of the nineteenth-century patent laws were very lax in checking the originality of the invention. Moreover, as mentioned in chapter 2, in most countries, including Britain (before 1852), the Netherlands, Austria and France, patenting by their nationals of imported inventions was often explicitly allowed. The cases of Switzerland and the Netherlands in relation to their patent laws deserve greater attention.[55]

As mentioned in Chapter 2 (section 2.2.6.B), the Netherlands abolished its 1817 patent law in 1869, as a result of both the rather deficient nature of the law (even by the standards of the time),[56] and the influence of the anti-patent movement that was sweeping Europe at the time.

Closely related to the free-trade movements, this condemned patents as being no different from other monopolistic practices.[57]

Switzerland did not acknowledge any IPR over inventions until 1888, when a patent law protecting only mechanical inventions ('inventions that can be represented by mechanical models')[58] was introduced. Only in 1907, partly prompted by the threat of trade sanctions from Germany in retaliation for Swiss use of its chemical and pharmaceutical inventions, did a patent law worth its name come into being. However, even this had many exclusions, in particular the refusal to grant patents to chemical substances (as opposed to chemical processes). It was only in 1954 that the Swiss patent law became comparable to those of other NDCs, although chemical substances remained unpatentable until 1978.[59]

With the introduction of IPR laws in an increasing number of countries, the pressures for an international IPR regime naturally began to grow from the late nineteenth century onward.[60] There was a series of meetings on this subject, beginning with the 1873 Vienna Congress; the Paris Convention of the International Union for the Protection of Industrial Property was finally signed by 11 countries in 1883. The original signatories were Belgium, Portugal, France, Guatemala, Italy, the Netherlands, San Salvador, Serbia, Spain and Switzerland.

The Convention covered not just patents but also trademark laws (which enabled Switzerland and Netherlands to sign up to it despite not having a patent law). In 1886 the Berne Convention on copyrights was signed. The Paris Convention was subsequently revised a number of times (notably 1911, 1925, 1934, 1958 and 1967) moving towards a strengthening of patentee rights; together with the Berne Convention, it formed the basis of the international IPR regime until the TRIPS agreement.[61] However, as we saw in Chapter 2 (section 2.3.3), despite the emergence of an international IPR regime, even the most developed NDCs were still routinely violating the IPR of other countries' citizens well into the twentieth century.

The above should show how deficient the IPR regimes of the NDCs were (when they were themselves developing countries) by the standards that are demanded of today's developing countries. There were widespread and serious violations by even the most advanced NDCs until the late nineteenth century and beyond, especially when it came to protecting the IPR of foreigners.

3.2.4. Corporate governance

A. Limited liability

These days, we tend to take the principle of limited liability for granted. However, for a few centuries after its invention in the sixteenth century for highly risky large-scale commercial projects (the British East India Company being the best-known early example), it tended to be regarded with great suspicion.

Many people believed that it led to excessive risk-taking (or what today we call 'moral hazard') on the part of both owners and managers. They regarded it as an institution that undermined what was then regarded – along with greed – as one of the key disciplinary mechanisms of capitalism, namely, fear of failure and destitution, especially given the harshness of bankruptcy laws at the time (see section 3.2.4.C).

Adam Smith argued that limited liability would lead to shirking by managers. The influential early nineteenth-century economist John McCulloch argued that it would make the owners lax in monitoring hired managers.[62] It was also believed, with some justification, to be an important cause of financial speculation. Britain banned the formation of new limited liability companies on these grounds with the Bubble Act in 1720, although with the repeal of the act in 1825 it was again allowed.[63]

However, as has been proven repeatedly over the last few centuries, limited liability provides one of the most powerful mechanisms to 'socialize risk', which has made possible investments of unprecedented scale. That is why, despite its potential to create 'moral hazard', all societies have come to accept limited liability as a cornerstone of modern corporate governance.[64]

In many European countries, limited liability companies – or joint stock companies as they were known in those days – had existed under *ad hoc* royal charters since the sixteenth century.[65] However, it was not until the mid-nineteenth century that it began to be granted as a matter of course, rather than as a privilege.

Generalized limited liability was first introduced in Sweden in 1844. England followed this closely with the 1856 Joint Stock Company Act, although limited liabilities for banks and insurance companies were introduced somewhat later (1857 and 1862 respectively), reflecting the then widespread concern that they could pose serious 'moral hazard'. Rosenberg and Birdzell document how, even a few decades after the introduction of generalized limited liability (the late nineteenth century), small businessmen 'who, being actively in charge of a business as well as its owner, sought to limit responsibility for its debts by the device of incorporation' were frowned upon.[66]

In Belgium, the first limited liability company was founded in 1822, and the 1830s saw the formation of a large number of such companies. However, it was not until 1873 that limited liability was generalized. During the 1850s in various German states, it was introduced in a restricted form, whereby the principal owners had unlimited liability but shares giving limited liability could be marketed. It was not until the 1860s that various German states scrapped or weakened traditional guild laws, thereby opening the door to the full institutionalization of limited liability (Saxony in 1861, Württemberg in 1862 and Prussia in 1868–9). In France, limited liability only became generalized in 1867, but in Spain, while joint-stock companies (*Sociedades Anónimas*) began to emerge from as early as 1848, it was not fully established until 1951. It is interesting to note that in Portugal limited liability was generalized as early as in 1863, despite the country's economic backwardness at the time.[67]

In the USA, the first general limited liability law was introduced in the state of New York in 1811. However, this fell into disuse around 1816, due to general apathy towards limited liability companies, and other states did not permit limited liability companies until 1837. Even after that, as in the European countries of the time, prejudice against limited liability companies prevailed until at least the 1850s. As late as the 1860s, most manufacturing was carried out by unincorporated companies, and there was still no federal law granting generalized limited liability.[68]

C. Bankruptcy Law

Bankruptcy laws have attracted an increasing amount of attention over the last two decades or so. The large-scale corporate failures that followed various economic crises during this period have made people more aware of the need for effective mechanisms to reconcile competing claims, transfers of assets and the preservation of employment. The industrial crises in the OECD countries during the 1970s and 1980s, the collapse of communism, the miserable failure of 'transition' since the late 1980s and the 1997 Asian crisis were particularly important in this regard.

While the debate is still unresolved as to what makes the best bankruptcy law – the USA's debtor-friendly law, the UK's creditor-friendly one, or the employee-protecting French one – there is little disagreement that an effective bankruptcy law is desirable.[69]

In pre-industrial Europe, bankruptcy law was mainly regarded as a means of establishing the procedures for creditors both to seize the assets of and to punish dishonest and profligate bankrupt businessmen. In the UK, the first bankruptcy law, applicable to traders with a certain amount of debt, was introduced in 1542, although it only became consolidated with the 1571 legislation. However, the law was very harsh on the bankrupt businessmen, as it deemed that all their future property was liable for former debts.[70]

With industrial development came an increasing acceptance that business can fail due to circumstances beyond individual control, not just as a result of dishonesty or profligacy. As a result, bankruptcy law also began to be seen as a way of providing a clean slate for bankrupts. This transformation of bankruptcy law was, together with generalized limited liability, one of the key elements in the development of mechanisms for 'socializing risk' that allowed the greater risk-taking necessary for modern large-scale industries. In 1705–6, for example, measures were introduced in the UK to allow cooperative bankrupts to keep five per cent of their assets and even discharged some from all future debts if the creditors consented.[71]

However, bankruptcy law in the UK remained highly deficient by modern standards up to the mid-nineteenth century. Until then, recovery from bankruptcy remained the privilege of a very small class of businessmen, the responsibility for prosecuting lay entirely with the creditors and the system was not uniform throughout the country. There were also problems involved in the granting of discharge, which could only be granted by creditors, not by courts, which deprived many businessmen of the opportunity to make a fresh start. There was also a lack of professionalism and a tendency to corruption among bankruptcy commissioners.[72]

The Victorian age saw a series of reforms of bankruptcy law, starting with the establishment of the Bankruptcy Court in 1831. In the 1842 amendment, discharge became the right of courts, not creditors, making it easier for bankrupts to get their second chance. However, the coverage of the law was still limited until 1849, when it became applicable to anyone who earned their living by 'the workmanship of goods or commodities'.[73] In the USA, early bankruptcy laws were modelled on the early (pro-creditor) English law and administered at the state level. However, until the late nineteenth century, only a few states had bankruptcy laws at all, and these varied from one state to another. A number of federal bankruptcy laws were introduced during the nineteenth century (1800, 1841 and 1867), but they were all short-lived due to their defective nature, and were repealed in 1803, 1841 and 1878 respectively. For example, the 1800 law discharged many from their just debts incurred in the turnpike and land speculation of late 1790s, and the relief it gave only led to further speculation. The 1841 law was censured for giving creditors just ten per cent of the estate, most of which was absorbed by legal and administrative costs. It was also criticized for the rule that property had to be sold immediately for cash, thus financially disadvantaging creditors. Moreover, courts could not cope with the heavy caseload; during the first four years after the 1867 law was passed, there were 25,000 cases per annum. Another point of contention surrounding the law was the relaxation of the requirement that bankrupts should repay at least half of their debts incurred before the Civil War, which attracted criticisms from creditors that the concession protected irresponsibility.[74]

It was not until 1898 that Congress was able to adopt a lasting federal bankruptcy law. The provisions in this law included relief of all debts, not just those after 1898; permission of involuntary and voluntary bankruptcies; exemption of farmers and wage-earners from involuntary bankruptcy; protection of all properties exempted from attachment under state law; and the granting of a grace period for insolvents to reorganize their affairs or reach compromises with creditors.

C. Audit, Financial Reporting and Information Disclosure

The importance of financial auditing and disclosure has attracted great attention since the recent crisis in the Asian economies. Many foreign lenders blame the opacity of company accounts, lax regulations about auditing and disclosure in the crisis countries for their bad loan decisions. One obvious counter to this argument is that, even before the crisis, it was widely accepted that company-level information in these countries had these problems; in such situations, the natural course of action for a prudent lender would have been not to lend to these companies. In this context, the 'lack of information' argument made by international lenders seems largely self-serving.[75]

Having said that, there seems to be little dispute that institutions which improve the quality and disclosure of corporate information are desirable. Even then, however, we need to set the human and financial resource costs of developing these institutions against their benefits, especially in developing countries which lack such resources.

Looking at the history of NDCs, we are struck by the fact that, even in these countries, institutions regulating company financial reporting and disclosure requirements were of still very poor quality well into the twentieth century.

The UK made external audit of companies a requirement through the 1844 Company Act, but this was made optional again by the Joint Stock Company Act of 1856 against the recommendation of critics such as John Stuart Mill.[76] Given that limited liability companies require more transparency to control opportunistic behaviour by their dominant shareholders and hired managers, this was a significant step backward.

With the introduction of the 1900 Company Act, external audit was again made compulsory for British companies. However, there was still no direct requirement for firms to prepare and publish annual accounts for shareholders, although this was required implicitly as the auditor had a duty to report to shareholders. Not until the 1907 Company Act was the publication of a balance sheet made compulsory. Even then, many companies exploited a loophole in the act, which did not specify a time period for this reporting, and filed the same balance sheet year after year. This loophole was only closed by an Act of 1928, by which companies were made to file and circulate ahead of annual general meetings up-to-date balance sheets and disclose more detailed information, such as the composition of assets.[77]

However, until the Companies Act of 1948, disclosure rules were still poor, turning the late Victorian market into a 'market for lemons'.[78] Crafts concludes that 'the development capital markets based on extensive shareholder rights and the threat of hostile takeover is a relatively recent phenomenon in the UK even though the British were pioneers of modern financial reporting and had the Common Law tradition'.[79]

In Germany, it was only through the company law of 1884 that regulations regarding the listing of companies in the stock markets were implemented. In Norway, legislation passed as late as 1910 forced companies to report their budgets and earnings twice a year to allow its shareholders, and the state, greater knowledge about the state of the business. The USA made the full disclosure of company information to investors in relation to public stock offerings compulsory only after the 1933 Federal Securities Act. In Spain, scrutiny of accounts by independent auditors was not made mandatory until as late as 1988.[80]

D. Competition law

Contrary to what is assumed in much current literature on the subject, corporate governance is not simply a matter internal to the corporation in question. Actions by very large firms with significant market power can have consequences for the whole economy (e.g., their bankruptcy can create financial panic) or undermine the basis of the market economy itself (for example, through the socially harmful exploitation of a monopoly position). In this context, corporate governance becomes a matter for society as a whole, not just for the particular company's shareholders.

Corporate governance in this sense does not simply involve company-level laws, for example, those specifying the duties of the board of directors to the shareholders. It also involves a wide range of other regulations – for instance sectoral regulations, regulations on foreign trade and investment – and informal norms that govern business practices, such as conventions regarding the treatment of subcontractors.

In this section, we review the evolution of the most easily identifiable institution of 'societal' corporate governance, namely, competition law (anti-monopoly and/or anti-trust legislation) in a number of NDCs. It should be emphasized that my discussion does not share the current orthodoxy, which assumes that the developing countries of today need a US-style anti-trust policy.[81]

As early as 1810, France adopted Article 419 of the Penal Code, which outlawed coalitions of sellers. These affiliations had resulted in the raising or lowering of prices above or below those of 'natural and free competition'. However, the law was unevenly implemented and by 1880 had fallen into disuse. From the 1890s, the French courts began to accept 'defensive' combinations (cartels) and to uphold their agreements. It was not until 1986 that France repealed Article 419 and adopted a 'modern' and more comprehensive anti-trust law.[82]

The USA was the pioneer in 'modern' competition law. The country introduced the Sherman Antitrust Act in 1890, although five years later the act was crippled by the Supreme Court in the notorious Sugar Trust case. Until 1902, when President Theodore Roosevelt used it against J P Morgan's railways holding company, the Northern Securities Company, it was in fact mainly used against labour unions rather than against large corporations. Roosevelt set up the Bureau of Corporations in 1905 to investigate corporate malpractice; the bureau was upgraded into the Federal

Trade Commission with the Clayton Antitrust Act of 1914, which also banned the use of the antitrust legislation against the unions.[83]

During the nineteenth century, the British state neither supported nor condemned trusts and other anticompetitive arrangements. However, until the First World War, the courts were quite willing to uphold the validity of restrictive trade agreements. The first anti-trust initiative to be taken was the short-lived Profiteering Act (1919, discontinued in 1921), created to cope with postwar shortages. During the Depression of the 1930s, the state endorsed rationalization and cartelization. It was only with the 1948 Monopolies and Restrictive Practices Act that serious antimonopoly/antitrust legislation was attempted, but this remained largely ineffective. The Restrictive Practices Act of 1956 was the first true antitrust legislation, in the sense that it assumed – for the first time – that restrictive practices were against the public interest unless industrialists could prove otherwise. The 1956 Act effectively countered cartels, but was less successful against monopolization through mergers.[84]

As already mentioned in Chapter 2 (section 2.2.3), the German state initially strongly supported cartels, and enforced their agreements during the early period of their existence (the late nineteenth and early twentieth centuries). The high point of this was a ruling in 1897 by the highest court in the country that cartels were legal. From the First World War onward, cartelization became widespread, and the means by which the government planned economic activities. The Cartel Law of 1923, which gave the court the power to nullify cartels, was the first general competition law in Europe. However, the law remained ineffective, as it defined cartels very narrowly, and those to whom this law gave the powers to control cartels – namely, the economic ministry and the cartel court – hardly used them anyway. The cartel court was abolished in 1930 when a series of emergency acts empowered the state to dissolve any cartel if deemed necessary. In 1933 the Minister for Economic Affairs was given the power to nullify any cartel or decree the formation of compulsory cartels.[85]

In Norway, a Trust Law was first introduced in 1926, but the trust board in charge of it operated from the standpoint that it should monitor, but not categorically prevent, monopolistic behaviour. Although the law was subsequently replaced by the Price Law and the Competition Law in 1953, which had somewhat more stringent provisions (for example, companies now had to report major mergers and acquisitions), the main thrust of the Norwegian anti-trust policy remained that of publicity and control, rather than the imposition of outright bans. The Danish competition law of 1955 (the Monopolies and Restrictive Practices Act) operated on the same principle of 'publicity and control'.[86]

3.2.5. Financial institutions

A. Banking and Banking Regulation

With a marked increase in banking crises across the world during the last two decades or so, especially in developing countries, establishing a good system of banking regulation has become a major theme in the push for institutional development by the IDPE. In the history of the NDCs, however, the establishment of institutions to regulate banking became an issue rather late, as the development of banking itself was a slow and uneven process, with the possible exception of Britain.

The banking system in the NDCs was only established slowly.[87] Even in England, a country with the most advanced banking system in the world until the mid-twentieth century, complete financial integration was only achieved in the 1920s, when deposit rates for town and country became uniform. In France, the development of the banking system was even more delayed, with widespread use of banknotes emerging in the mid-nineteenth century (as opposed to the eighteenth century in Britain) and with three quarters of the population still without access to banking as late as 1863. Prussia had no more than a handful of banks until the eighteenth century, while the first joint stock bank was only founded in 1848. In Sweden, banks only appeared in the late nineteenth century. They went through a major expansion in 1870, prior to which credits to producers and exporters were provided by merchant trading houses, and only became fully established in the 1890s. In Portugal, the banking industry only saw major development in the 1860s and 1870s, after the formation of joint-stock banks was allowed.[88]

In the NDCs, banks only became professional lending institutions after the early twentieth century. Before then, personal connections strongly influenced bank lending decisions. For example, throughout the nineteenth century, US banks lent the bulk of their money to their directors, their relatives, and those they knew.[89] Scottish banks in the eighteenth century and English banks in the nineteenth century were basically self-help associations for merchants wanting credit rather than banks in the modern sense.[90]

Banking regulation was highly inadequate. The USA permitted 'wildcat banking', which was 'little different in principle from counterfeiting operations'.[91] Wildcat banking was especially problematic during the 30-year period that saw the demise of the short-lived semi-central bank, the Second Bank of the USA, between 1836 and 1865 (see section 3.2.5.B). Although the overall cost of failures of unregulated banks at the time is estimated to have been small, such collapses were widespread.[92] As late as 1929, the US banking system was made up of 'thousands upon thousands of small, amateurishly managed, largely unsupervised banks and brokerage houses'. This meant that even during the prosperity of the Coolidge presidency (1923–9), 600 banks a year failed.[93]

In Italy, there was a huge scandal in the late nineteenth century (1889–92), where the bankruptcy of one of the six note-issuing banks, Banca Romana, revealed a web of corruption (extension of credit to important politicians and their relatives, including two former prime ministers), a defective accounting system, and 'irregular' issue of banknotes (e.g., duplicate notes) in the heart of the country's banking industry.[94]

In Germany, direct regulation of commercial banks was only introduced in 1934 with the Credit Control Act, while in Belgium, banking regulation was only introduced in 1935, with the establishment of the Banking Commission.[95]

B. Central banking

Today, the central bank – with its note-issue monopoly, money market intervention and lender-of-last-resort function – is regarded as a cornerstone of a stable capitalist economy. There is a heated debate on how politically independent the central bank should be, as well as on its appropriate goals, targets and instruments.[96] Heated though the debate may be, few people dispute the need for a central bank. However, this was not the case in the early days of capitalism.

From as early as the eighteenth century, dominant banks, such as the Bank of England or the large New York banks, were forced to play the role of lender-of-last-resort in times of financial crisis. The increased ability of such institutions to deal with systemic financial panic in the short term, and the consequent stability that this helped bring about in the long run, naturally pointed to the creation of a fully-fledged central bank.

However, many people at the time believed that creating a central bank

would encourage excessive risk-taking by bailing out imprudent borrow-
ers in times of financial turmoil (or what we these days call 'moral
hazard').[97] This sentiment is best summed up in Herbert Spencer's observation that '[t]he ultimate result of shielding man from the effects of
folly is to people the world with fools'.[98] As a result, the development of
central banking was a very slow and halting process in the NDCs.[99]

The Swedish Riksbank (established in 1688) was nominally the first
official central bank in the world. However, it could not function as a
proper central bank until the mid-nineteenth century because it did not
have, among other things, monopoly over note issue, which it gained
only in 1904.[100]

The Bank of England was established in 1694 and from the eighteenth century onward began to assume the role of lender-of-last-resort
(although some suggest that this only really took place in the first half
of the nineteenth century). However, it did not become a full central
bank until 1844. The French central bank, Banque de France, was
established in 1800, but only gained monopoly over note issue in 1848.
Until 1936, however, the Banque de France was basically controlled by
the bankers themselves rather than the government. The central bank
of the Netherlands, the Nederlandsche Bank, was established in 1814
by King William I, modelled on the Bank of England. However, it strug-
gled to circulate its notes widely until the 1830s, and remained an
Amsterdam-based 'local' bank until the 1860s.[101]

The Bank of Spain was established in 1829 but did not gain monopoly
over note issue until 1874, and was privately owned until 1962. The Bank
of Portugal was created in 1847, but its note-issue monopoly was
restricted to the Lisbon region. It legally gained full note-issue monopoly
in 1887 but, due to the resistance of the other note-issuing banks, it was
only in 1891 that the monopoly was achieved in practice. The Bank of
Portugal is still completely privately owned and cannot intervene in the
money market.[102]

The Belgian central bank, Banque National de Belgique, was created
as late as 1851; it was however one of the first genuine central banks
with note-issue monopoly, which was conferred at the time of its
creation.[103] Among the 11 countries we cover in this section, only the
British (1844) and the French (1848) central banks gained note issue
monopoly before Belgium's did. The German central bank was only
established in 1871, gaining monopoly over note issue in 1905. In Italy,
the central bank was only set up in 1893 and did not get monopoly over

note issue until 1926. The Swiss National Bank, not founded until 1907, was formed by merging the four note-issue banks.

In the USA, the development of central banking was even slower. Early attempts to introduce even a limited degree of central banking failed quite spectacularly. The First Bank of the USA (80 per cent of which was privately owned) was established in 1791 with strong support from Alexander Hamilton, then Treasury Secretary, over opposition from the then Secretary of the State, Thomas Jefferson. However, it failed to get its charter renewed in the Congress in 1811, and the Second Bank of the USA that was established in 1816 met the same fate twenty years later. In 1863, the USA finally adopted a single currency through the National Banking Act, but a central bank was still nowhere to be seen.[104]

Given this situation, as mentioned earlier, the large New York banks were compelled to perform the function of lender-of-last-resort to guarantee systemic stability, but this had obvious limitations. Finally, in 1913, the US Federal Reserve System came into being through the Owen-Glass Act, which was prompted by the spectacular financial panic of 1907. Until 1915, however, only 30 per cent of banks (with 50 per cent of all banking assets) were in the system and as late as 1929 65 per cent were still outside the system, although by this time they accounted for only 20 per cent of total banking assets. This meant that in 1929 the law 'still left some sixteen thousand little banks beyond its jurisdiction. A few hundred of these failed almost every year'.[105] Also, until the Great Depression, the Federal Reserve Board was de facto controlled by Wall Street.[106]

In table 3.3 below, we present a summary of the above descriptions of the evolution of central banking in the NDCs. The first column represents the year when various central banks were established; the second indicates when they became proper central banks by gaining note-issue monopoly and other legal endorsements. The table shows that the majority of the 11 countries in the table nominally had central banks by the late 1840s. However, it was not until the early twentieth century that these banks became true central banks in the majority of these countries. It was only in 1891, with the establishment of note-issue monopoly for the Bank of Portugal, that the majority of the 11 central banks in the table gained such monopoly.

Table 3.3
Development Central Banking in the NDCs

	Year of establishment	Year when note-issue monopoly was gained
Sweden	1688	1904
UK	1694	1844
France	1800	1848[1]
Netherlands	1814	After the 1860s
Spain	1829	1874
Portugal	1847	1891[2]
Belgium	1851	1851
Germany	1871	1905
Italy	1893	1926
Switzerland	1907	1907
USA	1913	After 1929[3]

1. Controlled by the bankers themselves until 1936.
2. Legally note-issue monopoly was established in 1887, but *de facto* monopoly was only achieved in 1891 due to the resistance of other note-issuing banks. The bank is still wholly privately owned and cannot intervene in the money market.
3. 65 per cent of the banks accounting for 20 per cent of banking assets were outside the Federal Reserve System until 1929.

C. Securities regulation

In the current phase of financial globalization led by the USA, the stock market has become the symbol of capitalism. When Communism was overthrown, many transition economies rushed to establish stock exchanges and sent promising young people abroad to train as stock-brokers, even before they had founded other more basic institutions of capitalism. Likewise, many developing country governments have tried very hard to establish and promote their stock markets, and to open them up to foreign investors, in the belief that this would allow them to tap into a hitherto unavailable pool of financial resources.[107]

Of course, many people, most famously John Maynard Keynes in the 1930s, have argued that capitalism functions best when the stock market plays a secondary role. Indeed, since the 1980s, there has been a heated debate on the relative merits of the stock-market-led financial systems of the Anglo-American countries, and the bank-led systems of Japan and the Continental European countries.[108] However, the orthodoxy remains that a well-functioning stock market is a key institution necessary for economic development – a view that was recently boosted thanks to the stock-market-led boom in the US, although this boom is fading fast due to the rapid slowing-down of the US economy.

Whatever importance one accords to the stock market and other securities markets, establishing institutions that regulate them effectively is unquestionably an important task. Given that stock markets recently became an extra source of financial instability in developing countries, especially when they were open to external flows, establishing the institutions to regulate them well is now an urgent task. So how did the NDCs manage the development of such institutions?

The early development of the securities market in Britain (established in 1692) led to a similarly early emergence of securities regulation. The first such attempt, made in 1697, limited the number of brokers through licensing and capped their fees. In 1734, the Parliament passed Barnard's Act, which tried to limit the more speculative end of the securities market by banning options, prohibiting parties from settling contracts by paying price differentials and stipulating that stocks actually had to be possessed if the contracts that had led to their sales were to be upheld in a court of law. However, this law remained ineffective and was finally repealed in 1860.[109]

Subsequently, except for the 1867 Banking Companies (Shares) Act forbidding the short-selling of bank shares – which in any case remained ineffective – there were few attempts at securities regulation until 1939, when the Prevention of Fraud (Investments) Act was legislated. The act introduced a licensing system for individuals and companies dealing with securities by the Board of Trade, which had the power to revoke, or to refuse the renewal of, a licence if the party gave false or inadequate information in their application for it or when trading. The act was strengthened over time, with the Board of Trade being granted the power to establish rules concerning the amount of information that dealers had to give in offers of sales (1944) and to appoint inspectors to investigate the administration of unit trusts (1958).[101]

It was only with the 1986 Financial Services Act that the UK introduced a comprehensive system of securities regulation (brought into force on 29 April 1988). This act required the official listing of investments on the stock exchange and the publication of particulars before any listing; it also established criminal liability of those who gave false or misleading information, and prohibited anyone from conducting investment business unless authorized to do so.[111]

In the USA, organized securities markets dated from the 1770s. Early attempts at regulation were directed against insider trading. In 1789, for example, Congress passed a bill banning treasury officials from speculating in securities; in introducing such legislation it was ahead of even the UK. Although the federal government made periodic threats to introduce securities regulation, such regulation was left to the individual states throughout the nineteenth century. However, not all states had laws regulating securities transaction (the best example being Pennsylvania, economically one of the most important states of the time), and what laws did exist were weak in theory and even weaker in enforcement.[112]

Fraud in securities transactions, especially misrepresentation of information, was made a property fraud in the mid-nineteenth century, but full information disclosure was not made mandatory until the 1933 Federal Securities Act. In the early twentieth century, 20 states instituted 'blue sky laws', which required investment bankers to register securities with state authorities before selling them, and which penalized misrepresentation, but the laws were ineffective and there were many loopholes. The first effective federal securities regulation came with the 1933 Federal Securities Act, which gave the Federal Trade Commission the authority to regulate security transactions – an authority that was then transferred to the new Securities and Exchange Commission in 1934.[113]

D. Public finance institutions

Continuing fiscal crisis in many developing countries has been a great obstacle to development since the 1970s at least. The IDPE believes that the nature of the fiscal problem in these countries stems from their profligacy, but in most cases there is a deeper problem, namely the incapacity to tax.[114] This argument is also supported by the fact that budgetary outlays in developing countries are proportionally much smaller than in developed countries, whose governments are able to spend – and tax – far more.

The ability to tax requires, at the deepest level, the ability to command political legitimacy, both for the government itself and for the particular taxes concerned. For example, the Community Charge ('Poll Tax') that Margaret Thatcher tried to introduce in the UK failed because most British taxpayers thought it was an 'unfair' (and thus illegitimate) tax, rather than because they thought they were being taxed at too high a rate, or because they thought her government was illegitimate.

However, ensuring the political legitimacy of a regime and of individual taxes is not enough to increase tax collection capability. It also requires the development of the requisite institutions, such as new taxes and administrative mechanisms for better tax collection. How then did the NDCs manage this process?

In the early days of their development, the NDCs suffered from very limited fiscal capabilities; in this regard they probably suffered even more than most developing countries suffer these days. Their power to tax was so limited that tax farming was widely accepted as a cost-effective means of raising government revenue in the seventeenth and eighteenth centuries. Many contemporaries justified it as a way of saving administrative costs, stabilizing revenue, and reducing corruption in tax collection; these were probably not unreasonable arguments, given how poorly developed public finance institutions were in these countries at the time.[115]

Overall, in many NDCs government finance – particularly local government finance – was in a mess during most of the period in question. A very telling example is that of the defaults by a number of US state governments on British loans in 1842. After these defaults, British financiers put pressure on the US federal government to assume the liabilities (which reminds us of the events in Brazil following the default of the state of Minas Gerais in 1999). When this pressure came to naught, *The Times* poured scorn on the US federal government's attempt to raise a new loan later in the year by arguing that '[t]he people of the United States may be fully persuaded that there is a certain class of securities to which no abundance of money, however great, can give value; and that in this class their own securities stand pre-eminent'.[116]

What especially exacerbated the problems in the public finance of the time was the combination of frequent wars, which required substantial extra public financing, and the inability to collect direct taxes, especially income tax.[117] The absence of income tax (some countries had had property tax and/or wealth tax from relatively early on) in part reflected the political under-representation of the poorer classes, but also the limited administrative capability of the bureaucracy. This restricted bureaucratic capacity was indeed one reason why tariffs (the easiest taxes to collect), were so important as a source of revenue in the NDCs in earlier times, and also for many of today's poorest developing countries.

Income tax was initially only used as an emergency tax intended for war financing. Britain introduced graduated income tax in 1799 to finance the war with France, but scrapped it with the end of the war in

1816. Denmark used income tax for emergency finance during the 1789 Revolutionary War and the 1809 Napoleonic War. The USA introduced a temporary income tax during the Civil War but repealed it soon after the war ended in 1872.[118]

In 1842 Britain became the first country to make income tax permanent. However, the tax was widely opposed as an unequal and intrusive measure; John McCulloch, one of the most influential economists of the time, argued that income taxes 'require a constant interference with, and inquiry into the affairs of individuals, so that, independent of their inequality, they keep up a perpetual feeling of irritation'.[119] As late as 1874, the abolition of income tax was a major plank of Gladstone's election platform, although he lost the election.[120]

Denmark introduced a permanent progressive income tax in 1903. In the USA, the income-tax law of 1894 was overturned as 'unconstitutional' by the Supreme Court. A subsequent bill was defeated in 1898, and the Sixteenth Amendment allowing federal income tax was only adopted in 1913. However, the tax rate was only one per cent for taxable net income above $3,000, rising to seven per cent on incomes above $500,000. In Belgium, income tax was introduced in 1919, while in Portugal, it was introduced in 1922, but abolished in 1928, and only reinstated in 1933. Depite being known later for its willingness to impose high rates of income tax, Sweden introduced it as late as 1932. In Spain, the first attempt to introduce income tax by the Finance Minister Calvo Sotelo in 1926 was thwarted by a campaign against it, 'led by the aristocracy of the banking world'.[121]

3.2.6. Social welfare and labour institutions

A. Social welfare institutions

With the progress in liberalization and deregulation that can bring about a large-scale economic dislocation, as well as the increasing frequency of economic crises, there is a greater concern with providing livelihoods for those worst affected by these processes in developing countries. Even the IMF and the World Bank, which used to be against the introduction into developing countries of what they regarded as 'premature' social welfare institutions (especially given their preoccupation with budget deficits), are now talking about the need to provide a 'safety net'. So, while the standards demanded tend to be quite low, there is now pressure on the developing countries to adopt some minimal social welfare institutions – although this pressure is much weaker than for most of the other items on the 'good governance' agenda.

Social welfare institutions are, however, much more than 'safety nets'; if carefully designed and implemented they can enhance efficiency and productivity growth.[122] Cost-effective public provision of health and education can bring about improvements in labour force quality that can, in turn, raise efficiency and accelerate productivity growth. Social welfare institutions reduce social tensions and enhance the legitimacy of the political system, thus providing a more stable environment for long-term investments. Inter-temporal smoothing of consumption through devices like unemployment benefit can even contribute to dampening the business cycle. And so on.

All these potential benefits of social welfare institutions have to be set against their potential costs. First, there are the potentially corrosive effects of social welfare institutions on the work ethic and the sense of self-worth felt by the recipients of benefits. Second, apparently technical issues can significantly determine the effectiveness and legitimacy of these institutions. These include assessing whether benefit and contribution levels are adequately set, whether the administration of the system is seen as fair and efficient, and whether there is an effective mechanism for checking frauds in the system. Third, trying to raise more taxes in order to finance a social welfare programme in a context where its political legitimacy is not firmly established may lead to 'investment strikes' by the rich – or even support for a violent reversal, as in the case of Chile under Allende.

Whatever the exact benefits and costs of a particular social welfare institution may be, the fact that all NDCs have developed a common set of social welfare institutions over time (except for the persistent and disturbing absence of comprehensive health care in the USA) suggests that there are some common needs that have to be addressed across countries. However, it is important to note that social welfare institutions tend to be established at quite a late stage in most countries' development.

Institutions that take some care of the weaker sections of a society have always been necessary to guarantee social stability. Before industrialization, this care was provided by extended families, local communities and religious organizations. In the NDCs, with the weakening of these institutions following industrialization and urbanization during the nineteenth century, social tensions began to rise, as can be seen from the constant fear of revolution that gripped many of these countries during the century.

However, before the 1870s, social welfare institutions in the NDCs were very poor, with the English Poor Law-type legislation at their core. The poor relief laws of the time stigmatized the recipients of state help, with many countries depriving them of voting rights. For example, Norway and Sweden introduced universal male suffrage in 1898 and 1918 respectively, but it was not until 1918 and 1921 respectively that those who had received state assistance were allowed to vote.[123]

As we can see in table 3.4 below, social welfare institutions in NDCs only started to emerge in the late nineteenth century. Their development was spurred on by the increasing political muscle-flexing of the popular classes after the significant extension of suffrage during this period (see section 3.2.1) and by union activism. There was, however, no fundamental relationship between the extension of suffrage and the extension of welfare institutions. While in countries like New Zealand there is a clear link between the early extension of suffrage and the development of welfare institutions, in cases like that of Germany welfare institutions grew quickly under relatively limited suffrage.

In fact, Germany was the pioneer in this area. It was the first to introduce industrial accident insurance (1871), health insurance (1883) and state pensions (1889), although France was the first country to introduce unemployment insurance (1905).[124] Germany's early welfare institutions were already very 'modern' in character (having, for example, universal coverage), and they apparently attracted great admiration from the French Left at the time. It is important to note that under the leadership of Gustav Schmoller, the scholars belonging to the German Historical School (see Chapter 1) formed the influential *Verein für Sozialpolitik* (Union for Social Policy) and pushed strongly for the introduction of social welfare legislation in Germany.[125]

Social welfare institutions made impressive progress in the NDCs during the fifty-year period between the last quarter of the nineteenth century and the first quarter of the twentieth century. In 1875, none of the 19 countries listed in table 3.4 had any of the four welfare institutions covered in the table, with the exception of Germany, which had introduced industrial accident insurance in 1871. However, by 1925, 16 countries had industrial accident insurance, 13 had health insurance, 12 had a pension system and 12 had unemployment insurance.

Table 3.4
Introduction of social welfare institutions in the NDCs

	Industrial Accident	Health	Pension	Unemployment
Germany	1871	1883	1889	1927
Switzerland	1881	1911	1946	1924
Austria	1887	1888	1927	1920
Norway	1894	1909	1936	1906
Finland	1895	1963	1937	1917
UK	1897	1911	1908	1911
Ireland*	1897	1911	1908	1911
Italy	1898	1886	1898	1919
Denmark	1898	1892	1891	1907
France	1898	1898	1895	1905
New Zealand	1900	1938	1898	1938
Spain	1900	1942	1919	n.a.
Sweden	1901	1891	1913	1934
Netherlands	1901	1929	1913	1916
Australia	1902	1945	1909	1945
Belgium	1903	1894	1900	1920
Canada	1930	1971	1927	1940
USA	1930	No	1935	1935
Portugal	1962	1984[+]	1984[+]	1984[+]

Sources: Pierson 1998, p. 104, table 4.1. The information on Spain is from Voltes 1979, Maza 1987 and Soto 1989. The information on Portugal is from Wiener 1977 and Magone 1997.

Notes:
1. The countries are arranged in the order in which they introduced industrial accident insurance (starting with Germany in 1871). If it was introduced in the same year in more than one country, we list the country that introduced health insurance earlier first.
2. The figures include schemes which were initially voluntary but state-aided, as well as those that were compulsory.
* Ireland was a UK colony during the years mentioned.
+ Although some social welfare institutions were introduced in Portugal from the 1960s, they remained very fragmented systems, consisting of partial regimes regulating the social insurance of certain social groups until 1984.

B. Institutions regulating child labour

Child labour has generated particularly heated debate since the early days of industrialization, as we shall soon see. More recently, however, the debate has taken on a new international dimension. There is now a demand that developed countries should put pressure on developing countries to eliminate child labour. Particularly controversial is the proposal to reduce child labour by imposing trade sanctions through the WTO on countries that violate 'international labour standards', including in particular those standards on child labour.[126]

There is widespread concern that such sanctions will impose institutional standards on developing countries that cannot afford them, although exactly what is 'affordable' is difficult to establish. Some are worried that such measures may be abused in the interests of 'unfair', covert protectionism; others argue that, whether or not they are economically viable, issues like child labour regulation should never be internationally sanctioned. Some commentators point out that it is unreasonable to expect a swift eradication of child labour in today's developing countries, when the NDCs took centuries to achieve it.

Child labour was widespread in the NDCs during the earlier days of their industrialization. In the 1820s, it was reported that British children were working between 12.5 and 16 hours per day. Between 1840 and 1846, children under 14 accounted for up to 20 per cent of the factory workforce in Germany. In Sweden, children as young as five or six years old could still be employed as late as 1837.[127]

In the USA, child labour was widespread in the early nineteenth century: in the 1820s, about half of cotton textile workers were under 16. At the time, it was very common for families to be hired as a complete unit. For example, in 1813 a cotton manufacturer advertised in a New York state provincial paper, the *Utica Patriot*, that '[a] few sober and industrious families of at least five children, each over the age of eight years are wanted at the Cotton Factory'.[128] As late as 1900, the number of children under 16 in the USA working full time (1.7 million) exceeded the whole membership of the American Federation of Labour (AFL), then the country's main trade union.[129]

In Britain, the first attempts to introduce institutions to regulate child labour met with stiff resistance. In the debate surrounding the 1819 Cotton Factories Regulation Act, which banned the employment of children under the age of nine and restricted children's working hours, some members of the House of Lords argued that 'labour ought to be free' while others argued that children are not 'free agents'. The earlier laws (1802, 1819, 1825 and 1831) remained largely ineffective, partly because Parliament would not vote to commit the money needed for its implementation. For example, the 1819 Act had secured only two convictions by 1825.[130]

The first serious attempt to regulate child labour in Britain was the

1833 Factory Act, but this only covered the cotton, wool, flax and silk industries.[131] This act banned the employment of children under nine; it also limited the working day of children between nine and 13 to eight hours and that for 'young persons' (those between 13 and 18) to 12 hours. Children were not allowed to work during the night (between 8.30 pm and 5.30 am). In 1844, another Factory Act reduced the working hours of children under 13 to six and a half (or seven under special circumstances), and made provisions for compulsory mealtimes. However, this was partly countered by a lowering of the minimum working age from nine to eight. The 1847 Factory Act (the 'Ten Hours Act') reduced the working day of children aged between 13 and 18 to 10 hours.

From 1853 onward, a series of other industries were brought under the acts, which all functioned simultaneously, with the 1867 Act the most significant in this respect. The working hours of children employed in the mines were, however, not brought under the Factory Act until 1872. However, even in the 1878 Factory and Workshop Act, children over the age of 10 were allowed to work up to 30 hours a week, while conditions were even less stringent in non-textile factories.[132]

In Germany, Prussia introduced the first law on child labour in 1839. This law forbade the 'regular' employment of children under nine and of illiterate children under 16 in factories and mines. In 1853–4, when factory inspection was instituted and the legal minimum age was raised to 12, the law became enforced to some extent. However, it was only in 1878, when the law strengthened inspection, that child labour under 12 finally became illegal. In Saxony, child labour under 10 was outlawed in 1861, and four years later the minimum working age for children was raised to 12. France introduced child labour regulation in 1841, and the following year Austria raised the working age at factories from nine (a level which had been set in 1787) to 12.[133]

A law was passed in Sweden in 1846 to ban labour by children under 12, while a law of 1881 restricted the working day for children to six hours. However, these laws were widely violated until 1900, when a special supervisory agency was established to enforce them; in the same year the maximum number of working hours for children aged between 13 and 18 were reduced to 10.[134]

In Denmark, the first regulation on child labour was introduced in 1873. This banned the employment of children under 10 in industry, with the maximum working hours of the 10–14 and 14–18 age groups set at six and a half and 12 respectively. In 1925, it was ruled that children under the age of 14 who had not legally finished their schooling could not be employed; however, this law exempted work in agriculture, forestry, fishing and sailing. The passing of this law was relatively easy, as the Danish parliament was at the time dominated by agricultural interest, who had no objections so long as the legislation didn't affect the agricultural sector.[135]

In Norway, the first legislation to regulate child labour was introduced in 1892.[136] This law forbade the employment of children below the age of 12 in industrial establishments, while work by children between 12 and 14 was heavily regulated, and the working day for those between 14 and 18 was restricted to 10 hours. Night shifts by those under 18 were banned, except in factories operating round the clock.

In 1873, the Spanish government passed a law banning the employment of children under 10, but it was ineffective. A new law, introduced in 1900, limited the working day of children between 10 and 14 to six hours in industrial establishments and to eight hours in commercial business. The first child labour regulations were introduced in 1874 in Holland and 1877 in Switzerland.[137]

In Belgium, the first attempt to regulate child labour was the 1878 law related to children employed in the mines. In 1909, children over the age of 12 were restricted to working 12 hours a day and six days a week. Employment of children below 12 was banned. In 1914, the minimum age for child labour was raised to 14. In Italy, a law prohibiting the employment of children under 12 was not introduced until 1902, while in Portugal, regulations on the working hours of children (and women) were only introduced in 1913.[138]

In the USA, some states introduced regulation on child labour as early as the 1840s – Massachusetts in 1842, New Hampshire in 1846 and Maine and Pennsylvania in 1848.[139] By the First World War, nearly every state had introduced laws banning the employment of young children and limiting the hours of older ones. In this transition, the initiative taken by the National Child Labour Committee is said to have been crucial. Unfortunately, the laws were still poorly enforced. The Congress passed a federal child labour law in 1916, but two years later the Supreme Court declared it unconstitutional. Another attempt in 1919 met with the same fate. A federal legislation banning child labour had to wait until 1938 and the introduction of the Fair Labour Standard Act.[140]

Table 3.5 provides a summary of the information presented above regarding the evolution of child labour regulation in the NDCs during the nineteenth and early twentieth centuries. While the information contained in the table is incomplete and the dating of events approximate, it seems clear that not until the mid-1870s did even cosmetic legislation on child labour exist in the majority of the 15 countries listed. Only in the early twentieth century have we come to see even 'reasonably serious' child labour regulation prevailing in the NDCs.

Table 3.5
Introduction of child labour regulation in the NDCs

	First Attempt at Regulation (mostly ineffective)	First 'Serious' Regulation	Relatively Comprehensive and Well-enforced Regulation
Austria	1787	1842?	?
UK	1802	1833	1878
Prussia	1839	1853–4	1878
France	1841	?	?
USA	1842*	1904–14	1938
Sweden	1846	1881	1900
Saxony	1861	?	?
Denmark	1873	1925	?
Spain	1873	1900	?
Holland	1874	?	?
Switzerland	1877	?	?
Belgium	1878	1909	1914?
Norway	1892	?	?
Italy	1902	?	?
Portugal	1913	?	?

Source: Text.

* When Massachusetts introduced its state regulation.

C. Institutions regulating adult working hours and conditions

Institutions that regulate the working hours and conditions of adult workers certainly do not attract as much comment as those regulating child labour. However, the substantive issues involved in their implementation are essentially the same as those to do with institutions regulating child labour.

In most NDCs, long working hours were common throughout the

nineteenth century. Prior to the 1844 Factory Act the normal working day in the UK exceeded 12 hours. In the USA, until as late as the 1890s, only a small number of enlightened employers were willing to go below the customary 10-hour working day. Many recent immigrant workers worked for up to 16 hours a day throughout the nineteenth century.[141] In Germany, the average working week was 75 hours between 1850 and 1870, 66 hours in 1890 and 54 in 1914, while the working day for bakers in Norway during the 1870s and the 1880s was often as long as 16 hours. Sweden's average working day was 11–12 hours until the 1880s, and until the 1900s could be as long as 17 hours in certain occupations, especially baking. Mørch estimates that in 1880 the Danish working week was about 70 hours spread over a six-and-a-half-day week.[142]

Despite these extremely long hours, legislation regulating the working hours of adults did not come into existence until the mid-nineteenth century (recall that some attempts to regulate child labour had been in place since the late eighteenth and early nineteenth centuries in some countries). One of the earliest to control adult working hours was the 1844 Factory Act in Britain. This act, among other things, restricted the working hours of women over 18 to 12 hours and banned them from night work.[143] Although not legally stipulated, the socially-acceptable working hours of adult male workers was also reduced to 12 after this act was introduced. The 1847 Factory Act, which came into force the following year, restricted the working day for women and children to 10 hours. However, various legal loopholes were exploited by many employers to minimise the impact of such legislation. For example, many employers did not allow mealtimes during the working day – between 9am and 7pm.[144]

In the USA, restrictions on working hours were first introduced at the state level. Massachusetts introduced pioneer legislation in 1874, which limited the working days of women and children to 10 hours.[145] It was not until the 1890s that such legislation became common across the US. Around the turn of the century, some states also restricted the length of the working day in special industries (like railways and mining), where fatigue led to major accidents. However, before 1900 'the collective impact of such legislation was not impressive', especially because many conservative judges tried to limit its application. In 1905, for example, the US Supreme Court declared in the famous Lochner vs. New York case that a 10-hour act for bakers, which was introduced by the New York state, was unconstitutional because it 'deprived the baker of the liberty of working as long as he wished'. As late as 1908, an Oregon law limiting women laundry workers to 10 hours' work a day was contested in the Supreme Court, although in this case the Court upheld the law.

It was only around 1910 that most US states 'modified the common-law tradition that a worker accepted the risk of accident as a condition of employment and was not entitled to compensation if injured unless it could be proved that the employer had been negligent'.[146] However, at the time safety laws were still very poorly enforced, and federal industrial accident insurance was not established until 1930 (see table 3.4).

The information on other NDCs is more fragmentary, but it seems reasonable to say that even minimal regulations on adult working hours and conditions did not come about in many NDCs until the late nineteenth, or even the early twentieth, century.

As early as 1848, France had a law limiting female working hours to 11 a day, yet the French elite was still strongly opposed to any regulation of the work of adult males in the early twentieth century. None of the Scandinavian countries had laws regulating hours of adult female labour before the start of the First World War. In Italy, the female working day was restricted to 11 hours in 1902, although a compulsory weekly rest day was not introduced until 1907. In Spain, it was not until 1904 that the rest day (Sunday) was established, while Belgium also only introduced the rest day in industrial and commercial enterprises in 1905.[147]

It was only well into the twentieth century that we begin to witness 'modern' regulations on working hours. In Spain, an eight-hour working day was introduced in 1902 – relatively early given its level of development – at regional levels, but this was not widely established until 1919. In Sweden, a 48-hour working week was introduced in 1920. Denmark also made the eight-hour working day compulsory in 1920, but agriculture and the maritime industry, which together employed about one third of the labour force, was exempt from the law. Belgium introduced a 48-hour working week in 1921 and a 40-hour week in 1936. It was only with the Fair Labour Standards Act in 1938 that the maximum working week of 40 hours was implemented in the USA.[148]

3.3. Institutional development in developing countries then and now

Given our discussion in this chapter, what can be said about institutional development among now-developed countries (NDCs) in the past? I realize that a generalization in this context is hazardous given the paucity of historical records (especially for the smaller countries) and the differences across countries. Nevertheless, such a generalization is necessary for the purpose of the present book, and I will attempt to address the question in this section.

I do this by first providing snapshot pictures for three different stages of development in the NDCs (section 3.3.1). I look at: (i) 1820, for the early days of industrialization even in the most advanced NDCs; (ii) 1875, for the height of industrialization in the more advanced NDCs and the beginning of industrialization in the less developed NDCs; and (iii) 1913, for the beginning of industrial maturity in the more developed NDCs and the height of industrialization in the less developed NDCs. In the following section, I point out that the process of institutional development in the NDCs has been slow and uneven (section 3.3.2). I then compare levels of institutional development in the NDCs in earlier times with those that are found in today's developing countries (section 3.3.3). I conclude that contemporary developing countries actually have much higher levels of institutional development than the NDCs did at comparable stages of development.

3.3.1. A bird's-eye view of historical institutional development in NDCs

A. 1820 – Early industrialization

In 1820, none of the NDCs even had universal male suffrage. When, if at all, the vote was extended, it was only to men with substantial property – and often to only those over 30. In all these countries, nepotism, spoils, sinecures and sales of office were common in bureaucratic appointments. Public office was often formally treated as private property, and in most countries salaried professional bureaucracy in the modern sense did not exist (Prussia and some other German states being notable exceptions).

Existing property rights had to be routinely violated to make room for new property rights, particularly in new countries like the USA. Only a handful of countries had patent laws (the UK, USA, France and Austria) and the quality of these laws was still very low, with virtually no checks on the originality of the inventions for which patents were sought. The emergence of something even approximating the 'modern' patent law had to wait another decade and a half, until the 1836 revision of the US patent law.

Limited liability, a key institutional condition for the development of the modern corporation, was not a generalized institution in any country, and was therefore a privilege rather than a right. Even those countries with the then most developed corporate financial systems did not have regulations demanding external audits or full information disclosure in place. Bankruptcy laws, if they existed at all, were highly deficient, covering only a limited class of business; moreover, they were restricted in their ability to 'socialise risk' by 'wiping the slate clean' for the bankrupts. Competition law was all but non-existent, a limited and poorly-enforced example being Article 419 in the French Penal Code legislated in 1810.

Banks were still for the most part a novelty, except perhaps in parts of Italy (Venice and Genoa, among others), the UK and to a lesser extent the USA; however, none of the countries had a proper central bank with monopoly over note issue and a formal lender-of-last-resort function. Securities market regulation existed in few countries, but was highly inadequate and rarely enforced. No country had income tax except as an 'emergency' measure during wars (e.g., Britain for the period 1799–1816, Denmark during the Napoleonic Wars).

In addition, none of the NDCs had social welfare institutions or labour regulations on working hours, child labour, or health and safety at work. The only exceptions were one or two minimal and ineffective laws regulating child labour in a few textile industries in the UK (the 1802 law and the 1819 law), and the restriction of the legal working age to nine and above in Austria, in a law introduced in 1787.

B. 1875 – Industrialization in full swing

By 1875, with the progress of industrialization, the NDCs experienced considerable institutional development, but the quality of their institutions was still well below what we expect from the developing countries of today at comparable levels of development (see section 3.3.3 for this comparison).

None of these countries had universal suffrage, although a few – such as France, Denmark and the USA – did, theoretically at least, achieve universal male suffrage; however, although it was subsequently reversed in the USA. Even in these countries, however, some basic institutions of democracy, for example secret balloting, were missing and electoral fraud was widespread. Bureaucracies had only just begun to adopt key modern features like meritocratic recruitment and disciplinary measures, but even then only in a few pioneer countries such as Prussia and Britain (but not, for example, in the USA), while the spoils system was still widely used in many countries.

Most NDCs may have instituted patent laws by this time (Switzerland and the Netherlands being the notable exceptions), but the quality of this legislation was poor. Protection of foreigners' intellectual property rights was particularly bad, partly because there was no international intellectual property rights system in place. For example, despite being a strong defender of an international patent system, the USA still did not recognize foreigners' copyrights, and many German firms were still busy producing counterfeit English goods.

Generalized limited liability may have come into being in a number of countries by this time (Sweden, Britain, Portugal, France and Belgium), but even these countries did not have regulations regarding the auditing and information disclosure procedures of limited liability companies. It had been barely three decades since the UK had established a relatively 'modern' bankruptcy law, thereby allowing some chance of a 'fresh start' to bankrupts (1849), and the USA still did not have a federal bankruptcy law. Competition laws were still non-existent, despite the rapid rise of large firms and trust activities (by this time, Article 419 of the French Penal Code of 1810 had fallen into disuse).

Banks were still new institutions in many NDCs, a number of which – notably Italy, Switzerland and the USA – still did not have a central bank. Even in countries which did nominally have central banks (e.g., Portugal, Sweden and Germany), their effectiveness was often highly limited because they did not have monopoly over note issue. Banking regulation was still a rarity, and there existed widespread 'cronyistic' lending and frequent bank failures. Even the UK, the country with the most developed securities market, did not have proper securities regulation, with the result that insider trading and price manipulation abounded in securities markets. A permanent income tax, first introduced in Britain in 1842, was still a novelty.

During this period, none of the NDCs had modern social welfare schemes, the only exception being the industrial accident insurance introduced in Germany in 1871. Institutions regulating child labour existed in a number of countries, such as the UK, Prussia and Sweden, but were usually very poorly enforced. In many countries, the employment of relatively young children, those between the ages of nine and 12, was still permitted. Other countries, for example Belgium, Italy and Norway, had no regulation whatsoever on child labour at this time. There was still no limit imposed on adult male working hours in any of the NDCs, although some countries passed legislation restricting female working hours; even then these were set at a relatively high 10–12 hours per day. Workplace safety laws, if they existed, were virtually unenforced.

C. 1913 – The beginning of industrial maturity

Even as late as 1913, when the richest of the NDCs reached the level of the richer of today's developing countries (Brazil, Thailand, Turkey, Mexico, Colombia), from whom 'world standard' institutions are expected, the then-developing NDCs had low-quality institutions by these standards.

Universal suffrage was still a novelty – it existed only in Norway and New Zealand – and even a genuine male universal suffrage in the sense of 'one man one vote' was not common. For example, the USA and Australia had racial qualifications, while the Germans had different numbers of votes according to property, education and age. Secret ballots had only just been introduced in France (1913); Germany still did not have them at all. Bureaucratic modernization had progressed quite significantly, especially in Germany, but a spoils system was still widespread in many countries (in particular the USA and Spain); meanwhile, bureaucratic professionalism was only just emerging even in countries like the USA – it had been barely three decades since even a minimal degree of competitive recruitment was introduced in the US federal bureaucracy in 1883.

Even in the UK and the USA, corporate governance institutions fell miserably short of modern standards. The UK had introduced compulsory auditing for limited liability companies just over a decade earlier (1900), but due to a loophole in legislation, the balance sheets companies provided did not have to be up-to-date. In both countries, full disclosure to investors on public stock offering was still not compulsory. Competition law was non-existent: although it had been addressed in the USA in the 1890 Sherman Act, it was not until the 1914 Clayton Act that the country had an antitrust law worthy of the name. Europe had to wait for another decade before it got its first competition law, in the shape of Germany's cartel law of 1923.

Banking continued to be underdeveloped – branch banking, for instance, was still not permitted in the USA. Banking regulation was still patchy in most countries. Central banks were becoming a common institution, but their quality was still far behind what we would expect these days. In the USA, for example, central banking had barely been born (1913) and covered only 30 per cent of the banks in the country. The Italian central bank was still fighting for monopoly over note issue. Insider trading and stock price manipulation was still not properly regulated. Neither the UK nor the USA, the two countries then with the most-developed securities markets, had securities regulation (they had to wait until 1939 and 1933 respectively). Income tax was still a novelty. The USA introduced it only in 1913 after two decades of political fights and legal wrangling, while Sweden, despite its extensive use of income tax in subsequent periods, still did not have one at all by this point.

Possibly the only area where the NDCs did well, compared to the currently developing countries at similar levels of development, was that of social welfare institutions, which saw quite impressive growth from the 1880s onward. By 1913, most NDCs (with the exception of Canada, the USA and Portugal) had – albeit highly incomplete – industrial accident insurance, health insurance (except the Netherlands, New Zealand, Spain, Finland, Australia and Portugal) and state pensions (with the exception of Norway, Finland, Switzerland, Spain and Portugal). Unemployment insurance was, however, still a novelty: it was first introduced in France in 1905, and in Ireland, UK, Denmark, and Norway by 1913. However, countries such as Norway and Sweden still disenfranchised the recipients of social welfare.

Much labour legislation regarding working hours, workplace safety, female labour and child labour had also been introduced by this time, but the standards were rather low, the coverage limited and enforcement poor. For example, in the USA, even a 10-hour limit to the working day was fiercely resisted by employers and conservative judges, and it would be another quarter century before child labour was banned at the federal level (1938). No country had attained even a 48-hour working week (let alone a 40-hour week) by this time.

3.3.2. The long and winding road to institutional development

The first thing that emerges from the detailed discussion in section 3.2, and the overview provided by section 3.3.1, is that it took the NDCs decades, if not centuries, to develop institutions from the time when the need for them began to be perceived. It should be also pointed out that the NDCs frequently experienced reversals in this process. Let us provide some examples to illustrate this point.

Democracy took long time to develop. Just to give a couple of examples, it took France and Switzerland almost 100 years (1848 to 1946 and 1879 to 1971, respectively) to move from universal male suffrage to universal suffrage. The need for a modern professional bureaucracy was widely perceived at early as the eighteenth century, but in many NDCs it was not until the early nineteenth century that such bureaucracy was actually instituted. The value of limited liability institutions had already been recognized by the end of the sixteenth century, when royal charters permitting limited liability were granted to big, risky ventures (e.g., the British East India Company); however, it did not come into general use until the mid-nineteenth century even in the most advanced countries. The need for central banking was acknowledged in some circles from as early as the seventeenth century, but the first 'real' central bank, the Bank of England, was not instituted until 1844. The USA felt the need for at least some degree of central banking from the very early days of its existence, as can be seen in the establishment of the (short-lived) First Bank of the USA in 1791, but it was only in 1913 that the Federal Reserve System was put in place, and even then its coverage was still highly limited.

The diffusion of new institutions from innovating countries to the rest of the NDCs also took a considerable time. Table 3.6 charts, whenever possible, where and when different institutions first emerged, when they were adopted by the majority of the NDCs and at what point they were accepted by all the NDCs. The table shows that, even when we exclude the exceptional case of the 'pre-modern' patent law, it took anything from 20 years, in the cases of state pension and unemployment insurance, to 150 years (for example, modern central banking) between an institutional innovation and its adoption by the majority of the NDCs. The table also shows that when it comes to the time period between an institutional innovation and its adoption as an 'international standard' among the NDCs (i.e., with the vast majority of countries espousing it), we are not even talking in decades but in generations. The reasons for this slow pace of institutional development in the NDCs were diverse.

First of all, especially in the earlier stages of development, many institutions did not get adopted or remained ineffective when adopted, because they were 'unaffordable'. The absence of social welfare and labour regulations are the most obvious examples in this regard, but many institutions of corporate governance and finance also remained ineffective in earlier times because there were not enough resources for their management and enforcement.

Second, in many cases institutions were not accepted, even when they had become 'affordable', because of the resistance from those who would (at least in the short run) lose out from the introduction of such institutions. The resistance to democracy, labour regulation, or income tax by the propertied classes are probably the best examples in this regard.

Third, institutions were sometimes not adopted because the economic logic behind them had not been properly understood by their contemporaries. Resistance to limited liability or central banking, even by those who would have benefited from such institutions, are good examples of this.

Fourth, there were also institutions that were not adopted because of certain 'epochal prejudices', even when they had become obviously 'affordable' and the logic behind them had been understood. The late introduction of professional bureaucracy in the USA due to the Jacksonian prejudice against professionalism, or the late introduction of female suffrage in Switzerland are probably the best examples.

Fifth, institutional development was sometimes delayed because of the interdependence between certain institutions, so it was necessary for related institutions to develop simultaneously. For example, without the development of public finance institutions to collect taxes, it was difficult to pay properly for a modern professional bureaucracy, but without a developed tax bureaucracy it was difficult to develop public finance institutions. It is no coincidence that the development of modern bureaucracy went hand in hand with the development of the fiscal capacity of the state.

More detailed historical knowledge is required to explain why a particular institution was not adopted in a particular country at a particular time; unfortunately, there is no space in this book to engage in such discussion. However, what seems clear from our analysis here is that institutions have typically taken decades, if not generations, to develop. In this context, the currently popular demand that developing countries should adopt 'world standard' institutions right away, or at least within the next 5 to 10 years, or face punishments for not doing so, seems to be at odds with the historical experiences of the NDCs that are making these very demands.

Table 3.6
Summary of institutional Evolution in the NDCs

	First Adoption	Majority Adoption	Last Adoption	UK	US
Democracy					
Male Suffrage	**1848 (France)**	1907[a]	**1925 (Japan)**[a]	**1918**	**1870**
Universal Suffrage	1907 (New Zealand)	1946[a]	1971 (Switzerland)[a]	1928	1965
Modern Bureaucracy	early 19th C. (Prussia)			mid-1800s	early-1900s
Modern Judiciary				1930s?	
Intellectual Property Rights					
Patent Law	**1474 (Venice)**	1840s[b]	**1912 (the Netherlands)**[b]	**1623**	**1793**
'Modern' Patent Law[1]	1836 (USA)			1852	1836
'Modern' Copyright Law[2]		1960s[b]	1990s (Spain, Canada)[b]		1891 (1988)[3]
Trademark Law	1862 (UK)			1862	
Corporate Governance Institutions					
Generalized Limited Liability	1844 (Sweden)			1856 (1862)[4]	1800
Bankruptcy Law				**1542**	
'Modern' Bankruptcy Law[5]				1849	1898
'Modern' Auditing and Disclosure[6]				1948	1933
Competition Law	**1890 (USA)**			**1919**	**1890**
Effective Competition Law	1914 (USA)			1956	1914
Financial Institutions					
'Modern' Banking[7]	mid-1920s (UK)			mid-1920s	
Central Banking	**1688 (Sweden)**	1847[c]	**1913 (USA)**[c,9]	**1694**	**1913**
'Modern' Central Banking[8]	1844 (UK)	1891[c]	1929 (USA)[c,9]	1844	1929
Securities Regulation	**1679 (UK)**			**1679**	
'Modern' Securities Regulation[10]				1939	1933
Income Tax	1842 (UK)			1842	1913
Social Welfare and Labour Institutions					
Industrial Accident Insurance	1871 (Germany)	1898[d]	1930 (USA, Canada)[d]	1897	1930

	First Adoption	Majority Adoption	Last Adoption	UK	US
Health Insurance	1883 (Germany)	1911[d]	Still absent in the USA[d]	1911	Still absent
State Pension	1889 (Germany)	1909[d]	1946 (Switzerland)[d]	1908	1946
Unemployment Insurance	1905 (France)	1920[d]	1945 (Australia)[d]	1911	1935
Child Labour Regulation	*1787 (Austria)*	*1873[e]*	*1913 (Portugal)[e]*	*1802*	*1904*
'Modern' Child Labour Regulation[11]	1878 (UK/Prussia)			1878	1938

Source: The text.

* The institutions entered in italics denote 'pre-modern' varieties, which fell so short of modern standards in terms of coverage and enforcement that they are usually better regarded in a different category to their 'modern' descendants.

a. Out of the 19 countries for which the information is available (Australia, Austria, Belgium, Canada, Denmark, Finland, France, Germany, Italy, Japan, the Netherlands, New Zealand, Norway, Portugal, Spain, Sweden, Switzerland, UK, USA).

b. Out of the 17 countries for which the information is available (Austria, Belgium, Canada, Denmark, Finland, France, Germany, Italy, Japan, the Netherlands, Norway, Portugal, Spain, Sweden, Switzerland, UK, USA). At this time, the German states that had patent law were Prussia, Bavaria, Württemberg, and Saxony. The Italian states that had it were Sardinia and the Vatican State.

c. Out of the 11 countries for which information is available (Belgium, France, Germany, Italy, the Netherlands, Portugal, Spain, Sweden, Switzerland, UK, USA).

d. Out of the 17 countries for which information is available (Australia, Austria, Belgium, Canada, Denmark, Finland, France, Germany, Ireland, Italy, the Netherlands, New Zealand, Norway, Sweden, Switzerland, UK, USA).

e. Out of the 15 countries for which information is available (Austria, Belgium, Denmark, France, the Netherlands, Italy, Norway, Portugal, Prussia, Saxony, Spain, Sweden, Switzerland, UK, USA).

1. 'Modern' patent law is defined as a patent law that has provisions such as strict checks on originality of the invention, equal protection of foreign citizens' invention, and patents on chemical and pharmaceutical substances.

2. 'Modern' copyright law is defined as a copyright law that, above all, provides equal protection of foreign citizens' copyrights.

3. Until 1988, the USA did not acknowledge foreign citizens' copyrights unless the material had been printed in the USA.

4. Banks were only given limited liability in 1857 and insurance companies in 1862.

5. 'Modern' bankruptcy law is defined as a bankruptcy law that applies to everyone without any asset threshold and gives the debtors a second chance.

6. 'Modern' auditing and disclosure rules require external auditing, reporting of up-to-date balance sheets, and the disclosure of detailed information.

7. 'Modern' banking is defined as banking with very wide coverage, little insider lending, and one price across regions.

8. 'Modern' central banking applies to central banks with a note issue monopoly, acting as lender-of-last-resort, and having control over all banks.

9. Although the USA established the Federal Reserve System in 1913, even in 1915 only 30 per cent of the banks (accounting for 50 per cent of total banking assets) were under the system. Until 1929, the Federal Reserve System still did not cover 65 per cent of the banks (although with only 20 per cent of total banking assets).

10. 'Modern' securities regulation is defined as regulation requiring the faithful representation of information, full information disclosure, licensing of traders and power of the regulatory authority to initiate investigation.

11. 'Modern' child labour regulation is defined as child labour regulation with comprehensive coverage and effective enforcement.

3.3.3. Comparisons with currently developing countries

We have seen that institutional development in the NDCs in the past was a long and winding process. What is even more pertinent here is the fact that, in general, the NDCs were institutionally much less advanced in those times than the currently developing countries are at similar stages of development.

To make this point, we first need to compare the levels of development of the then-developing NDCs with today's developing countries. In table 3.7, we compare the per capita incomes of the NDCs during the nineteenth and early twentieth centuries (in 1990 international dollars) with the 1992 incomes of today's developing countries. Obviously, this is only a very rough-and-ready comparison, given that there are well-known problems with using income figures to measure a country's level of development, especially when it involves using historical statistics over two centuries. However, the table does give us a rough idea as to where the NDCs were when they were developing, in relation to those of today's developing countries.

The comparison shows that, in the 1820s, most of the NDCs were, broadly speaking, at a level of development somewhere between Bangladesh ($720 per capita income) and Egypt ($1,927 per capita income) of today – such a group includes countries like Burma (Myanmar), Ghana, Côte d'Ivoire, Kenya, Nigeria, India and Pakistan. By 1875, most NDCs had moved beyond the Nigeria–India level of income, but even the richest ones (the UK, New Zealand and Australia) were at the level of today's China ($3,098) or Peru ($3,232). The rest, including the USA, Germany and France, were between today's Pakistan ($1,642) and Indonesia ($2,749). By 1913, the wealthiest NDCs (the UK, the USA, Australia and New Zealand) had reached the level of the richer of today's developing countries (for example, Brazil, Mexico, Colombia and Thailand). However, the majority, from Finland to France and Austria, were still at the level of today's middle-income developing countries (such as the Philippines, Morocco, Indonesia, China and Peru).

When we match these income comparisons with the three historical snapshots of the NDCs provided above (section 3.3.1), we can see at once that NDCs in earlier times had relatively low levels of institutional development compared to the countries that are at comparable levels of development today. For example, the UK in 1820 was at a somewhat higher level of development than India today, but it did not have many of even the most 'basic' institutions that exist in India, such as universal suffrage (the UK did not at that point even have universal male suffrage), a central bank, income tax, generalized limited liability, a 'modern' bankruptcy law, a professional bureaucracy or meaningful securities regulations. Except for a couple of minimal and hardly-enforced regulations on child labour in a few industries, the UK in 1820 did not possess even minimal labour regulations.

Similarly, in 1875, Italy was at a level of development comparable to Pakistan today. However, it did not have universal male suffrage, a professional bureaucracy, even a remotely independent and professional judiciary, a central bank with a note issue monopoly or competition law – institutions that Pakistan has had for decades. (Democracy is an obvious exception, but despite frequent suspension of electoral politics, suffrage in Pakistan, when allowed, has remained universal.)

To give another example, the USA in 1913 was at a level of development similar to that of Mexico today, yet its level of institutional development was well behind: women were still formally disenfranchised, as de facto were blacks and other ethnic minorities in many parts of the country. It had been just over a decade since a federal bankruptcy law had appeared (1898) and barely two decades since the country recognized foreigners' copyrights in 1891. At this stage, moreover, the USA still had a highly-incomplete central banking system, while income tax had only just come into being (1913), and the establishment of a meaningful competition law had to wait until the Clayton Act of 1914. There was also no federal regulation on federal securities trading or on child labour, and what little state legislation existed in these areas was of low quality and very poorly enforced.

From these examples we can conclude that, in the early days of their economic development, the NDCs were operating with much less developed institutional structures than those which exist in today's developing countries at comparable levels of development. Needless to say the level of institutional development in the NDCs fell well short of the even higher 'global standards' to which today's developing countries are being told to conform.

Table 3.7
Where were the now-developed countries when they were developing?
(figures are given in 1990 dollars)

Per Capita Income Band	Now-Developed Countries (1750)	Now-Developed Countries (1820)	Now-Developed Countries (1875)	Now-Developed Countries (1913)	Developing Countries (1992)
Below 1,000	France (921)	Japan (704) Finland (759) Canada (893) Ireland (954)			Ethiopia (300) Bangladesh (720) Burma (748)
1,000–1,500	UK (1,328)	Norway (1,002) Spain (1,063) Italy (1,092) Germany (1,112) Sweden (1,198) France (1,218) Denmark (1,225) USA (1,287) Belgium (1,291) Austria (1,295)	Finland (1,176) Norway (1,469)	Japan (1,334) Portugal (1,354)	Ghana (1,007) Kenya (1,055) Côte d'Ivoire (1,134) Nigeria (1,152) India (1,348)
1,500–2,000		Australia (1,528) The Netherlands (1,561) UK (1,756)	Italy (1,516) Canada (1,690) Sweden (1,835) Austria (1,986)	Greece (1,621)	Pakistan (1,642) Egypt (1,927)

Table 3.7 contd.

Per Capita Income Band	Now-Developed Countries (1750)	Now-Developed Countries (1820)	Now-Developed Countries (1875)	Now-Developed Countries (1913)	Developing Countries (1992)
2,000–3,000			Denmark (2,031) France (2,198) Germany (2,198) USA (2,599) Belgium (2,800) The Netherlands (2,829)	Finland (2,050) Spain (2,255) Norway (2,275) Italy (2,507) Ireland (2,733)	Philippines (2,213) Morocco (2,327) Indonesia (2,749)
3,000–4,000			New Zealand (3,707) UK (3,511)	Sweden (3,096) France (3,452) Austria (3,488) Denmark (3,764) Germany (3,833) The Netherlands (3,950)	Peru (3,232) China (3,098)
4,000–5,000			Australia (4,433)	Belgium (4,130) Switzerland (4,207) Canada (4,231)	Turkey (4,422) Thailand (4,422) Brazil (4,862)
5,000–6,000				UK (5,032) New Zealand (5,178) USA (5,307) Australia (5,505)	Mexico (5,098) Colombia (5,359)

Source: Maddison 1995. The 1750 figures are extrapolated from 1820 data, with annual growth rate taken as 0.4 per cent for both the UK and France. 0.4 per cent is the weighted average of estimates by economic historians of England (de Vries 1984). It is widely accepted among economic historians that the French growth rate at the time was similar to that of England (Crouzet 1967).

Chapter 4

Lessons for the Present

4.1. Introduction

The discussion so far shows how the policies and institutions used by now-developed countries in the early stages of their development differ significantly from those that have commonly assumed to have been used by them, and even more from the guidelines recommended to, or rather more frequently demanded of, today's developing countries.

In the next two sections of this chapter, I summarize the principal conclusions of chapters 2 and 3, and discuss whether we can really conclude that the current push for 'good policies' and 'good governance' by the developed countries amounts in fact to 'kicking away the ladder'. Section 4.4 then considers some possible objections to my argument, while the final section draws some conclusions, and suggests new directions of research that have emerged from the present study.

4.2 Rethinking Economic Policies for Development

In Chapter 2, I looked at the policies that had been used by the now-developed countries (NDCs) during their development, from fourteenth-century England down to the East Asian NICs in the late twentieth century.

My discussion confirms to a remarkable extent the observation made by List 150 years ago – a time when many would have laughed at the suggestion that, within two generations, Germany would be economically challenging Britain or that the USA would become the world's leading industrial power. A consistent pattern emerges, in which all the catching-up economies use activist industrial, trade and technology (ITT) policies – but not simply tariff protection, as I have repeatedly pointed out – to promote economic development, as had been the case since before List's time. The policy tools involved in such promotional efforts may have become more varied, complex and effective since List's time, but the general pattern has remained remarkably true to type.

Whatever the exact policy method used, there seems to be a number of common principles that run through the lengthy series of successful development strategists starting from Edward III in the fourteenth century, through to Robert Walpole, Frederick the Great and Alexander Hamilton in the eighteenth century, to the nineteenth century US, German, or Swedish policy-makers, right down to their twentieth century East Asian or French counterparts.

As has been repeatedly observed over the last few centuries, the common problem faced by all catch-up economies is that the shift to higher-value-added activities, which constitutes the key to the process of economic development, does not happen 'naturally'.[1] This is because, for a variety of reasons, there exist discrepancies between social and individual returns to investments in the high-value-added activities, or infant industries, in the catch-up economies.[2]

Given such discrepancies, it becomes necessary to establish some mechanisms to socialize the risk involved in such investments. Contrary to the popular view, this does not have to involve direct policy intervention such as tariff protection or subsidies, but could be done by establishing institutions which can socialize the risk involved in such projects (more on this later – see section 4.3). However, the institutional solution has significant limitations. First of all, institutions are by nature embodiments of general rules, and therefore may not be effective in addressing problems related to particular industries. Second, establishing new institutions can take a long time, as we argued in Chapter 3, and this is therefore likely to limit the ability of countries to respond quickly to new challenges. As a result, a more focused and quick-footed policy intervention may in many cases be preferable to institutional solutions.

However, the fact that direct state intervention, especially in the form of ITT policies, is often necessary for socializing the risks involved in the development of infant industries, does not mean that there is only one way of doing it – that is to say, by means of tariff protection.[3] As my discussion in Chapter 2 shows, there were many different policy tools used for the purpose across different countries, as a result of the differences in their relative technological backwardness, international conditions, human resource availability and so on. Needless to say, even within the same country the focus of promotion can – indeed has to – evolve over time with changing domestic and international conditions. Typically, the successful countries have been those that were able skilfully to adapt their policy focus to changing conditions.

Of course, the fact that the use of activist ITT policies is necessary does not imply that all countries that use such policies are guaranteed economic success. As we know from the experiences of a range of developing countries during the postwar period, the success of these policies is critically determined one the one hand by the detailed forms of these policies, and on the other by the ability and the willingness of the state to implement these policies.[4]

The picture that emerges from our historical survey seems clear enough. In trying to catch-up with the frontier economies, the NDCs used interventionist industrial, trade and technology policies in order to promote their infant industries. The forms and emphases of these policies may have been varied according to different countries, but there is no denying that they actively used such policies. In relative terms (that is, taking into account the productivity gap with the more advanced countries), many of them actually protected their industries far more strongly than the currently developing countries have done.

If this is the case, the currently recommended package of 'good policies', which emphasizes the benefits of free trade and other *laissez-faire* ITT policies, seems at odds with historical experience. With one or two exceptions (e.g., the Netherlands and Switzerland), the NDCs did not succeed on the basis of such a policy package. The policies they had used in order to get where they are now – that is, activist ITT policies – are precisely those that the NDCs say the developing countries should not use because of their negative effects on economic development.

So are the developed countries, and the international development policy establishment (IDPE) that they control, recommending policies that they find beneficial for themselves, rather than those beneficial for the developing countries? Is there any parallel between this and the nineteenth-century British push for free trade against the protectionist policies of the USA and other NDCs which were trying to catch up with it? Is it fair to say that the WTO agreement that puts restrictions on the ability of the developing countries to pursue activist ITT policies is only a modern, multilateral version of the 'unequal treaties' that Britain and other NDCs used to impose on semi-independent countries? In other words, are the developed countries 'kicking away the ladder' by which they climbed up to the top beyond the reach of the developing countries? The answer to all these questions, unfortunately, is yes.

The only possible way for the developed countries to counter the accusation that they are 'kicking away the ladder' would be to argue that the activist ITT policies which they had previously pursued used to be beneficial for economic development but are not so any more, because 'times have changed'. In other words, it may be argued, the 'good policies' of yesterday may not be 'good policies' of today.

Apart from the paucity of convincing reasons as to why this may be the case,[5] the poor growth records of the developing countries over the last two decades suggest that this line of defence is simply untenable. During this period, most developing countries have gone through 'policy reforms' and implemented 'good' – or at least 'better' – policies, which were supposed to promote growth. Put simply, the result has been very disappointing.

The plain fact is that the Neo-Liberal 'policy reforms' have not been able to deliver their central promise – namely, economic growth. When they were implemented, we were told that, while these 'reforms' might increase inequality in the short term and possibly in the long run as well, they would generate faster growth and eventually lift everyone up more effectively than the interventionist policies of the early postwar years had done. The records of the last two decades show that only the negative part of this prediction has been met. Income inequality did increase as predicted, but the acceleration in growth that had been promised never arrived. In fact, growth has markedly decelerated during the last two decades, especially in the developing countries, when compared to the 1960–1980 period when 'bad' policies prevailed.

According to the data provided by Weisbrot et al. in the 116 (developed and developing) countries for which they had data, GDP per capita grew at the rate of 3.1 per cent p.a. between 1960 and 1980, while it grew at the rate of only 1.4 per cent p.a. between 1980 and 2000. In only 15 of the 116 countries in the sample – 13 of the 88 developing countries[6] – did the growth rate rise by more than 0.1 percentage points p.a. between these two periods.[7]

More specifically, according to Weisbrot et al., GDP per capita grew at 2.8 per cent p.a. in Latin American countries during the period 1960–1980, whereas it was stagnant between 1980 and 1998, growing at 0.3 per cent p.a. GDP per capita fell in Sub-Saharan Africa by 15 per cent (or grew at the rate of -0.8 per cent p.a.) between 1980 and 1998, whereas it had risen by 36 per cent between the period 1960–1980 (or at the rate of 1.6 per cent p.a.). The records in the former Communist economies (the 'transition economies') – except China and Vietnam, which did not follow Neo-Liberal recommendations – are even more dismal. Stiglitz points out that, of the 19 transition economies of Eastern Europe and the former Soviet Union,[8] only Poland's 1997 GDP exceeded that of 1989, the year when the transition began. Of the remaining 18 countries, GDP per capita in 1997 was less than 40 per cent that of 1989 in four countries (Georgia, Azerbaijan, Moldova and Ukraine). In only five of them was GDP per capita in 1997 more than 80 per cent of the 1989 level (Romania, Uzbekistan, Czech Republic, Hungary and Slovakia).

So we have an apparent 'paradox' here – at least if you are a Neo-Liberal economist. All countries, but especially developing countries, grew much faster when they used 'bad' policies during the 1960–1980 period than when they used 'good' ones during the following two decades. The obvious answer to this paradox is to accept that the supposedly 'good' policies are in fact not beneficial for the developing countries, but rather that the 'bad' policies are actually likely to do them good if effectively implemented.

Now, the interesting thing is that these 'bad' policies are basically those that the NDCs had pursued when they were developing countries themselves. Given this, we can only conclude that, in recommending the allegedly 'good' policies, the NDCs are in effect 'kicking away the ladder' by which they have climbed to the top.

4.3 Rethinking Institutional Development

The process of institutional development, and the role that it plays in overall economic development, is still a poorly understood subject. While we need further research on the role of institutions in economic development in order to arrive at more definite conclusions – something beyond the scope of this book – the following points emerge from our discussion in Chapter 3.

Most of the institutions that are currently recommended to the developing countries as parts of the 'good governance' package were in fact the results, rather than the causes, of economic development of the NDCs. In this sense, it is not clear how many of them are indeed 'necessary' for today's developing countries – are they so necessary that, according to the view of the IDPE, they have to be imposed on these countries through strong bilateral and multilateral external pressures?

Moreover, even when we agree that certain institutions are 'good' or even 'necessary', we have to be careful in specifying their exact shapes. In Chapter 3, I have shown that for just about every institution, there is a debate on what exact form it should take. What type of bureaucracy is good for development? How strongly should property rights regimes protect existing property rights? How debtor-friendly should a bankruptcy law be? How independent should the central bank be? The questions could go on. Deciding exactly which variety of which institution is necessary for which type of country is beyond the scope of this book. However, I hope my discussion in Chapter 3 has shown that the currently dominant view that there is only one set of 'best practice' institutions (which usually mean Anglo–American institutions) which everyone has to adopt is highly problematic.

However, arguing that many of the institutions currently recommended by the 'good governance' discourse may not be necessary or even beneficial for the currently developing countries should not be interpreted as saying that institutions do not matter, or that developing countries do not need improvements to their institutions. On the contrary, improvements to the quality of institutions seem historically to have been associated with better growth performance, an observation that we can easily support with historical and contemporary evidence.

As we can see from table 4.1, annual per capita income growth rates among the 11 NDCs for which data are available during the 1820–75 period ranged between 0.6 per cent (Italy) and 2 per cent (Australia), with the unweighted average and the median values both at 1.1 per cent. The table also shows that, between 1875 and 1913, per capita income growth rates ranged between 0.6 per cent (Australia) and 2.4 per cent (Canada), with the unweighted average at 1.7 per cent and the median at 1.4 per cent. Given that the NDCs had seen a significant development in their institutions since the mid-nineteenth century (see section 3.3.1 of Chapter 3), it is very plausible that at least a part of this growth acceleration was due to the improvements in the quality of their institutions.

The vastly superior economic performance of the NDCs during the so-called 'Golden Age of Capitalism' (1950–1973), when compared to that of the periods before and after, also highlights the importance of institutions in generating economic growth and stability. During the Golden Age, the NDCs typically grew at 3–4 per cent p.a. in per capita terms, in contrast to the 1–2 per cent rate that had prevailed before it (see table 4.1) and also in contrast to the 2–2.5 per cent rate that has been typical since its end (see table 4.3 – more on this later). According to the estimate by Maddison (1989), per capita income in the 16 largest NDCs grew at 3.8 per cent p.a. during this period, with countries like Japan (eight per cent), Germany, Austria (both at 4.9 per cent) and Italy (4.8 per cent), notching up previously unimaginable growth rates.[9] Most commentators attribute the Golden Age in the NDCs to the introduction of better institutions following Second World War, such as activist (Keynesian) budgetary institutions, fully-fledged welfare states, stricter financial market regulations, corporatist wage-bargaining institutions, institutions of investment coordination and in some cases nationalized industries (especially in France and Austria). It is widely agreed that these institutions helped the NDCs to grow quickly by providing them with greater macroeconomic and financial stability, better resource allocation and greater social peace.[10]

Table 4.1
Per capita annual growth performance among the NDCs in earlier times

	1820–1875 (per cent)	1875–1913 (per cent)
Australia	2.0	0.6
Austria	0.8	1.5
Belgium	1.4	1.0
Canada	1.2	2.4
Denmark	0.9	1.6
Finland	0.8	1.5
France	1.1	1.2
Germany	1.2	1.5
Italy	0.6	1.3
Netherlands	1.1	0.9
Norway	0.7	1.2
Sweden	0.8	1.4
UK	1.3	1.0
USA	1.3	1.9
Unweighted Average	1.1	1.7
Median	1.1	1.4

Source: Calculated from Maddison 1995.

The comparison of growth performance in the NDCs in earlier times with that of the developing countries during the postwar period also provides us with some important insights into the relationship between policies, institutions and economic growth.

I would argue that the developing countries were able to grow faster in the early postwar period (1960–1980) than the NDCs had done at comparable stages of development, partly because they had much better institutions than the latter countries had had (see section 3.3.3 in chapter 3).[11] Table 4.2 shows that, during the period 1960–1980, today's developing countries grew at about three per cent p.a. in per capita terms. This is a far superior growth performance to that which the NDCs managed during their 'century of development' (1820–1913), shown in table 4.1, when the average growth rates in the NDCs were around 1–1.5 per cent p.a..

Table 4.2
Per capita GNP growth performance of the developing countries, 1960–1980

	1960–1970 (per cent)	1970–1980 (per cent)	1960–1980 (per cent)
Low-income countries	1.8	1.7	1.8
Sub-Saharan Africa	1.7	0.2	1.0
Asia	1.8	2.0	1.9
Middle-income countries	3.5	3.1	3.3
East Asia and Pacific	4.9	5.7	5.3
Latin America and the Caribbean	2.9	3.2	3.1
Middle East and North Africa	1.1	3.8	2.5
Sub-Saharan Africa	2.3	1.6	2.0
Southern Europe	5.6	3.2	4.4
All Developing Countries	3.1	2.8	3.0
Industrialised Countries	3.9	2.4	3.2

Source: World Bank 1980, appendix table to part I.
Note: The 1979 and 1980 figures used are not final, but World Bank estimates. Given that the estimates were supposed to be on the optimistic side, the actual growth figures for 1970–1980 and 1960–1980 would have been slightly lower than those reported in this table.

All the above figures suggest that improving the quality of their institutions is an important task for developing countries wanting to accelerate their economic growth and development. However, two significant qualifications need to be made.

First of all, in pushing for institutional improvement in developing countries, we should accept that it is a lengthy process and be more patient with it. The discussion in Chapter 3 shows that it took the NDCs decades, if not centuries, to develop institutions, and that there were frequent setbacks and reversals during the course of the process. Seen from this perspective, the 5 to 10-year transition periods currently being given to the developing countries to bring their institutions up to 'global standards' are highly inadequate. Moreover, given that today's developing countries are already institutionally more advanced than were the NDCs at comparable stages of development, asking these countries to install a whole range of new 'global standard' institutions in short periods of time seems unrealistic. This, of course, should not mean that developing countries should adopt institutional standards of the last century. Nor should it make developed countries accept any 'we-are-not-ready-yet' argument put forward by governments of developing nations (more on this point later in section 4.4). However, it is clear that there should be a keener recognition of the speed – or lack of it – with which institutional development can be achieved in developing countries.

The second qualification I wish to make is that 'good' institutions produce growth only when they are combined with 'good' policies. As the reader can probably guess, when I say 'good' policies here, I mean the policies that most NDCs were using when they were developing, rather than the ones that they are now recommending to the developing countries. The fact is that, despite the continuous, and presumably accelerating, improvements in the quality of their institutions, today's developing countries have experienced marked slowdowns in growth during the last two decades (see section 4.2). In my view, this was because the ability of these countries to pursue the '(genuinely) good' policies was significantly curtailed as a result of the 'policy reforms' implemented during this period.

Table 4.3 shows that the average per capita growth rate among developing countries has fallen from around three per cent p.a. during the period 1960–1980 (see table 4.1) to 1.5 per cent p.a. for 1980–1999.[12] The latter is basically the rate of growth that the NDCs achieved during the late nineteenth and early twentieth centuries (1875–1913) when they were hampered by less favourable institutional conditions than those experienced by the developing countries of today (see table 4.2). The only sub-groups which achieved growth rates above that level during this period were East Asia (and Pacific) and South Asia, whose growth rates are dominated by those of China and India respectively.

The interesting thing to note is that both these countries are frequent lambasted by the IDPE for the poor quality of their institutions and policies. If we had excluded these two countries from our calculation of developing country average, we would have ended up with a much lower growth rate still.[13]

Table 4.3

Per capita annval GDP growth rates (per cent) in developing countries during the 'Age of Institutional Reform'

	1980–1990	1990–1999	1980–1999
Developing Countries	1.4	1.7	1.5
East Asia and Pacific	6.4	6.1	6.3
Europe and Central Asia	1.5	-2.9	-0.6
Latin America and the Caribbean	-0.3	1.7	0.6
Middle East and North Africa	-1.1	0.8	-0.2
South Asia	3.5	3.8	3.6
Sub-Saharan Africa	-1.2	-0.2	-0.7
Developed Countries	2.5	1.8	2.2

Notes: The data is from **World Bank 2001**. The figures are only approximate, as they were constructed by subtracting the population growth rates from GDP growth rates. This had to be done because the World Bank stopped publishing 10-year per capita GDP growth rates from its 1998 **World Development Report**. For country classification, see the table in p. 334 of the report.

It therefore seems quite plausible to argue that, during the period 1960–1980, partly thanks to their better institutional foundations compared to those possessed by the NDCs at comparable stages of development, the currently developing countries grew much faster than the NDCs had done, because they were being allowed to pursue 'bad policies'. However, when such policies were discontinued in the 1980s, better – and presumably improving – institutions were not enough to allow them to notch up better performances than those of the NDCs in the early days of their development, not to mention letting them improve over their own performance of the 1960–1980 period.[14]

What do all these mean for the 'kicking away the ladder' argument? I would agree that, if done in a realistic way and if combined with the right policies, international pressures for institutional improvements can play a positive role in the developmental process. However, the current push for institutional improvements in developing countries is not done in this way and is likely to end up as another 'ladder-kicking' exercise.

By demanding from developing countries institutional standards that they themselves had never attained at comparable levels of development, the NDCs are effectively adopting double standards, and hurting the developing countries by imposing on them many institutions that they neither need nor can afford.[15] For example, maintaining 'global standard' property rights and corporate governance institutions would require the developing countries to train (or even worse, to hire from abroad) a large army of world-class lawyers and accountants. This means that they will inevitably have less money (their own or donors') to spend on, say, the training of schoolteachers or of industrial engineers, which may be more necessary given their stages of development. In this sense, the NDCs are 'kicking away the ladder', not only in the area of policies but also in the area of institutions.

However, the picture in relation to institutions is more complicated than that in relation to policies. Unlike in the case of policies, many of the institutions that are recommended can bring benefits to the developing countries, although their exact forms do matter. However, these potential benefits can only be fully realized when combined with the 'right' policies. There are, too, genuine costs to institutional improvements. Therefore, whether the campaign for 'good institutions' will in effect turn into an act of 'kicking away the ladder' greatly depends on the exact forms and quality of the institutions demanded, and on the speed with which such demands are expected to be met. On both accounts, the current push for institutional reform does not look very positive for the developing countries.

4.4. Possible Objections

There are at least three objections that could be raised against my argument in this book. The first, and most obvious, is the argument that developing countries need to adopt the policies and institutions recommended by developed countries whether they like them or not, because that is how the world works – the strong calling the shots and the weak following orders.

At one level, it is difficult to deny the force of this argument. Indeed, my discussion in section 2.3 of Chapter 2 on the 'pulling away' tactics used by the NDCs in earlier times (e.g., colonialism, unequal treaties, bans on machinery exports) provides ample support for this argument. There is, too, plenty of evidence that even in the present age, when colonialism and unequal treaties are no longer acceptable, the developed countries can exercise enormous influence on developing ones. The NDCs exercise direct bilateral influence through their aid budgets and trade policies; they also maintain collective influence on developing countries through their control of the international financial institutions, on which developing countries are dependent. And they have disproportionate influence in the running of various international organizations, including even the ostensibly 'democratic' WTO, which is run on the one-country-one-vote principle (unlike the UN, in which the permanent members of the security council have veto power – or the World Bank and the IMF where voting power roughly corresponds to share capital). Moreover, during the last two decades or so, the collapse of the Soviet Union, which had provided some counterbalance to the power of the developed countries, and the demise of the so-called 'non-aligned' movement among developing countries, have further weakened the bargaining positions of the developing countries.

However, at another level, the argument that developing countries should follow the 'new rules' of the world economy because that this is what the developed countries, and the IDPE that they control, want is beside the point. What I am arguing is precisely that these 'new rules' should be changed. I do agree that the chance of these rules being changed in the near future is very small. However, this does not mean that therefore it is not worth discussing how they should be changed. If we think these rules need changing, we need to debate how best this can be achieved, however small the chance of change may be. By identifying the 'rules' by which the NDCs had developed, this book is intended to contribute to precisely this debate.

The second possible objection is the argument that the policies and institutions recommended by the IDPE to the developing countries have to be adopted because they are what the international investors want. It it may be argued that it is irrelevant whether or not the developing countries like these 'new rules', or even whether the IDPE is willing to change them, because in this globalized age it is the international investors who are calling the shots. Countries that do not adopt policies and institutions that international investors want, it is argued, will be shunned by them and suffer as a result.

However, there are many problems with this argument. First of all, it is not clear whether international investors do necessarily care so much about the policies and institutions promoted by the IDPE. For example, China has been able to attract a huge amount of foreign investment despite the proliferation of what are by current definition 'bad policies' and 'poor institutions'. This suggests that what the investors really want is often different from what they say they want or what the IDPE says they want – democracy and the rule of law being the best examples in this regard. Empirical studies show that most institutional variables are much less important than factors such as market size and growth in determining international investment decisions.[16]

Second, even if the conformity to international standards in policies and institutions were to bring about increased foreign investment, foreign investment is not going to be the key element in most countries' growth mechanisms. In other words, the potential value of a policy or an institution to a country should be determined more by what it will do to promote internal development than by what the international investors will think about it. This book demonstrates that many of the institutions currently being promoted by the proponents of the 'good governance' framework may not be necessary for development. Some of them (e.g., the protecting of certain property rights) may not even be good for it. Especially when taking into account their set-up and maintenance costs, establishing such institutions can easily have a negative impact overall, even if this were to lead to higher foreign investment.

Third, specifically in relation to institutions, I would argue that, even if certain 'good' institutions are introduced under global pressure, they may not deliver the expected results if they cannot be effectively enforced. It is possible to argue that we should welcome a certain degree of external pressure in situations where the government of a developing country is resisting the introduction of certain institutions that are obviously 'affordable' and compatible with the prevailing political and cultural norms in their society. However, we should also recognize that the introduction of institutions in countries that are not 'ready' to receive them can mean that the institutions will not function well or may even be undermined altogether. Examples include democracies undermined by military coups, electoral frauds and vote buying, or income taxes routinely and openly evaded by the rich. There will also be problems with institutional changes that are imposed from outside without 'local ownership', as the current jargon has it. If that is the case, clever international investors will figure out that possessing certain institutions on paper is not the same as really having them, which means that the formal introduction of 'global standard' institutions will in fact make little difference to the country's attractiveness to foreign investors.

Fourth, as long as the international development policy establishment is able to influence the way in which 'good policies' and 'good institutions' are defined, interpreted and promoted, there is still some value in discussing what policies and institutions should be asked of which developing countries. The 'follow the global norm or perish' argument assumes that the IDPE is a weather vane blindly following the winds of international investors' sentiments. However this establishment can, and to a great extent does, actively decide how strongly which policies and institutions are pushed.

The third possible objection to my argument, which particularly concerns the issue of institutional development, is that the 'world standard' in institutions has risen over the last century or so, and therefore that the current developing countries should not consider the NDCs of 100 and 150 years ago their role models.

I must say that I agree with this point wholeheartedly. On one level, it would be absurd to argue otherwise. In terms of per capita income, India may be at a similar level of development to that of the USA in 1820, but that should not mean that it should re-introduce slavery, abolish universal suffrage, de-professionalize its bureaucracy, abolish generalized limited liability, abolish the central bank, abolish income tax, abolish competition law, and so on.

Indeed, in many respects, the heightened global standard in institutions has been a good thing for the developing countries, or at least for the reformers in them. Unlike their counterparts in the NDCs of yesteryear, the reformers in today's developing countries do not have to struggle too hard against views that the introduction of things like female suffrage, income tax, restrictions on working hours, and social welfare institutions would spell the end of civilization as we know it. They also don't have to re-invent certain institutions like central banking and limited liability, the logic behind which the NDCs in earlier times had found difficult to understand.

Therefore, the developing countries should exploit to the utmost these advantages of being latecomers and try to achieve the highest level of institutional development possible. Moreover, as I have pointed out earlier in this chapter (section 4.2), the higher levels of institutional development may indeed be the reason why today's developing countries could, when they were allowed to use 'bad policies' during the 1960s and 1970s, generate much higher growth rates than the NDCs had managed at comparable stages of development.

What I am worried about, however, is the view that institutions are simply matters of choice and therefore all countries should try to reach the (quite highly-set) 'minimum global standard' right away or after a minimal transition period. While accepting that latecomer countries do not have to spend as much time as the pioneer countries had done in developing new institutions, we should not forget that it took the NDCs typically decades, and sometimes even generations, to establish certain institutions whose need had already been perceived. It usually took them another few decades to make them work properly by improving administration, closing various loopholes and strengthening enforcement. In addition, we should not forget that, when compared to the NDCs in earlier times, today's developing countries already have high standards of institutional development, which in the 1960s and 1970s proved quite capable of supporting high rates of economic growth. Given this, it may be unreasonable to ask them to raise the quality of their institutions dramatically in a short time span.

4.5 Concluding Remarks

Why do the international development policy establishment, and the NDCs that control it, not recommend the policies that were used over the last several centuries by most of the successful developers? Why do they try to impose on today's developing countries certain 'best practice' institutions, which had not been used by the NDCs at comparable stages of development?

Why then are the advanced countries so ignorant of their own historical development? Is it because of the natural tendency for people to interpret history from the viewpoint of their current intellectual and political agenda, which can often obscure the historical perspective? Or is it because, as it has happened repeatedly, countries have vested interests in imposing policies and institutions which they themselves had not used during their own development, but which are beneficial for them once they have reached the technological frontier? In short, are the developed countries trying to 'kick away the ladder' by insisting that developing countries adopt policies and institutions that were *not* the ones that they had used in order to develop?

The discussion in this book proposes that this is indeed what they are doing. I do accept that this 'ladder-kicking' may be done out of genuine (if misinformed) goodwill. Some of those NDC policymakers and scholars who make the recommendations may be genuinely misinformed: thinking that their own countries developed through free trade and other *laissez-faire* policies, they want developing countries to benefit from these same policies. However, this makes it no less harmful for developing countries. Indeed, it may be even more dangerous than 'ladder-kicking' based on naked national interests, as self-righteousness can be a lot more stubborn than self-interest.

Whatever the intention behind the 'ladder-kicking' may be, the fact remains that these allegedly 'good' policies and institutions have not been able to generate the promised growth dynamism in the developing countries during the last two decades or so when they have been strongly promoted by the IDPE. Indeed, in many developing countries growth has simply collapsed.

So what is to be done? While spelling out a detailed agenda for action is beyond the scope of this book, the following points may be made.

To begin with, the historical facts about the developmental experiences of the developed countries should be more widely publicized. This is not only a matter of 'getting history right', but also of allowing the developing countries to make informed choices about the policies and institutions that may be appropriate for them. There should be greater intellectual effort towards a better understanding of the role of policies and institutions – especially the latter – in economic development, by throwing out historical myths and overly abstract theories that are blinding many theoreticians and policymakers.

More specifically, in terms of policies, the 'bad policies' that most NDCs used so effectively when they themselves were developing should at least be allowed, if not actively encouraged, by the developed countries and the IDPE that they control. While it is true that the activist ITT policies can sometimes degenerate into a web of red tape and corruption, this should not mean that therefore such policies should never be used. After all, we do not stop flying aeroplanes because there is a chance that they might crash, or abandon all vaccination programmes because some children may die from allergic reactions.

The upshot of all this is that we need an approach to international development policymaking that is very different from that which is being pursued by the developed countries and the international development policy establishment.

In terms of policies, I would first of all argue for a radical change to the policy-related conditionalities attached to financial assistance from the IMF and the World Bank or from the developed country governments. These conditionalities should be based on the recognition that many of the policies that are considered 'bad' are in fact not so, and that there can be no 'best practice' policy to which everyone should adhere. Second, the WTO rules and other multilateral trade agreements should be rewritten in such a way that a more active use of infant industry promotion tools (e.g., tariffs and subsidies) is allowed.

Institutional improvement should be encouraged, especially given the enormous growth potential that a combination of (truly) good policies and good institutions can bring about. However, this should not be equated with imposing a fixed set of contemporary Anglo-American institutions on all countries. There also need to be more serious attempts, both at the academic and the practical levels, to explore exactly which institutions are necessary or beneficial for what types of countries, given their stages of development and specific economic, political, social and even cultural conditions. Particular care has to be taken not to demand an excessively rapid upgrading of institutions by developing countries, especially given that they already have quite developed institutions when compared to the NDCs at comparable stages of development, and given that establishing and running new institutions is very costly.

Allowing developing countries to adopt policies and institutions that are more suitable to their stages of development and to other conditions they experience will enable them to grow faster, as indeed was the case during the 1960s and 1970s. This will benefit not only the developing countries, but also the developed nations in the long term, as it will increase the trade and investment opportunities available.[17] That the developed countries are not able to see this is the tragedy of our time. To use a classic Chinese adage, they may be 'missing larger, longer-term gains by too eagerly seeking smaller, short-term ones'. It is time to think again about which policies and institutions will help today's developing countries to develop faster; this will in turn bring greater benefits to the developed countries as well.

References

Abramovitz, M, 1986, 'Catching Up, Forging Ahead, and Falling Behind', *Journal of Economic History*, vol. 46, no. 2.

———— 1989, 'Thinking about Growth', in *Thinking About Growth*, Cambridge, Cambridge University Press.

Agarwala, A N and Singh, S P, 1958, *The Economics of Underdevelopment*, Delhi, Oxford University Press.

Akyuz, Y, Chang, H J and Kozul-Wright, R, 1998, 'New Perspectives on East Asian Development', *Journal of Development Studies*, vol. 34, no. 6.

Allen, G C, 1981, *A Short Economics History of Modern Japan*, 4th edition, London and Basingstoke, Macmillan.

Amsden, A, 1989, *Asia's Next Giant*, New York, Oxford University Press.

———— 2000, 'Industrialisation under New WTO Law', a paper presented at the UNCTAD X meeting, 12–19 February 2000, Bangkok, Thailand.

———— 2001, *The Rise of 'The Rest' – Challenges to the West from Late-Industrialising Economies*, Oxford, Oxford University Press.

Amsden, A and Singh, A, 1994, 'The Optimal Degree of Competition and Dynamic Efficiency in Japan and Korea', *European Economic Review*, vol. 38, nos. 3, 4.

Amsler, C, Bartlett, R and Bolton, C, 1981, 'Thoughts of Some British Economists on Early Limited Liability and Corporate Legislation', *History of Political Economy*, vol. 13, no. 4.

Anderson, E and Anderson, P, 1978, 'Bureaucratic Institutionalisation in 19th Century Europe', in A Heidenheimer et al., 1978, eds., *Political Corruption: A Handbook*, New Brunswick, Transaction Publishers.

Armstrong, J, 1973, *The European Administrative Elite*, Princeton, Princeton University Press.

Armstrong, P, Glyn, A and Harrison, J, 1991, *Capitalism since 1945*, Oxford, Blackwell.

Aron, J, 2000, Growth and Institutions: A Review of the Evidence, *The World Bank Research Observer*, vol. 15, no. 1.

Atack, J and Passell, P, 1994, *A New Economic View of American History*, 2nd ed., New York, Norton.

Baack, B and Ray, E, 1985, 'Special Interests and the Adoption of the Income Tax in the United States', *Journal of Economic History*, vol. 45, no. 3.

Bairoch, P, 1993, *Economics and World History – Myths and Paradoxes*, Brighton, Wheatsheaf.

Balabkins, N, 1988, *Not by Theory Alone . . .: The Economics of Gustav von Schmoller and Its Legacy to America*, Berlin, Duncker and Humblot.

Banner, S, 1998, *Anglo-American Securities Regulation: Cultural and Political Roots, 1690–1860*, Cambridge, Cambridge University Press.

Bardhan, P, 1993, 'Symposium on Democracy and Development, *Journal of Economic Perspectives*, vol. 7, no. 3.

Basu, K, 1999a, 'Child Labor: Cause, Consequence and Cure with Remarks on International Labor Standards', *Journal of Economic Literature*, vol. 37, no. 3.

———— 1999b, 'International Labor Standards and Child Labor', *Challenge*, September/October 1999, vol. 42, no. 5.

Baudhuin, F, 1946, *Histoire Economique de la Belgique, 1914–39*, vol. 1, 2nd edition, Bruxelles, Etablissements Emile Bruylant.

Baumol, W, Wolff, E and Blackman, S, 1989, *Productivity and American Leadership*, Cambridge, Massachusetts, The MIT Press.

Benson, G, 1978, *Political Corruption in America*, Lexington, Lexington Books.

Berg, M, 1980, *The Machinery Question and the Making of Political Economy, 1815–1848*, Cambridge, Cambridge University Press.

Bhagwati, J, 1985, *Protectionism*, Cambridge, Massachusetts, The MIT Press.

———— 1998, 'The Global Age: From Skeptical South to a Fearful North', in *A Stream of Windows – Unsettling Reflections on Trade, Immigration, and Democracy*, Cambridge, Massachusetts, The MIT Press.

Bhagwati, J, and Hirsch, M, 1998, *The Uruguay Round and Beyond – Essays in Honour of Arthur Dunkel*, Ann Arbor, The University of Michigan Press.

Bils, M, 1984, 'Tariff Protection and Production in the Early US Cotton Textile Industry', *Journal of Economic History*, vol. 44, no. 4.

Biucchi, B, 1973, 'The Industrial Revolution in Switzerland', in C Cipolla, 1973, ed., *The Fontana Economic History of Europe, vol. 4: The Emergence of Industrial Societies – Part Two*, Glasgow, Collins.

Blackbourn, D, 1997, *The Fontana History of Germany, 1780–1918*, London, Fontana Press.

Blanpain, R, 1996, *Labour Law in Belgium*, Rotterdam, Kluwer Law International Publishers.

Blaug, M, 1958, 'The Classical Economists and the Factory Acts: A Re-examination', *Quarterly Journal of Economics*, vol. 72, no. 2.

Bohlin, J, 1999, 'Sweden: The Rise and Fall of the Swedish Model', in J Foreman-Peck and G Federico, eds., *European Industrial Policy – The Twentieth-Century Experience*, Oxford, Oxford University Press.

Bollen, K, 1995, 'Measuring Democracy', *The Encyclopaedia of Democracy*, London, Routledge.

Bonney, R, 1995, *Economic Systems and State Finance*, Oxford, Clarendon Press.

Borit, G, 1966, 'Old Wine Into New Bottles: Abraham Lincoln and the Tariff Reconsidered', *The Historian*, vol. 28, no. 2.

Boxer, C, 1965, *The Dutch Seaborne Empire, 1600–1800*, London, Hutchinson.

Briggs, R, 1998, *Early Modern France 1560–1715*, 2nd ed., Oxford, Oxford University Press.

Brisco, N, 1907, *The Economic Policy of Robert Walpole*, New York, The Columbia University Press.

Brogan, H, 1985, *The Penguin History of the United States of America*, London, Penguin.

Bruck, W, 1962, *Social and Economic History of Germany from William II to Hitler, 1888–1938*, New York, Russell and Russell.

Bruland, K, 1991, ed., *Technology Transfer and Scandinavian Industrialisation*, New York, Berg.

Bury, J, 1964, *Napoleon III and the Second Empire*, London, The English University Presses Ltd.

Cairncross, F and Cairncross, A, 1992, eds., *The Legacy of the Golden Age – The 1960s and Their Economic Consequences*, London, Routledge.

——— 1953, 'The Crédit Mobilier and the Economic Development of Europe', *Journal of Political Economy*, vol. 61, no. 6.

Cameron, R, 1993, *A Concise Economic History of the World*, 2nd ed., Oxford, Oxford University Press.

Carr, R, 1980, *Modern Spain, 1875–1980*, Oxford, Oxford University Press.

Carruthers, B, 2000, 'Institutionalising Creative Destruction: Predictable and Transparent Bankruptcy Law in the Wake of the East Asian Financial Crisis', a paper presented at the UNRISD (United Nations Research Institute for Social Development) conference, 'Neoliberalism and Institutional Reform in East Asia', 12–13 May 2000, Bangkok, Thailand.

Carruthers, B and Halliday, T, 1998, *Rescuing Business – The Making of Corporate Bankruptcy Law in England and the United States*, Oxford, Oxford University Press.

Carson, C, 1991, 'Income Tax', in E Foner and J Garraty, 1991, eds., *The Reader's Companion to American History*, Boston, Houghton Mifflin Company.

Chang, H-J, 1993, 'The Political Economy of Industrial Policy in Korea', *Cambridge Journal of Economics*, vol. 17, no. 2.

——— 1994, *The Political Economy of Industrial Policy*, London, Macmillan Press.

——— 1997, 'Luxury Consumption and Economic Development', a report prepared for UNCTAD, *Trade and Development Report, 1997*.

——— 1998a, 'Globalisation, Transnational Corporations, and Economic Development', in D Baker, G Epstein, and R Pollin, 1998, eds., *Globalisation and Progressive Economic Policy*, Cambridge, Cambridge University Press.

———— 1998b, Korea – The Misunderstood Crisis, *World Development*, vol. 26, no. 8.

———— 2000, 'The Hazard of Moral Hazard – Untangling the Asian Crisis', *World Development*, vol. 28, no. 4.

———— 2001a, 'Intellectual Property Rights and Economic Development – Historical Lessons and Emerging Issues', *Journal of Human Development*, vol. 2, no. 2.

———— 2001b. 'Rethinking East Asian Industrial Policy – Past Records and Future Prospects', in P-K Wong and C-Y Ng, eds., *Industrial Policy, Innovation and Economic Growth: The Experience of Japan and the Asian NIEs*, Singapore, Singapore University Press.

———— forthcoming (2002), 'Breaking the Mould – An Institutionalist Political Economy Alternative to the Neo-Liberal Theory of the Market and the State', *Cambridge Journal of Economics,* vol. 26, no. 5.

Chang, H-J and Cheema, A, 2002, 'Economic, Political and Institutional Conditions for Effective Technology Policy in Developing Countries', *Journal of Economic Innovation and New Technology.*

Chang, H-J, and Kozul-Wright, R, 1994, 'Organising Development: Comparing the National Systems of Entrepreneurship in Sweden and South Korea', *Journal of Development Studies*, vol. 30, no. 4.

Chang, H-J, Park, H-J and Yoo, C G, 1998, 'Interpreting the Korean Crisis: Financial Liberalisation, Industrial Policy, and Corporate', *Cambridge Journal of Economics*, vol. 22, no. 6.

Chang, H-J and Rowthorn, B, 1995, eds., *The Role of the State in Economic Change*, Oxford, Oxford University Press.

Chang, H-J and Singh A, 1993, 'Public Enterprises in Developing Countries and Economic Efficiency – A Critical Examination of Analytical, Empirical, and Policy Issues', *UNCTAD Review*, no. 4.

Clark, M, 1996, *Modern Italy, 1871–1995*, 2nd ed., London and New York, Longman.

Clarke, P, 1999, 'Joseph Chamberlain: The First Modern Politician', in *A Question of Leadership – From Gladstone to Blair*, London, Penguin Books.

Cochran, T and Miller, W, 1942, *The Age of Enterprise: A Social History of Industrial America*, New York, The Macmillan Company.

Cohen, S, 1977, *Modern Capitalist Planning: The French Model*, 2nd edition, Berkeley, University of California Press.

Coleman, P, 1974, *Debtors and Creditors in America*, Madison, State Historical Society of Wisconsin.

Conkin, P, 1980, *Prophets of Prosperity: America's First Political Economists*, Bloomington, Indiana University Press.

Corden, M, 1974, *Trade Policy and Economic Welfare*, Oxford, Oxford University Press.

Cornish, W, 1979, 'Legal Control over Cartels and Monopolisation, 1880–1914: A

Comparison', in N Horn and J Kocka, 1979, eds., *Law and the Formation of Big Enterprises in the 19th and the Early 20th Centuries*, Göttingen, Vandenhoeck and Ruprecht.

Cottrell, P, 1980, *Industrial Finance, 1830–1914*, London, Methuen.

Cox, A, 1986, *State, Finance, and Industry in Comparative Perspective*, Brighton, Wheatsheaf Books.

Crafts, N, 2000, 'Institutional Quality and European Development before and after the Industrial Revolution', a paper prepared for World Bank Summer Research Workshop on Market Institutions, 17–19 July 2000, Washington, DC.

Crouzet, F, 1967, 'England and France in the 18th Century: A Comparative Analysis of Two Economic Growths', as reprinted in P K O'Brien, 1994, ed., *The Industrial Revolution in Europe, vol. 2*, Oxford, Blackwells.

Dahl, B, 1981, 'Antitrust, Unfair Competition, Marketing Practices, and Consumer Law', in H Gammeltoft-Hansen, B Gomard and A Phillips, 1981, eds., *Danish Law: A General Survey*, Copenhagen, GEC Gads Publishing House.

Daunton, M, 1998, *Progress and Poverty*, Oxford, Oxford University Press.

Davids, K, 1995, 'Openness or Secrecy? – Industrial Espionage in the Dutch Republic', *The Journal of European Economic History*, vol. 24, no. 2.

Davies, N, 1999, *The Isles – A History*, London and Basingstoke, Macmillan.

Davis, R, 1966, 'The Rise of Protection in England, 1689–1786', *Economic History Review*, vol. 19, no. 2.

De Clercq, W, 1998, 'The End of History for Free Trade?', in J Bhagwati and M Hirsch, 1998, eds., *The Uruguay Round and Beyond – Essays in Honour of Arthur Dunkel*, Ann Arbor, The University of Michigan Press.

De Soto, H, 2000, *The Mystery of Capital*, London, Bantam Books.

De Vries, J, 1984, 'The Decline and Rise of the Dutch Economy, 1675–1900', *Research in Economic History*, Supplement 3.

De Vries, J and Van der Woude, A, 1997, *The First Modern Economy – Success, Failure, and Perseverance of the Dutch Economy, 1500–1815*, Cambridge, Cambridge University Press.

Deane, P, 1979, *The First Industrial Revolution*, 2nd ed., Cambridge, Cambridge University Press.

Dechesne, L, 1932, *Histoire Economique et Sociale de la Belgique depuis les Origines jusqu'en 1914*, Paris, Librairie du Recueil Sirey.

Defoe, D, 1728, *A Plan of the English Commerce*, published by C Rivington: repr. Basil Blackwell, Oxford, 1928.

Dhondt, J and Bruwier, M, 1973, 'The Low Countries' in C Cipolla, 1973, ed., *The Fontana Economic History of Europe, vol. 4: The Emergence of Industrial Societies – Part One*, Glasgow, Collins.

di John, J and Putzel, J, 2000, 'State Capacity Building, Taxation, and Resource Mobilisation in Historical Perspective', a paper presented at the conference, 'New Institutional Economics, Institutional Reform, and Poverty Reduction',

7–8 September 2000, Development Studies Institute, London School of Economics and Political Science.

Doi, T, 1980, *The Intellectual Property Law of Japan*, The Netherlands, Sijthoff and Noordhoff.

Dore, R, 1986, *Flexible Rigidities: Industrial Policy and Structural Adjustment in the Japanese Economy 1970–80*, London, The Athlone Press.

——— 2000, *Stock Market Capitalism: Welfare Capitalism – Japan and Germany versus the Anglo-Saxons*, Oxford, Oxford University Press.

Dorfman, J, 1955, 'The Role of the German Historical School in American Economic Thought', *American Economic Review*, vol. 45, no. 1.

Dorfman, J and Tugwell, R, 1960, *Early American Policy – Six Columbia Contributors*, New York, Columbia University Press.

Dormois, J-P, 1999, 'France: The Idiosyncrasies of *Volontarisme*', in J Foreman-Peck and G Federico, 1999, eds., *European Industrial Policy – The Twentieth-Century Experience*, Oxford, Oxford University Press.

Dorwart, R, 1953, *The Administrative Reforms of Frederick William I of Prussia*, Cambridge, MA Harvard University Press.

Duffy, I, 1985, *Bankruptcy and Insolvency in London during the Industrial Revolution*, New York, Garland Publishing.

Edquist, C and Lundvall, B-A, 1993, 'Comparing the Danish and Swedish Systems of Innovation', in R Nelson, 1993, ed., *National Innovation Systems*, New York, Oxford University Press.

Edwards, J, 1981, *Company Legislation and Changing Patterns of Disclosure in British Company Accounts, 1900–1940*, London, Institute of Chartered Accountants in England and Wales.

Elections since 1945, London, Longman.

Elkins, S and McKitrick, E, 1993, *The Age of Federalism*, New York and Oxford, Oxford University Press.

Elton, G, 1997, *England Under the Tudors*, London, The Folio Society.

Engerman, S, 2001, 'The History and Political Economy of International Labour Standards', mimeo., Department of Economics, University of Rochester.

Engerman, S and Sokoloff, K, 2000, 'Technology and Industrialisation, 1790–1914', in S Engerman and R Gallman, 2000, eds., *The Cambridge Economic History of the United States, vol. 2: The Long Nineteenth Century*, Cambridge, Cambridge University Press.

Evans, P, 1995, *Embedded Autonomy – States and Industrial Transformation*, Princeton, Princeton University Press.

Falkus, M, 1968, ed., *Readings in the History of Economic Growth – A Study of Successful and Promising Beginnings, of Special Relevance for Students in Underdeveloped Countries*, Nairobi, Oxford University Press.

Fei, J and Ranis, G, 1969, 'Economic Development in Historical Perspective', *American Economic Review*, vol. 59, no. 2.

Feuchtwanger, E, 1970, *Prussia: Myth and Reality – The Role of Prussia in German History*, London, Oswald Wolff.

Fielden, K, 1969, 'The Rise and Fall of Free Trade' in C Bartlett, 1969, ed., *Britain Pre-eminent: Studies in British World Influence in the Nineteenth Century*, London, Macmillan.

Finer, S, 1989, 'Patronage and Public Service in Britain and America' in A Heidenheimer et al., 1989, eds., *Political Corruption: A Handbook*, New Brunswick, Transaction Publishers.

Fohlen, C, 1973, 'France' in C Cipolla, 1973, ed., *The Fontana Economic History of Europe, vol. 4: The Emergence of Industrial Societies-Part One*, Glasgow, Collins.

Foner, E, 1998, *The Story of American Freedom*, New York, WW Norton and Company.

Fransman, M and King, K, 1984, *Technological Capability in the Third World*, London and Basingstoke, Macmillan.

Fraysse, O, 1994, *Lincoln, Land, and Labour*, trans. S Neely from the original French edition published in 1988 by Paris, Publications de la Sorbonne, Urbana and Chicago, University of Illinois Press.

Freeman, C, 1989, 'New Technology and Catching-Up', *European Journal of Development Research*, vol. 1, no. 1.

Gallagher, J and Robinson, R, 1953, 'The Imperialism of Free Trade', *Economic History Review*, vol. 6, no. 1.

Garraty, J and Carnes, M, 2000, *The American Nation – A History of the United States*, 10th edition, New York, Addison Wesley Longman.

Geisst, C, 1997, *Wall Street: A History*, Oxford, Oxford University Press.

Gerber, D, 1998, *Law and Competition in the 20th Century Europe*, Oxford, Clarendon Press.

Gerschenkron, A, 1962, *Economic Backwardness in Historical Perspective*, Cambridge, MA, Harvard University Press.

Gillman, M and Eade, T, 1995, The Development of the Corporation in England, with emphasis on Limited Liability', *International Journal of Social Economics*, vol. 22, no. 4.

Glasgow, G, 1999, 'The Election of County Coroners in England and Wales, c. 1800–1888', *Legal History*, vol. 20, no. 3.

Gothelf, R, 2000, 'Frederick William I and the Beginning of Prussian Absolutism, 1713–1740 (chapter 2)', in P Dwyer, 2000, ed., *The Rise of Prussia, 1700–1830*, Harlow, Longman.

Grabel, I, 2000, 'The Political Economy of 'Policy Credibility': The New-classical Macroeconomics and the Remaking of Emerging Economies', *Cambridge Journal of Economics*, vol. 24, no. 1.

Gunn, S, 1995, *Early Tudor Government, 1485–1558*, Basingstoke, Macmillan.

Gustavson, C, 1986, *The Small Giant: Sweden Enters the Industrial Era*, Athens, OH, Ohio State University Press.

Hadenius, S, Nilsson, T and Aselius, G, 1996, *Sveriges Historia*, Stockholm, Bonnier Alba.

Hall, P, 1986, *Governing the Economy – The Politics of State Intervention in Britain and France*, Cambridge, Polity Press.

Hammond, J and Hammond, B, 1995, *The Town Labourer*, Oxford, Alan Sutton Publishing.

Hannah, L, 1979, 'Mergers, Cartels, and Cartelisation: Legal Factors in the US and European Experience', in N Horn and J Kocka, 1979, eds., *Law and the Formation of Big Enterprises in the 19th and the Early 20th Centuries*, Göttingen, Vandenhoeck and Ruprecht.

Harnetty, P, 1972, *Imperialism and Free Trade: Lancashire and India in the Mid-Nineteenth Century*, Vancouver, University of British Columbia Press.

Heckscher, E, 1954, *An Economic History of Sweden*, Cambridge, MA, Harvard University Press.

Helleiner, E, 2001, 'The South Side of Embedded Liberalism: The Politics of Postwar Monetary Policy in the Third World', mimeo., Department of Political Science, Trent University, Canada.

Henderson, W, 1963, *Studies in the Economic Policy of Frederick the Great*, London, Frank Cass and Co., Ltd.

——— 1972, *Britain and Industrial Europe, 1750–1870*, 3rd edition, Leicester, Leicester University Press.

——— 1983, *Friedrich List – Economist and Visionary, 1789–1846*, London, Frank Cass.

Hens, L and Solar, P, 1999, 'Belgium: Liberalism by Default in Model', in J Foreman-Peck and G Federico, 1999, eds., *European Industrial Policy – The Twentieth-Century Experience*, Oxford, Oxford University Press.

Hirschman, A, 1958, *The Strategy of Economic Development*, New Haven, Yale University Press.

Hobsbawm, E, 1999, *Industry and Empire*, new edition, London, Penguin Books.

Hodgson, G, 2001, *How Economics Forgot History: The Problem of Historical Specificity in Social Science*, London, Routledge.

Hodne, F, 1981, *Norge Økonomiske Historie, 1815–1970*, Oslo, JW Cappelen Forlag.

Hood, C, 1995, 'Emerging Issues in Public Administration', *Public Administration*, vol. 73, Spring 1995.

——— 1998, *The Art of the State: Culture, Rhetoric and Public Management*, Oxford, Clarendon Press.

Hoppit, J, 1987, *Risk and Failure in English Business, 1700–1800*, Cambridge, Cambridge University Press.

Hou, C-M and Gee, S, 1993, 'National Systems Supporting Technical Advance in Industry: The Case of Taiwan', in R Nelson, 1993, ed., *National Innovation Systems*, New York, Oxford University Press.

Howe, J, 1979–80, 'Corruption in British Elections in the Early 20th Century', *Midland History*, vol. V.

Hughes, O, 1994, *Public Management and Administration*, New York, St. Martin's Press.

Hutchison, T, 1988, 'Gustav Schmoller and the Problem of Today', *Journal of Institutional and Theoretical Economics*, vol. 144, no. 3.

Hutton, W, 1995, *The State We're In*, London, Jonathan Cape Ltd.

Irwin, D, 1993, 'Free Trade and Protection in Nineteenth-Century Britain and France Revisited: A Comment on Nye', *Journal of Economic History*, vol. 53, no. 1.

Irwin, D and Temin, P, 2000, 'The Antebellum Tariff on Cotton Textiles Revisited', mimeo., Cambridge, MA, National Bureau of Economic Research.

Johnson, C, 1982, *The MITI and the Japanese Miracle*, Stanford, Stanford University Press.

—— 1984, ed., *The Industrial Policy Debate*, San Francisco, Institute for Contemporary Studies.

Jonker, J, 1997, 'The Alternative Road to Modernity: Banking and Currency, 1814–1914', in M T Hart, J Jonker, J van Zanden, 1997, eds., *A Financial History of The Netherlands*, Cambridge, Cambridge University Press.

Kaplan, A, 1931, *Henry Charles Carey – A Study in American Economic Thought*, Baltimorie, The Johns Hopkins Press.

Kapur, D and Webber, R, 2000, 'Governance-related Conditionalities of the IFIs', G-24 Discussion Paper Series, no. 6, Geneva, UNCTAD.

Kaufmann, D, Kraay, A and Zoido-Lobaton, P, 1999, 'Governance Matters', Policy Research Working Paper, no. 2196, Washington, DC, World Bank.

Kennedy, W, 1987, *Industrial Structure, Capital Markets, and the Origins of British Economic Decline*, Cambridge, Cambridge University Press.

Kent, S, 1939, *Electoral Procedure under Louis Philippe*, New Haven, Yale University Press.

Kim, L, 1993, 'National System of Industrial Innovation: Dynamics of Capability Building in Korea', in R Nelson, 1993, ed., *National Innovation Systems*, New York, Oxford University Press.

Kindleberger, C, 1958, *Economic Development*, New York, McGraw-Hill.

—— 1964, *Economic Growth in France and Britain, 1851–1950*, Cambridge, MA, Harvard University Press.

—— 1975, 'The Rise of Free Trade in Western Europe, 1820–1875', *Journal of Economic History*, vol. 35, no. 1.

—— 1978, 'Germany's Overtaking of England, 1806 to 1914', in *Economic Response: Comparative Studies in Trade, Finance, and Growth*, Cambridge, MA, Harvard University Press.

—— 1984, *A Financial History of Western Europe*, Oxford, Oxford University Press.

—— 1990a, 'Commercial Policy between the Wars', in *Historical Economics*, Hemel Hempstead, Harvester Wheatsheaf.

—— 1990b, 'America in Decline? – Possible Parallels and Consequences', in *Historical Economics*, Hemel Hempstead, Harvester Wheatsheaf.

———— 1996, *World Economic Primacy: 1500 to 1990*, New York, Oxford University Press.

Korpi, W, 1983, *The Democratic Class Struggle*, London, Routledge and Kegan Paul.

Kossmann, E, 1978, *The Low Countries, 1780—1940*, Oxford, Clarendon Press.

Kozul-Wright, R, 1995, 'The Myth of Anglo-Saxon Capitalism: Reconstructing the History of the American State', in H-J Chang and R Rowthorn, 1995, eds., *Role of the State in Economic Change*, Oxford, Oxford University Press.

Kravis, I, 1970, 'Trade as a Handmaiden of Growth: Similarities between the Nineteenth and Twentieth Centuries', *Economic Journal*, vol. 80, no. 6.

Kruezer, M, 1996, 'Democratisation and Changing Methods of Electoral Corruption in France from 1815 to 1914', in W Little and E Posada-Carbo, 1996, ed., *Political Corruption in Europe and Latin America*, London and Basingstoke, Macmillan.

Kruman, M, 1991, 'Suffrage', in E Foner and J Garraty, 1991, eds., *The Reader's Companion to American History*, Boston, Houghton Mifflin Company.

Kuisel, R, 1981, *Capitalism and the State in Modern France*, Cambridge, Cambridge University Press.

Kuznets, S, 1965, *Economic Growth and Structure*, London, Heinemann Educational Books.

Kuznets, S, 1973, *Population, Capital, and Growth – Selected Essays*, London, Heinemann Educational Books.

Lall, S, 1992, 'Technological Capabilities and Industrialisation', *World Development*, vol. 20, no. 2.

———— 1994, 'Does the Bell Toll for Industrial Policy?', *World Development*, vol. 22, no. 4.

Lall, S and Teubal, M, 1998, 'Market stimulating Technology Policies in Developing Countries: A Framework with Examples from East Asia', *World Development*, vol. 26, no. 8.

Lamoreaux, N, 1996, *Insider Lending*, Cambridge, Cambridge University Press.

Landes, D, 1965, 'Japan and Europe: Contrasts in Industrialistion', in W Lockwood, 1965, ed., *The State and Economic Enterprise in Japan*, Princeton, Princeton University Press.

———— 1969, *The Unbound Prometheus – Technological Change and Industrial Development in Western Europe from 1750 to the Present*, Cambridge, Cambridge University Press.

———— 1998, *The Wealth and Poverty of Nations*, New York, WW Norton and Company.

Larsson, M, 1993, *En Svensk Ekonomisk Historia, 1850–1985*, 2nd edition, Stockholm, SNS Fölag.

Lee, J, 1978, 'Labour in German Industrialisation', in P Mathias and M Postan, 1978, eds., *Cambridge Economic History of Europe, vol. II*, Cambridge, Cambridge University Press.

Lewis, WA, 1955, *Theory of Economic Growth*, London, George Allen and Unwin Ltd.

—— 1980, 'The Slowing Down of the Engine of Growth', *American Economic Review*, vol. 70, no. 4.

Linz, J, 1995, 'Spain', *The Encyclopaedia of Democracy*, London, Routledge.

Lipsey, R, 2000, 'US Foreign Trade and the Balance of Payments', in S Engerman and R Gallman, 2000, eds., *The Cambridge Economic History of the United States, vol. 2: The Long Nineteenth Century*, Cambridge, Cambridge University Press.

List, F, 1885, *The National System of Political Economy*, translated from the original German edition published in 1841 by Sampson Lloyd, London, Longmans, Green, and Company.

Little, I, Scitovsky, T and Scott, M, 1970, *Industry in Trade in Some Developing Countries – A Comparative Study*, London, Oxford University Press.

LO (Landsorganisationen i Sverige), 1963, *Economic Expansion and Structural Change*, ed. and trans. T Johnston, London, George Allen and Unwin.

Luedde-Neurath, R, 1986, *Import Controls and Export-Oriented Development; A Reassessment of the South Korean Case*, Boulder and London, Westview Press.

Luthin, R, 1944, Abraham Lincoln and the Tariff, *The American Historical Review*, vol. 49, no. 4.

Machlup, F and Penrose, E, 1950, 'The Patent Controversy in the Nineteenth Century, *Journal of Economic History*, vol. 10, no. 1.

Maddison, A, 1989, *The World Economy in the 20th Century*, Paris, OECD.

—— 1995, *Monitoring the World Economy*, Paris, OECD.

Magone, J, 1997, *European Portugal: The Difficult Road to Sustainable Democracy*, London, Macmillan Press.

Marglin, S and Schor, J, 1990, eds., *The Golden Age of Capitalism*, Oxford, Oxford University Press.

Marriner, S, 1980, 'English Bankruptcy Records and Statistics before 1850', *Economic History Review*, vol. 33, no. 3.

Marx, K, 1976, *Capital, vol. 1*, London, Penguin Books.

Mata, E, 1987, *Pobreza y Asistencia Social en España, siglos XVI al XX: Aproximación Histórica*, Valladolid, Secretriado de Publicaciones Universidad de Valladolid.

Mata, E and Valerio, N, 1994, *Historia Economica de Portugal: Uma Perspectiva Global*, Lisbon, Editorial Presenca.

Mathias, P, 1969, *The First Industrial Nation*, London, Methuen and Co.

McCusker, J, 1996, 'British Mercantilist Policies and the American Colonies', in S Engerman and R Gallman, 1996, eds., *The Cambridge Economic History of the United States, vol. 1: The Colonial Era*, Cambridge, Cambridge University Press.

McLeod, C, 1988, *Inventing the Industrial Revolution: the English Patent System, 1660–1800*, Cambridge, Cambridge University Press.

McPherson, W J, 1987, *The Economic Development of Japan, 1868–1941*, London and Basingstoke, Macmillan Press (Cambridge University Press edition, 1995).

Mercer, H, 1995, *Constructing a Competitive Order: The Hidden History of British Antitrust Policy*, Cambridge, Cambridge University Press.

Milward, A and Saul, S, 1979, *The Economic Development of Continental Europe, 1780–1870*, 2nd edition, London, George Allen and Unwin.

—— 1977, *The Development of the Economies of Continental Europe, 1850–1914*, London, George Allen and Unwin.

Montgomery, G, 1939, *The Rise of Modern Industry in Sweden*, London, P S King and Son Ltd.

Mørch, S, 1982, *Den Ny Danmarkshistorie: 1880–1960*, Copenhagen, Gyldendal.

Morishima, M, 1982, *Why Has Japan Succeeded?*, Cambridge, Cambridge University Press.

Mowery, D and Rosenberg, N, 1993, 'The US National Innovation System', in R Nelson, 1993, ed., *National Innovation Systems – A Comparative Analysis*, Oxford, Oxford University Press.

Munn, C, 1981, 'Scottish Provincial Banking Companies: An Assessment', *Business History*, vol. 23.

Musson, A, 1978, *The Growth of British Industry*, London, BT Batsford Ltd..

National Law Centre for Inter-American Free Trade, 1997, 'Strong Intellectual Property Protection Benefits the Developing Countries', http://www.natlaw.com/pubs/spmxip11.htm.

Nerbørvik, J, 1986, *Norsk Historie, 1870–1905: Frå jordbrukssamfunn mot organisasjonssamfunn*, Oslo, Det Norske Samlaget.

Newton, M and Donaghy, P, 1997, *Institutions of Modern Spain: A Political and Economic Guide*, Cambridge, Cambridge University Press.

North, D, 1965, 'Industrialisation in the United States', in H Habakkuk and M Postan, 1965, eds., *The Cambridge Economic History of Europe, vol. VI. The Industrial Revolutions and After: Incomes, Population and Technological Change (II)*, Cambridge, Cambridge University Press.

Nye, J, 1991, 'The Myth of Free-Trade Britain and Fortress France: Tariffs and Trade in the Nineteenth Century', *Journal of Economic History*, vol. 51. no. 1.

—— 1993, 'Reply to Irwin on Free Trade', *Journal of Economic History*, vol. 53, no. 1.

O'Leary, C, 1962, *The Elimination of Corrupt Practices in British Elections, 1868–1911*, Oxford, Clarendon Press.

O'Rourke, K, 2000, 'Tariffs and Growth in the Late 19th Century', *Economic Journal*, vol. 110, no. 4.

O'Rourke, K and Williamson, J, 1999, *Globalisation and History: The Evolution of Nineteenth-Century Atlantic Economy*, Cambridge, MA, The MIT Press.

Ocampo, J 2001, 'Rethinking the Development Agenda', a paper presented at the American Economic Association annual meeting, 5–7 January 2001, New Orleans, USA.

Ohnesorge, J. 2000, 'Asia's Legal Systems in the Wake of the Financial Crisis: Can the Rule of Law Carry any of the Weight?', a paper presented at the UNRISD (United Nations Research Institute for Social Development) conference on 'Neoliberalism and Institutional Reform in East Asia', 12–14 May, 2000, Bangkok.

Owen, G, 1966, *Industry in the USA*, London, Penguin Books.

Palacio, V, 1988, *Manual de Historia de España 4: Edad Contemporánea I (1808–1898)*, 2nd edition, Madrid, Espasa Calpe.

Patel, S, 1989, 'Intellectual Property Rights in the Uruguay Round – A Disaster for the South?', *Economic and Political Weekly*, 6 May 1989.

Pekkarinen, J, Pohjola, M and Rowthorn, B, 1992, eds., *Learning from Corporatist Experiences*, Oxford, Clarendon Press.

Pennington, R, 1990, *The Law of the Investment Markets*, Oxford, Basil Blackwell.

Penrose, E, 1951, *The Economics of the International Patent System*, Baltimore, The Johns Hopkins Press.

Perelman, M, 2000, *The Invention of Capitalism – Classical Political Economy and the Secret History of Primitive Accumulation*, Durham, NC Duke University Press.

Pérez, S, 1997, *Banking on Privilege: The Politics of Spanish Financial Reform*, Ithaca, NY, Cornell University Press.

Pierson, C, 1998, *Beyond the Welfare State – The New Political Economy of Welfare*, 2nd edition, Cambridge, Polity Press.

Plessis A, 1994, 'The History of Banks in France', in M Pohl, ed., *Handbook of the History of European Banks*, Aldershot, Edward Elgar.

Polanyi, K, 1957 (1944), *The Great Transformation*, Boston, Beacon Press.

Pomeranz, K, 2000, *The Great Divergence – China, Europe and the Making of the Modern Western Europe*, Princeton, Princeton University Press.

Pontusson, J, 1992, *The Limits of Social Democracy – Investment Politics in Sweden*, Ithaca, NY, Cornell University Press.

Pryser, T, 1985, *Norsk Historie, 1800–1870: Frå standssamfunn mot dlassesamfunn*, Oslo, Det Norske Samlaget.

Przeworkski, A and Limongi, F, 1993, 'Political Regimes and Economic Growth', *Journal of Economic Perspectives*, vol. 7, no. 3.

Ramsay, GD, 1982, *The English Woollen Industry, 1500–1750*, London and Basingstoke, Macmillan.

Rauch, J and Evans, P, 2000, 'Bureaucratic Structure and Bureaucratic Performance in Less Developed Countries', *Journal of Public Economics*, vol. 75, no. 1.

Reinert, E, 1995, 'Competitiveness and Its Predecessors – a 500-year Cross-national Perspective', *Structural Change and Economic Dynamics*, vol. 6, no. 1.

———— 1996, 'Diminishing Returns and Economic Sustainability: The Dilemma of Resource-based Economies under a Free Trade Regime', in H

Stein et al., eds., *International Trade Regulation, National Development Strategies and the Environment – Towards Sustainable Development?*, Centre for Development and the Environment, University of Oslo.

——— 1998, 'Raw Materials in the History of Economic Policy – Or why List (the protectionist) and Cobden (the free trader) both agreed on free trade in corn', in G Cook, 1998, ed., *The Economics and Politics of International Trade – Freedom and Trade, vol. 2*, London, Routledge.

Rodrik, D, 1999, 'Institutions for High-Quality Growth: What They Are and How to Acquire Them', a paper prepared for the IMF conference on Second-Generation Reform, Washington, DC, 8–9 November 1999.

Rosenberg, N and Birdzell, L, 1986, *How the West Grew Rich*, London, IB Tauris and Co. Ltd.

Rosenstein-Rodan, P, 1943, 'Problems of Industrialisation of Eastern and South-Eastern Europe', *Economic Journal*, vol. 53, no. 3.

Rostow, WW, 1960, *The Stages of Economic Growth*, Cambridge, Cambridge University Press.

Rueschemeyer, D, Stephens, E and Stephens, J, 1992, *Capitalist Development and Democracy*, Cambridge, Polity Press.

Ruggiero, R, 1998, 'Whither the Trade System Next?', in J Bhagwati and M Hirsch, 1998 eds., *The Uruguay Round and Beyond – Essays in Honour of Arthur Dunkel*, Ann Arbor, The University of Michigan Press.

Sachs, J and Warner, A, 1995, 'Economic Reform and the Process of Global Integration', *Brookings Papers on Economic Activity*, 1995, no. 1.

Samuelsson, K, 1968, *From Great Power to Welfare State*, London, Allen and Unwin.

Schiff, E, 1971, *Industrialisation without National Patents – the Netherlands, 1869–1912 and Switzerland, 1850–1907*, Princeton, Princeton University Press.

Searle, G, 1987, *Corruption in British Politics, 1895–1930*, Oxford, Clarendon Press.

Semmel, B, 1970, *The Rise of Free Trade Imperialism: Classical Political Economy, the Empire of Free Trade, and Imperialism, 1750–1850*, Cambridge, Cambridge University Press.

Senghaas, D, 1985, *The European Experience – A Historical Critique of Development Theory*, translated from the original German edition published in 1982 by KHK Kimmig, Leamington Spa, Berg Publishers.

Serrao, J, 1979, *Historia de Portugal, vol. 9*, Lisbon, Editorial VERBO.

Shafaeddin, M, 2000, 'What did Frederick List Actually Say? – Some Clarifications on the Infant Industry Argument', Discussion Paper, no. 149, Geneva, UNCTAD.

Shapiro, H and Taylor, L, 1990, 'The State and Industrial Strategy', *World Development*, vol. 18, no. 6.

Shin, K, 1994, *An International Comparison of Competition Policy: USA, Japan, and Germany* (in Korean), Seoul, Korea Development Institute.

Shonfield, A, 1965, *Modern Capitalism*, Oxford, Oxford University Press.

Silbey, J, 1995, 'United States of America', *The Encyclopaedia of Democracy*, London, Routledge.

Singh, A, 1994, "Openness' and the 'Market-friendly' Approach to Development: Learning the Right Lessons from Development Experience', *World Development*, vol. 22, no. 12.

———— 1997, 'Financial Liberalisation, the Stockmarket and Economic Development', *Economic Journal*, vol. 107, no. 442.

Singh, A and Dhumale, R, 1999, 'Competition Policy, Development, and Developing Countries', T.R.A.D.E. Working Paper, no. 7, Geneva, South Centre.

Smith, A, 1937 [1776], *An Inquiry into the Nature and Causes of the Wealth of Nations*, edited with an introduction, notes, marginal summary and an enlarged index by Edwin Cannan, with an introduction by Max Lerner, originally published in 1776, New York, Random House.

Smith, T, 1955, *Political Change and Industrial Development in Japan: Government Enterprise, 1868–1880*, Stanford, Stanford University Press.

Sokoloff, K and Kahn, BZ, 2000, 'Intellectual Property Institutions in the United States: Early Development and Comparative Perspective', a paper prepared for World Bank Summer Research Workshop on Market Institutions, 17–19 July 2000, Washington, DC.

Soto, A, 1989, *El Trabajo Industrial en la España Contemporánea, 1874–1936*, Barcelona, Editorial Anthropos.

Spiegel, H, 1971, *The Growth of Economic Thought*, Englewood Cliffs, NJ, Prentice Hall.

Stiglitz, J, 1996, 'Some Lessons from the East Asian Miracle', *World Bank Research Observer*, August, 1996.

———— 2001a, 'More Instruments and Broader Goals: Moving Toward the Post-Washington Consensus', in H-J Chang, 2001, ed., *The Rebel Within: Joseph Stiglitz at the World Bank*, London, Anthem Press.

———— 2001b, 'Whither Reform? – Ten Years of the Transition', in H-J Chang, 2001, ed., *The Rebel Within: Joseph Stiglitz at the World Bank*, London, Anthem Press.

Supple, B, 1963, ed., *The Experience of Economic Growth*, New York, Random House.

'T Hart, M, 1997, 'The Merits of a Financial Revolution: Public Finance, 1550–1700', in M 'T Hart, J Jonker, J van Zanden, 1997, eds., *A Financial History of The Netherlands*, Cambridge, Cambridge University Press.

'T Hart, M, Jonker, J and van Zanden, J, 1997, 'Introduction', in M 'T Hart, J Jonker, J van Zanden, 1997, eds., *A Financial History of The Netherlands*, Cambridge, Cambridge University Press.

Taussig, F, 1892, *The Tariff History of the United States*, New York, G Putnam.

Taylor, A J P, 1955, *Bismarck – The Man and the Statesman*, London, Penguin Books.

Therborn, G, 1977, 'The Rule of Capital and the Rise of Democracy', *New Left Review*, no. 103, May–June.

Thompson, G, 1989, ed., *Industrial Policy: US and UK Debates*, London, Routledge.

Tilly, R, 1991, 'Germany', in R Sylla and G Toniolo, eds., *Patterns of European Industrialisation – The Nineteenth Century*, London, Routledge.

———— 1994, 'A Short History of the German Banking System', in M Pohl, 1994, ed., *Handbook of the History of European Banks*, Aldershot, Edward Elgar.

———— 1996, 'German Industrialisation', in M Teich and R Porter, 1996, eds., *The Industrial Revolution in National Context – Europe and the USA*, Cambridge, Cambridge University Press.

Toye, J, 2000, 'Fiscal Crisis and Fiscal Reform in Developing Countries', *Cambridge Journal of Economics*, vol. 24, no. 1.

Trebilcock, C, 1981, *The Industrialisation of the Continental Powers, 1780–1914*, London and New York, Longman.

Tribe, K, 1995, *Strategies of Economic Order: German Economic Discourse, 1750–1959*, Cambridge, Cambridge University Press.

Upham, F, 2000, 'Neoliberalism and the Rule of Law in Developing Societies', a paper presented at the UNRISD (United Nations Research Institute for Social Development) conference on 'Neoliberalism and Institutional Reform in East Asia', 12–14 May 2000, Bangkok.

Van der Wee, H, 1987, 'The Economic Challenge Facing Belgium in the 19th and 20th Centuries', in Van der Wee et al., 1987, eds., *The Economic Development of Modern Europe since 1870*, vol. 8, Cheltenham, Edward Elgar.

———— 1996, 'The Industrial Revolution in Belgium', in M Teich and R Porter, 1996, eds., *The Industrial Revolution in National Context – Europe and the USA*, Cambridge, Cambridge University Press.

Van Zanden, J, 1996, 'Industrialisation in the Netherlands', in M Teich and R Porter, 1996, eds., *The Industrial Revolution in National Context – Europe and the USA*, Cambridge, Cambridge University Press.

———— 1999, 'The Netherlands: The History of an Empty Box', in J Foreman-Peck and G Federico, 1999, eds., *European Industrial Policy: The Twentieth Century Experience*, Oxford, Oxford University Press.

Voltes, P, 1979, *Historia de la Empresarial Española, la Evolución Empresairal dentro de la Economía Española*, Barcelona, Editorial Hispano Europea.

Wade, R, 1990, *Governing the Market*, Princeton, Princeton University Press.

———— 1996, 'Japan, the World Bank, and the Art of Paradigm Maintenance: The *East Asian Miracle* in Political Perspective', *New Left Review*, no. 217, May–June 1996.

Weber, M, 1968 (originally 1904–1911), *Economy and Society*, edited by Gηnter Roth and Claus Wittich, New York, Bedminster Press.

Weisbrot, M, Naiman, R and Kim, J, 2000, 'The Emperor Has No Growth:

Declining Economic Growth Rates in the Era of Globalisation', Briefing Paper, September 2000, Washington, DC, Center for Economic and Policy Research.

Weiss, L and Hobson, J, 1995, *States and Economic Development – A Comparative Historical Analysis*, Cambridge, Polity Press.

Westney, E, 1987, *Imitation and innovation: The Transfer of Western Organizational Patterns to Meiji Japan*, Cambridge, Massachusetts, Harvard University Press.

Westphal, L, 1978, 'The Republic of Korea's Experience with Export-Led Industrial Development', *World Development*, vol. 6, no. 3.

Westphal, L, 1990, 'Industrial Policy in an Export-Propelled Economy: Lessons from South Korea's Experience', *Journal of Economic Perspectives*, vol. 4, no. 3.

Wiarda, H, 1977, *Corporatism and Development: The Portugese Experience*, Amherst, University of Massachusetts Press.

Williams, E, 1896, '*Made in Germany*', London, William Heinemann, the 1973 edition with an introduction by Austen Albu, Brighton, The Harvester Press.

Williamson, J, 1990, 'What Washington Means by Policy Reform', in J Williamson, ed., *Latin American Adjustment: How Much Has Happened?*, Washington, DC, Institute for International Economics.

Wilson, C, 1984, *England's Apprenticeship, 1603–1763*, 2nd ed., London and New York, Longman.

World Bank, 1991, *World Development Report, 1991 – The Development Challenge*, New York, Oxford University Press.

———— 1993, *The East Asian Miracle*, New York, Oxford University Press.

———— 1997, *World Development Report, 1997 – The State in a Changing World*, New York, Oxford University Press.

———— 2001, *World Development Report, 2000/2001 – Attacking Poverty*, New York, Oxford University Press.

———— 2002, *World Development Report, 2001/2002 – Institutions for Markets*, New York, Oxford University Press.

Wright, H, 1955, *Free Trade and Protectionism in the Netherlands, 1816–1830: A Study of the First Benelux*, Cambridge, Cambridge University Press.

You, J and Chang, H-J, 1993, 'The Myth of Free Labour Market in Korea', *Contributions to Political Economy*, vol. 12.

Zysman, J, 1983, *Governments, Markets, and Growth*, Oxford, Martin Robertson.

Notes

Chapter 1. Introduction: How did the Rich
Countries *Really* Become Rich?

1. So in addition to the conventional 'economic conditionalities' attached to multilateral and bilateral financial assistance to developing countries, we now have 'governance-related conditionalities' (see Kapur and Webber 2000).
2. Williamson 1990 is the classic statement of this. For some recent criticisms see Stiglitz 2001a; Ocampo 2001.
3. Bhagwati 1985, p. 22, n. 10.
4. National Law Center for Inter-American Free Trade 1997, p. 1.
5. The book was translated in the USA as early as 1856 (Henderson 1983, p. 214), reflecting the then close intellectual affinity between the USA and Germany as the two centres of 'nationalistic' economics (also see Dorfman 1955; Balabkins 1988; Hodgson 2001). However, its British translation, the version that I have used for this book, did not appear until 1885, reflecting the dominance of free trade doctrine in Britain during the middle of the nineteenth century.
6. They are also interesting for the amazing degree of sophistication in understanding the role of public policy and institutions in economic development. For example, List states: 'However industrious, thrifty, inventive, and intelligent individual citizens might be, they could not make up for the lack of free institutions. History also teaches that individuals derive the greater part of their productive powers from the social institutions and conditions under which they are placed' (p. 107).
7. List 1885, p. 39.
8. He then goes on to argue: 'This policy was pursued with greater or lesser, with speedier or more tardy success, just in proportion as the measures adopted were more or less judiciously adapted to the object in view, and applied and pursued with more or less energy and perseverance' (p. 111).
9. List 1885, pp. 295–6.
10. List 1885, p. 99.
11. Smith 1937 (1776), pp. 347–8.
12. List 1885, pp. 99–100.
13. Polanyi 1957 (1944); Shonfield (1965). It is also found in certain strands in Marxism – for example, in Marx's theory of history rather than in his labour theory of value.
14. Wagner's Law states that there is a natural tendency for the relative size of the government to grow with the development of human society.

15. See Balabkins 1988, chapter 6; Tribe 1995; Hodgson 2001.
16. Marshall, *Principles of Economics*, 8th edition, p. 768; as cited in Hutchison, 1988, p. 529.
17. Balabkins 1988, chapter 6; Hodgson 2001; Dorfman 1955. Balabkins cites a survey conducted in 1906 that shows that half of the Americans who studied social sciences in Europe studied in Germany (1988, p. 95).
18. Balabkins 1988, p. 95; Conkin 1980, p. 311.
19. Balabkins 1988, p. 95; Cochran and Miller 1942, p. 260; Conkin 1980, p. 311; Garraty and Carnes 2000, p. 562.
20. For a selection of the early key works in the field, see Agarwala and Singh 1958.
21. For deployment of these theories, see Lewis 1955; Rostow 1960; Kuznets 1965, idem. 1973.
22. Gerschenkron 1962; Hirschman 1958; Kindleberger 1958.
23. See for example Supple 1963; Falkus 1968.
24. Fei and Ranis 1969.
25. Such as Senghaas 1985; Bairoch 1993; Weiss and Hobson 1995; Amsden 2001. However, the first three of these studies are not as comprehensive as this book. Bairoch, while covering a wider range of countries, mainly focuses on trade policy. Senghass looks at an even wider range of countries, but his discussion of them, except for the Scandinavian nations, is rather brief. Weiss and Hobson cover a wider range of policies – industrial, trade and fiscal – but cover a relatively limited range of countries – Britain, France, Prussia, Japan, Russia, and the USA. The study by Amsden has many spot-on references to the historical experiences of the developed countries, but its main focus is actually on the historical experience of the developing countries.
26. For example, few people will dispute that achieving macroeconomic stability through appropriate budgetary and monetary policies is a pre-condition for development, although I object to defining it narrowly as merely achieving very low rates of inflation (say, below five per cent), as in the current orthodoxy (also see Stiglitz 2001a, pp. 23–5).

Chapter 2. Policies for Economic Development: Industrial, Trade and Technology Policies in Historical Perspective

1. Sachs and Warner 1995 is one of the more balanced and better informed, but ultimately flawed, versions of this. Bhagwati (1985, 1998) offer a less balanced but probably more representative version. Essays by leading international policy makers espousing this view can be found in Bhagwati and Hirsch 1998, a volume of essays compiled in honour of Arthur Dunkel, who oversaw the Uruguay Round (1986–93) during his tenure as the Director-General of the GATT (General Agreement on Tariffs and Trade). The articles by de Clercq and by Ruggiero cited below are from this collection.
2. De Clercq 1998, p. 196.
3. De Clercq 1998, pp. 201–2.
4. This unfortunate link between state interventionism and autocracy, according to this version of the story, was subsequently broken after the end of the Second World War, when the American Occupation Authorities in these countries, realising them to be the root cause of fascism, disbanded the cartels.
5. Sachs and Warner 1995, pp. 11–21.

6. Bhagwati 1998, p. 37.
7. The phrase is taken from Sachs and Warner 1995, p. 3.
8. Sachs and Warner 1995 date this 'golden age' to the period 1850–1914.
9. Ruggiero 1998, p. 131.
10. For classic discussions of catching up, see Abramovitz, 1986, id.. 1989.
11. I put the word 'illegal' in quotation marks, since the 'legality' in this case was in terms of British laws, whose legitimacy may not be (and in practice certainly was not) accepted by other countries.
12. Kindleberger 1996, p. 109.
13. Ramsay 1982, p. 59; Davies 1999, p. 348.
14. Ramsay, 1982, p. 59.
15. This is reminiscent of the policies used by Japan and Korea during the postwar period to control 'luxury consumption', especially concerning imported luxury goods. On this, see Chang 1997.
16. Davies 1999, p. 349; also see Davis 1966, p. 281.
17. I must thank Erik Reinert for drawing my attention to this book both through his work (e.g., Reinert 1996) and personally.
18. Defoe 1728, pp. 81–101.
19. Defoe 1728, p. 94. However, Defoe got his facts wrong here. Prior to his coronation in 1485, Henry VII spent his exile years in Brittany and France, not in Burgundy (Gunn 1995, p. 9). Given that Burgundy had a long association with the Yorkists (Elton 1997, pp. 5–6), it would in any case have been impossible for the young Henry, a Lancastrian fleeing the Yorkist regime, to seek exile in Burgundy. Of course, this factual mistake by Defoe does not change the basic point that the focus of the British catch-up effort under Henry VII was the Low Countries, including Burgundy. I thank Tom Penn for raising this important point.
20. According to Defoe, Henry VII 'set the Manufacture of Wool on Foot in several Parts of his Country, as particularly as *Wakefield, Leeds*, and *Hallifax*, in the West Riding of *Yorkshire*, a Country pitch'd upon for its particular Situation, adapted to the Work, being fill'd with innumerable Springs of Water, Pits of Coal, and other Things proper for carrying on such a Business'. (Defoe 1728, p. 95).
21. According to Defoe, Henry VII 'secretly procured a great many Foreigners, who were perfectly skill'd in the Manufacture, to come over and instruct his own People here in their Beginnings' (Defoe 1728, p. 96).
22. Ramsay 1982, p. 61.
23. Henry VII realised 'that the *Flemings* were old in the business, long experience'd, and turn'd their Hands this Way and that Way, to new Sorts and Kinds of Goods, which the *English* could not presently know, and when known, had not Skill presently to imitate: And that therefore he must proceed gradually' (Defoe 1728, p. 96). So he 'knew . . . that it was an Attempt of such a Magnitude, as well deserv'd the utmost Prudence and Caution, that it was not to be attempted rashly; so it was not to be push'd with too much Warmth' (ibid., p. 96).
24. Henry VII 'did not immediately prohibit the exporting the Wool to the *Flemings*, neither did he, till some Years after, load the Exportation of it with any more Duties than he had before' (Defoe 1728, p. 96). As for the ban on raw wool export, Defoe says Henry VII was 'so far . . . from being able to compleat his Design, that he could never come to a total Prohibition of exporting the Wool in this Reign (ibid., p. 96). Thus, although Henry VII 'did once pretend to stop the Exportation of the Wool, he conniv'd at the Breach of his Order, and afterwards took off the Prohibition entirely' (ibid., p. 97).
25. Defoe 1728, pp. 97–8.
26. Defoe 1728, pp. 97–101.

27. Cloth exports (mostly woollen) accounted for around 70 per cent of English exports in 1700 and was still over 50 per cent of total exports until the 1770s (Musson 1978, p. 85).

28. See Wilson 1984, pp. 164–5, on the evolution of early Navigation Acts.

29. As cited in List 1885, p. 40. In List's view, this 'for centuries had been the ruling maxim of English commercial policy, as formerly it had been that of the commerical policy of the Venetian Republic' (ibid., p. 40).

30. For details see Brisco 1907, pp. 131–3, 148–55, 169–71; McCusker 1996, p. 358; Davis 1966, pp. 313–14; Wilson 1984, p. 267.

31. Interestingly, in the case of the drugs for dyeing, import duties were abolished in order to help the dyeing industries, while export duty was introduced 'in order that their exportation might not assist foreign manufacturers' (Brisco 1907, p. 139).

32. Brisco points out that the first duty drawback was granted under William and Mary to the exportation of beer, ale, mum, cider and perry (1907, p. 153). This is a policy that has been made famous by its successful use in the East Asian countries after the Second World War (see section 2.2.7 below).

33. Brisco 1907, p. 132.

34. Up to the late seventeenth century, most exports, like most imports, were taxed at 5 per cent. William III raised import taxes to 15–25 per cent, but kept the export tax at 5 per cent for most products (Davis, 1966, pp. 310–11). The exceptions to the subsequent abolition of export duties under Walpole included alum, lead, lead ore, tin, tanned leather, coals, white woollen cloths, skins, and hairs (for further details see Brisco 1907, p. 131, n. 1).

35. Brisco points out that export subsidies under Walpole were *not* granted to infant industries, but to industries that had already been established (1907, p. 152).

36. In Brisco's words, 'Walpole understood that, in order successfully to sell in a strongly competitive market, a high standard of goods was necessary. The manufacturer, being too eager to undersell his rival, would lower the quality of his wares which, in the end, would reflect on other English-made goods. There was only one way to secure goods of a high standard, and that was to regulate their manufacture by governmental supervision' (1907, p. 185). Once again, we find the modern version of such policy in countries like Japan and Korea during the postwar period, whose state trading agencies not only acted as information sources and marketing channels but also as a monitor of export product quality.

37. Brisco 1907, p. 129.

38. Davis 1966 argues that the period between 1763 and 1776 saw a particular proliferation of protectionist measures, which he believes was influential in shaping Adam Smith's view on mercantilism in his *Wealth of Nations*, published in 1776.

39. The British export of cotton textile products to the East Indies, most of which went to India, increased from 6 per cent of total cotton textile exports after the Napoleonic Wars (c. 1815) increased to 22 per cent in 1840 and anything up to 60 per cent after 1873. (see Hobsbawm 1999, p. 125).

40. Of course, in most cases, the manufacturers' support for free trade was a self-centred one, rather than out of their intellectual conversion to lofty principle of free trade – while supporting the repeal of the Corn Law, the cotton manufacturers remained opposed to free export of cotton machinery right until the end of the ban (first imposed in 1774) in 1842 (Musson 1978, p. 101; see section 2.3.3.).

41. Bairoch 1993, pp. 20–1.

42. The term comes from Gallagher and Robinson 1953.

43. Kindleberger 1978, p. 196. See Semmel 1970 for a classic study of the role of economic theory in the development of British trade policy between 1750 and 1850.

44. Kindleberger 1975; Reinert 1998. In 1840, Bowring advised the member states of

German *Zollverein* to grow wheat and sell it to buy British manufactures (Landes 1998, p. 521).

45. *The Political Writings of Richard Cobden*, 1868, William Ridgeway, London, vol. 1, p. 150; as cited in Reinert 1998, p. 292.

46. Fielden 1969, p. 82.

47. Bairoch 1993, p. 46.

48. See Polanyi 1957 [1944], chapters 12–13. Polanyi argues that 'there was nothing natural about *laissez-faire*; free markets could never have come into being merely by allowing things to take their course. Just as cotton manufacturers – the leading free trade industry – were created by the help of protective tariffs, export bounties, and indirect wage subsidies, *laissez-faire* itself was enforced by the state. The thirties and forties saw not only an outburst of legislation repealing restrictive regulations, but also an enormous increase in the administrative functions of the state, which was now being endowed with a central bureaucracy able to fulfil the tasks set by the adherents of liberalism. To the typical utilitarian . . . *laissez-faire* was not a method to achieve a thing, it was the thing to be achieved' (1957 [1944], p. 139). Also see Perelman 2000 on how the Classical economists endorsed state intervention that was deemed necessary for the establishment of the market system, especially the creation of wage labourers through the destruction of small-scale rural production.

49. Fielden 1969, p. 82.

50. See Clarke 1999, on the rise and fall of the Tariff Reform League and Chamberlain's role in it.

51. Bairoch 1993, pp. 27–8.

52. Bairoch 1993, p. 30.

53. Trebilcock 1981, p. 83.

54. North 1965, p. 694.

55. Of course, there is no simple one-to-one correspondence between someone's 'material' position and his/her intellectual position. Despite being a Southern slave-owner, Jefferson was strongly in favour of infant industry protection. In contrast, despite being from the Northern manufacturing part of the country and being a famous industrial inventor, Benjamin Franklin was not a supporter of infant industry protection. However, Franklin still supported protection of American manufacturing industry on the ground that the American industry would never be able to compete with European industry that could get away with paying subsistence wage, whereas the American industry could not, given the abundance of land and shortage of labour. See Kaplan (1931, pp. 17–27).

56. Corden 1974, chapter 8; Freeman 1989; Reinert 1996. Of course, there were thinkers before Hamilton who had elements of the infant industry argument in their writings. For these, see Reinert 1995. According to Bairoch 1993, between Hamilton's *Reports* and List's *National System of Political Economy*, there were other writings advocating infant industry protection by authors such as the German Adam Müller and the Frenchmen Jean-Antoine Chaptal and Charles Dupin (p. 17).

57. Henderson 1983; Reinert 1998. For further details on List's life and work, see Henderson 1983. List's full argument was published in *The National System of Political Economy* in 1841. However, according to Spiegel (1971), the earliest version of his argument for the development of national 'productive power' was made in a book that he wrote for the Pennsylvania protectionists in 1827, *Outlines of American Political Economy* (pp. 362–3).

58. Bairoch (1993, p. 17) credits Hamilton for inventing the term, 'infant industry'.

59. Dorfman and Tugwell 1960, pp. 31–2; Conkin 1980, pp. 176–7.

60. According to Elkins and McKitrick, '[a]s the Hamiltonian progress revealed itself

– a sizeable funded debt, a powerful national bank, excises, nationally subsidized manufactures, and eventually even a standing army – the Walpolean point was too obvious to miss. It was in resistance to this, and everything it seemed to imply that the 'Jeffersonian persuasion' was erected' (1993, p. 19).

61. Garraty and Carnes 2000, pp. 139–40.
62. Garraty and Carnes 2000, pp. 153–5, 210; Bairoch 1993, p. 33.
63. Garraty and Carnes, 2000, p. 210; Cochran and Miller, 1942, pp. 15–16.
64. Bairoch 1993, p. 33.
65. Garraty and Carnes 2000, p. 210.
66. Cochran and Miller 1942, p. 16.
67. Garraty and Carnes, pp. 219, 221.
68. Bairoch 1993, p. 34; Garraty and Carnes 2000, pp. 262–3, 328; Cochran and Miller 1942, p. 18.
69. Garraty and Carnes, p. 335; Bairoch 1993, pp. 34–5; Luthin 1994, p. 611.
70. Although a regular transatlantic steam service was inaugurated in 1838, steamships only came to replace sailboats as the major means of sea transportation in the 1870s (O'Rourke and Williamson 1999, pp. 33–4).
71. Garraty and Carnes 2000, p. 405.
72. Luthin 1944, pp. 614–24. It should be remembered that, as a coalition between the protectionst Whigs and the western Democrats who wanted free distribution of public land but in general wanted free trade, the Republican party in its early days was *not* an openly protectionist party.
73. The plank read '[t]hat, while providing revenue for the support of the general government by duties upon imports, sound policy requires such an adjustment of these imports as to encourage the development of the industrial interests of the country; and we commend that policy of national exchanges, which secures to the working man liberal wages, to agriculture remunerative prices, to mechanics and manufacturers an adequate reward for their skill, labor, and enterprise, and to the nation commercial prosperity and independence' (cited in Borit 1966, p. 309).
74. Luthin 1944, pp. 617–18; Borit 1966, pp. 302, 309–31. One eyewitness records: 'The Pennsylvania and New Jersey delegations were terrific in their applause over the tariff resolution, and their hilarity was contagious, finally pervading the whole vast auditorium'. Another wrote: 'The scene this evening upon the reading of the 'Protection to Home Industries' plank in the platform was beyond precedent. One thousand tongues yelled, ten thousand hats, caps and handkerchiefs waving with the wildest fervor. Frantic jubilation'. Both are cited in Luthin 1944, p. 617.
75. Luthin 1944, pp. 610–11; Frayssé 1986, pp. 99–100. One of Lincoln's economic advisors was the famous protectionist economist Henry Carey (see below). Lincoln even appointed a close associate of Carey to a post in the Treasury in charge of tariffs, although Carey is known to have been frustrated by Lincoln's unwillingness to take things as far as he wanted (Luthin 1944, pp. 627–9). Carey is reported to have said: 'Protection made Mr. Lincoln president. Protection has given him all the success he has achieved, yet has he never, so far as I can recollect, bestowed upon her a single word of thanks. When he and she part company, he will go to the wall' (his letter to Noah Swayne, enclosed as a copy in Swayne to Carey, February 4th, 1865, *Carey Papers*, Box 78; cited in Luthin 1944, p. 629).
76. The Republican Party was only formed in 1856 out of an alliance between Northern manufacturing interests and small farmers of the West.
77. Luthin 1944, pp. 624–5; Borit 1966, pp. 310–12.
78. Garraty and Carnes 2000, pp. 391–2, 414–15; Foner 1998, p. 92. In response to a newspaper editorial urging immediate slave emancipation, Lincoln wrote: 'If I could save the Union without freeing any slave, I would do it; and if I could save it

by freeing all the slaves, I would do it; and if I could do it by freeing some and leaving others alone, I would also do that' (Garraty and Carnes 2000, p. 405).

79. Cochran and Miller 1942, p. 106.

80. However, the increase was considered so exceedingly high that even Congressman Justin Morrill, one of the architects of the 1862 Tariff Act, is reported to have commented in 1870 that '[i]t is a mistake of the friends of a sound tariff to insist on the extreme rates imposed during the war' (originally cited in F Taussig, *The Tariff History of the United States*, Putnam, 1903; as cited in Cochran and Miller 1942, p. 106).

81. And at least for the earlier period, we cannot underestimate the natural protection accorded to the US manufacturing producers by the sheer distance from Europe, given high transportation costs (Bairoch 1993, p. 35).

82. Bairoch 1993, p. 37.

83. Bairoch 1993, pp. 37–8.

84. Bhagwati 1985, p. 22, n. 10.

85. Kindleberger 1990a, pp. 136–7.

86. I would like to thank Irfan ul Haque for raising this point.

87. Lipsey 2000, pp. 726–7.

88. Bairoch 1993, pp. 51–2.

89. Bairoch 1993, pp.52–3. According to Bairoch, the third fastest-growing 20-year period was that of 1850–70 (1.8 per cent). However, the record for this period is more difficult to assess than those of the other two periods. First of all, 1850–61 was a period of relatively (but relatively) low protectionism, while 1862–70 witnessed a marked increase in protection. Moreover, this period contains the periods of the Civil War (1861–5) and the postwar reconstruction, and thus cannot be treated in the same way as other periods.

90. See O'Rourke 2000. The 10 countries are: Austria, Canada, Denmark, France, Germany, Italy, Norway, Sweden, the UK and the USA.

91. The role of tariffs in the development of cotton textile has generated a heated debate. Taussig was the first to argue that '[p]robably as early as 1824, and almost certainly by 1832, the industry had reached a firm position, in which it was able to meet foreign competition on equal terms' (1892, p. 136). Bils disputed this and concluded his study with the statement that '[t]he removal of tariff . . . would have reduced value added in textiles by, at a minimum, three-quarters. The implication is that about half of the industrial sector of New England would have been bankrupted' (1984, p. 1,045). Irwin and Temin 2000 sided with Taussig on the ground that the American cotton textile producers would have survived the abolition of tariff because they specialised in different products from those of the British producers. However, the difference between them and Bils is actually not as striking as it first seems. Irwin and Temin do not disagree with Bils's view that the American producers could not compete with the British producers in high-value-added segments of the market. They merely make the point that most American producers were *not* actually in those segments.

92. Engerman and Sokoloff 2000, p. 400; Lipsey 2000, p. 726. This is presumably why on the eve of the Civil War the New England woollen textile industry was in general quite content with the moderate protection accorded by the 1857 Tariff Act, inasmuch as the tariff on raw materials remained low. In contrast, states like Pennsylvania, New Jersey, parts of Maryland, and West Virginia (with its mining interests), where the new generation of heavy industries were growing around the iron-coal axis, were very strongly protectionist (see Luthin 1944, pp. 615–20).

93. Kozul-Wright 1995, pp. 100–2, esp. p. 101, n. 37.

94. Shapiro and Taylor 1990, p. 866; Owen 1966, chapter 9; Mowery and Rosenberg 1993.
95. Owen 1966, pp. 149–50.
96. Mowery and Rosenberg 1993, table 2.3.
97. Shapiro and Taylor sum this up nicely: 'Boeing would not be Boeing, nor would IBM be IBM, in either military or commercial endeavours without Pentagon contracts and civilian research support' (1990, p. 866).
98. See http://www.phrma.org/publications.
99. Spiegel 1971, p. 364.
100. Conkin 1980, p. 188. The best example of such extreme protectionist was Willard Philips, who, together with Calvin Colton, was one of the most famous campaigners for infant industry protection in the early nineteenth century. Philips published one of the two or three earliest American economics textbooks, *A Manual of Political Economy* (Conkin 1980, p. 178).
101. See above; see also Kaplan 1931, on Carey's life and work.
102. Letter to Weydemeyer, 5 March 1852, in K Marx and F Engels, *Letters to Americans, 1848–95: A Selection* (New York, International Publishers, 1953, cited in Fraysse 1994, p. 224, n. 46.
103. Reinert 1996, p. 5.
104. Reinert 1998, p. 296. The original source is F List, *Gesammelte Werke*, vol. V, p. 338.
105. Conkin 1980, pp. 287–8.
106. Luthin 1944, p. 616.
107. Trebilcock 1981, p. 41; see also Blackbourn 1997, p. 117. However, Tilly cites the Ph.D. thesis written in German by T Ohnishi at the University of Göttingen, which demonstrates what he calls 'surprisingly significant (and rising) protective effects' of the Prussian Commercial Union tariff, which formed the basis of *Zollverein* tariff (Tilly 1991, p. 191).
108. Kindleberger 1978, p. 196; Fielden 1969, pp. 88–90.
109. Taylor 1955, is a classic text on Bismarck's politics.
110. Blackbourn 1997, p. 320.
111. Trebilcock 1981, p. 26.
112. Henderson 1963, pp. 136–52.
113. Trebilcock 1981, pp. 26–7.
114. Henderson 1963; Trebilcock 1981, pp. 27–9.
115. Trebilcock 1981, pp. 27–8; Kindleberger 1978, p. 192; id. 1996, p. 153. Especially successful was support for the production of locomotives. In 1841, when August Borsig established his locomotive factory with Beuth's help, all 20 of the locomotives in service in Germany were imported. By 1854, no locomotive was imported. Borsig produced 67 out of 69 locomotives bought in Germany and exported six to Poland and four to Denmark – 'a classic example of effective import subsitution leading to exports' (Kindleberger 1996, p. 153).
116. Trebilcock 1981, pp. 28–9, 76. It is worth noting that scarcity of such talent was also one of the things that motivated the establishment of state-owned enterprises in many developing countries in the immediate postwar period (see Chang and Singh 1993, for further discussion on this point).
117. Milward and Saul 1979, p. 417.
118. Kindleberger 1978, p. 191; Balabkins 1988, p. 93. The reorientation of teaching is similar to what happened in Korea during the 1960s. During this time, the Korean government increased university places for science and technology subjects vis-à-vis humanities and social sciences. As a result, the ratio between these two subject groups changed from around 0.6 in the early 1960s to around one by the early 1980s. See You and Chang 1993 for further details.

119. Kindleberger 1978, pp. 199–200.
120. Milward and Saul 1979, p. 418.
121. Trebilcock 1981, pp. 77–8.
122. On the role of the *Junkers* in the Prussian bureaucracy, see Dorwart 1953; Feuchtwanger 1970; Gothelf 2000.
123. Trebilcock 1981, pp. 79–80.
124. Tilly 1996, p. 116.
125. However, this attempt, organized by the legeadary Scottish Fiancier John Law of Mississippi Company Fame, backfired and prompted the British in 1719 to introduce a ban on the emigration of skilled workers, and especially on the attempt to recruit such workers for jobs abroad ('suborning') (see section 2.3.3 for further details).
126. See Milward and Saul 1979, pp. 270, 284; Fohlen 1973, pp. 68–9.
127. Milward and Saul 1979, p. 284.
128. Milward and Saul 1979, pp. 284–5.
129. See for example Trebilcock 1981; Kuisel 1981.
130. Nye 1991, p. 25.
131. In apparent contradiction to table 2.1, table 2.2 shows that there was still some protection left in the British economy. This is because total free trade prevailed only for manufactured products (as shown in table 2.1) and there were still some 'revenue tariffs' for luxury goods left (which are reflected in table 2.2). See the first quote from Fielden 1969 towards the end of section 2.2.1 for further details.
132. Irwin 1993 questions Nye's conclusion on a number of grounds. The most important of his criticisms is that most British tariffs that remained after the 1840s were 'revenue tariffs' imposed on luxury items, and therefore had little impact on industrial incentives. However, in his reply, Nye 1993 points out that even revenue tariffs can have a significant impact on industrial structure and that it was only in the 1860s that British tariffs became mainly revenue tariffs, thus making his claim valid at least until 1860.
133. Trebilcock 1981, p. 184; Bury 1964, chapter 4; Cameron 1953. Cameron describes *Crédit Foncier* as being 'virtually an agency of the government' (1963, p. 462).
134. See Kindleberger 1975 for further details on the making of the treaty.
135. Kuisel 1981, p. 18.
136. Kuisel 1981, pp. 9–10, 12–13.
137. Kuisel 1981, p. 14.
138. Kuisel 1981, p. 18; Dormois 1999, p. 71.
139. For the postwar French experience, see, among others, Shonfield 1965; Cohen, 1977; Hall 1986. It is probably as a result of this bitter experience of being overtaken by its century-long rival that many British commentators (whether pro-French or otherwise) highlight the contrast between their own *laissez-faire* approach and France's *étatisme* or *dirigisme*, and therefore ignore the fact that the French state had been almost as non-interventionist (and in some respects even more so) as the British state for the century and a half between the French Revolution and the Second World War.
140. Gustavson 1986, pp. 15, 57.
141. Gustavson 1986, p. 65.
142. Bohlin 1999, p. 155.
143. Chang and Kozul-Wright 1994, p. 869; Bohlin 1999, p. 156.
144. Liepman 1938, as cited by Bairoch 1993, p. 26, table 2.3. The original source is H Liepmann, *Tariff Levels and the Economic Unity of Europe*, London, 1938. The countries included are Austria-Hungary, Belgium, Bulgaria, Finland, France, Germany, Italy, Romania, Russia, Serbia, Spain, Sweden, Switzerland, and the

UK. Those excluded were Denmark, Norway, Portugal, and the Netherlands. Of these, Portugal and the Netherlands were far less protectionist than Sweden. Overall Denmark was less protectionist but had quite high industrial tariffs. Norway had high tariffs.

145. Baumol et al. 1990, p. 88, table 5.1. The 16 countries, in alphabetical order, are Australia, Austria, Belgium, Canada, Denmark, Finland, France, Germany, Italy, Japan, the Netherlands, Norway, Sweden, Switzerland, the UK, and the USA.
146. Chang and Kozul-Wright 1994, p. 871; Heckscher 1954, p. 259; Bohlin 1999, p. 158.
147. Samuelsson 1968, pp. 71–6; Bohlin 1999, p. 153.
148. Chang and Kozul-Wright 1994, pp. 869–70; Bohlin 1999, pp. 153–5. However, in the telephone industry there erupted a 'telephone war' in the Stockholm area between 1903 and 1918 between the state-owned company, *Telegrafverket*, and the private company, *Stockholm allmäna*, which ended only when the former took the latter over (Bohlin 1999, p. 154).
149. Gustavson 1986, pp. 71–2; Chang and Kozul-Wright 1994, p. 870. For public-private collaboration in the East Asian economies, see the classic work by Evans (1995).
150. Chang and Kozul-Wright 1994, p. 870.
151. For pioneering works on 'technological capabilities', see Fransman and King 1984; Lall 1992.
152. See Korpi 1983; Pekkarinen et al. 1992; Pontusson 1992. However, Pontusson (1992) points out that the work of the Rationalisation Commission (1936–9) established some principles underlying the so-called 'active labour market policy' of the postwar years (pp. 46–7).
153. LO 1963, is the document that set out the strategy in detail.
154. Edquist and Lundvall 1993, p. 274.
155. Milward and Saul 1979, pp. 437, 441, 446; Hens and Solar 1999, p. 195.
156. Hens and Solar 1999, pp. 194, 197.
157. Dhondt and Bruwier 1973, pp. 350–1; Van der Wee 1996, p. 65.
158. Milward and Saul 1977, p. 174; Fielden 1969, p. 87.
159. Boxer 1965, chapter 10. Kindleberger estimates that the Netherlands' economic strength had peaked by 1730 (1990b, p. 258).
160. Schmoller of the German Historical School provides a brief, but illuminating discussion of the Dutch policies used in order to establish its commercial supremacy – colonial policy, navigation policy, the regulation of the Levant trade, and the regulation of the herring and whale fisheries (see Schmoller 1884, esp. pp. 52–3).
161. Kindleberger 1990b, p. 259; id. 1996, pp. 100–4; Milward and Saul 1977, p. 201.
162. List 1885, pp. 33–4; Wright 1955.
163. Dhondt and Bruwier 1973, p. 329, 355.
164. van Zanden 1996, pp. 84–5.
165. Kossmann 1978, pp. 136–8; Henderson 1972, pp. 198–200.
166. For further details, see Schiff 1971.
167. van Zanden 1999, pp. 179–80.
168. Maddison 1995.
169. van Zanden 1999, pp. 182–4.
170. Biucchi 1973, pp. 464, 628.
171. Milward and Saul 1979, pp. 454–5.
172. Biucchi 1973, p. 629.
173. Biucchi 1973, p. 455.
174. Biucchi 1973, pp. 628, 630–1.
175. For further details see Schiff 1971.
176. See Smith 1955 and Allen 1981 for further details.
177. McPherson 1987, pp. 31, 34–5.

178. 'So cautious were private investors that capital was raised in 1881 for the first private railway, between Tokyo and Aomori, only after the government promised to build the line for the owners with engineers from the Department of Industry, to make the land owned by the company tax-free, and to guarantee the company a net return of 8 percent per annum for ten years on the line between Tokyo and Sendai and for fifteen years on the line from Sendai to Aomori' (Smith, 1955, p. 43).
179. McPherson 1987, p. 31; Smith 1955, pp. 44–5.
180. e.g., Landes 1965, pp. 100–6.
181. Smith 1955, p. 103.
182. Of these, 205 were technical advisers, 144 teachers, 69 managers and administrators and 36 skilled workmen (Allen 1981, p. 34).
183. McPherson 1987, p. 30.
184. See Westney 1987, chapter 1, and McPherson 1987, p. 29 for details.
185. Allen 1981, p. 133; McPherson 1987, p. 32.
186. Allen 1981, pp. 133–4.
187. Johnson 1982, pp. 105–6; McPherson 1987, pp. 32–3.
188. Johnson 1982, pp. 105–15.
189. McPherson 1987, pp. 35–6.
190. Maddison 1989. The 16 countries are Australia, Austria, Belgium, Canada, Denmark, Finland, France, Germany, Italy, Japan, the Netherlands, Norway, Sweden, Switzerland, the UK and the USA.
191. Japanese GDP (not per capita) in 1945 is estimated to have fallen to 48 per cent of the peak reached in 1943. This was, however, somewhat less dramatic than what Germany experienced, where 1946 GDP was only 40 per cent of the peak reached in 1944 or Austria, where the 1945 GDP was only 41 per cent of the peaks reached in 1941 and 1944. See Maddison 1989, pp. 120–1, table B-2).
192. All the information in this paragraph comes from Maddison 1989, p. 35, table 3.2.
193. For the earlier phase of this debate, see Johnson 1982, id. 1984; Dore 1986; Thompson 1989; Amsden 1989; Westphal 1990; Wade 1990; and Chang 1993. For the more recent phase, see World Bank 1993; Singh 1994; Lall 1994; Stiglitz 1996; Wade 1996; and Chang 2001b.
194. Westphal 1978; Luedde-Neurath 1986; Amsden 1989; World Bank 1993.
195. Westphal 1978; Luedde-Neurath 1986; Chang 1993.
196. Chang 1993; id. 1994.
197. Amsden and Singh 1994; Chang 1994; id. 1999.
198. Dore 1986; Chang 2001b.
199. You and Chang 1993.
200. Chang 1998a.
201. Kim 1993; Hou and Gee 1993; Lall and Teubal 1998; Chang and Cheema, 2002.
202. For further criticism of this view, see Chang 1999; id. 2000.
203. See Chang 1998b; Chang et al. 1998.
204. List 1885, p. 95.
205. Brisco 1907, p. 165.
206. Brisco 1907, p. 157.
207. Garraty and Carnes 2000, pp. 77–8.
208. Lipsey 2000, p. 723.
209. Even after the USA had become independent, Britain still wanted to keep it as a supplier of raw materials (especially cotton), which is why it supported the South in the Civil War.
210. The industry was finally destroyed during the first half of the nineteenth century by the flooding of markets by the then superior British products, following the end in 1813 of the East India Company's monopoly (Hobsbawm 1999, p. 27).

211. Ramsay 1982, p. 66; Rinert 1995, p. 32 for Ireland; Garraty and Carnes 2000, pp. 77–8 for the USA.
212. Brisco 1907, p. 60.
213. Bairoch 1993, p. 89.
214. For further details, see Harnetty 1972, chapter 2.
215. Hobsbawm 1999, p. 129.
216. Bairoch 1993, pp. 41–2.
217. Little et al. 1970, pp. 163–4; World Bank 1991, p. 102.
218. Bairoch 1993, pp. 41–2; Gallagher and Robinson 1953, p. 11. The 1838 Convention of Balta Liman with Turkey bound Turkish import duties at three per cent (Fielden 1969, p. 91).
219. Johnson 1982, p. 25.
220. Bairoch 1993, p. 42. Eyüp Özveren has pointed out to me that the 1923 granting of tariff autonomy to Turkey took effect only in 1929.
221. Amsden, 2001.
222. Kindleberger 1990b, p. 260.
223. See Jeremy 1977; Harris 1998, chapter 18, for further details.
224. Landes 1969, p. 148.
225. On the Tools Act and the ban on suborning, see Harris 1998, pp. 457–62; Jeremy 1977. On the loosening and abolition of the ban, see Kindleberger, p. 132; Landes 1969, p. 148. Berg 1980, chapter 9 provides an informative discussion of the political and academic debates surrounding the abolition of the ban on export of machinery.
226. Davids 1995; De Vries and Van der Woude 1997, pp. 348–9.
227. For example, in the 1750s, John Holker, a former Manchester textile finisher and Jacobite officer, was appointed as Inspector-General of Foreign Manufactures in the French government. While also advising French producers on technological problems, his main activity under this euphemistic job title consisted of industrial espionage and the suborning of British skilled workers (Harris 1998, p. 21).
228. See Landes 1969; Harris 1991; Bruland 1991.
229. Landes 1969.
230. On the issue of technological capabilities in developing countries, see Fransman and King 1984; Lall 1992; Lall and Teubal 1998.
231. See Landes 1969, pp. 150–1, for further details.
232. On the controversy surrounding TRIPS, see Chang 2001a. Obviously, exactly what aspect of these laws is considered 'deficient' will depend on one's view. For example, there are good arguments for and against the product patent in the chemical and pharmaceutical industries.
233. For further details, see Williams 1896; Penrose 1951; Schiff 1971; McLeod 1988; Crafts 2000; and Sokoloff and Khan 2000.
234. The USA did not fully conform to the Berne Convention on international copyright (1886) until 1988, when the country finally abolished the requirement that copyrighted books had to be printed in the USA or typeset with US plates (Sokoloff and Khan 2000, p. 9).
235. See Landes 1969, p. 328. It is interesting to note that at the time the British were criticising Germany not only for using industrial espionage and the violation of trademark law but also for exporting goods made with convict labour (recall the recent US dispute with China on this account).
236. Kindleberger 1978, p. 216.
237. Williams 1896, p. 137.
238. Kindleberger 1978, p. 216.
239. Williams 1896, p. 138.

240. Kindleberger 1964, chapter 15, provides a classic discussion of this issue. Indeed, just about everything from patterns of coal deposits in the case of Western Europe (Pomeranz 2000) to varieties of Confucian culture in the case of Japan (Morishima, 1982) have been used to explain industrial success.
241. Little et al. 1970, pp. 162–9 and World Bank 1991, pp. 97–8, are the two notable exceptions.
242. Little et al. 1970, pp. 163–4.
243. World Bank 1991, p. 97, box 5.2. The twelve countries in question are Austria, Belgium, Denmark, France, Germany, Italy, the Netherlands, Spain, Sweden, Switzerland, the UK and the USA.
244. For an assessment of the additional constraints imposed by the WTO agreement on policy choice by developing country governments, see Akyuz et al. 1998; Amsden 2000; Chang and Cheema 2002.
245. Note that up to Second World War, virtually none of today's developing countries had trade policy autonomy due to their colonial status or unequal treaties. So it is meaningless to discuss them at the same level as today's developing countries. See section 2.3.2 for further details.
246. See Maddison 1995.
247. For example, per capita incomes measured in 1990 dollars in Japan and Finland in 1820 were $704 and $759 respectively, while those in the UK and the Netherlands were $1,756 and $1,561 – a ratio of less than 2.5 to 1. By 1913, the gap between Japan ($1,334) or Portugal ($1,354) and the UK ($5,032) or the USA ($5,505) increased to a ratio of around 4 to 1. For further details from Maddison's historical income estimates, see table 3.7 in Chapter 3 of the present volume.
248. In purchasing power parity terms (in 1999 dollars), per capita income in the USA, Switzerland, and Japan were $31,910, $28,760, and $25,170 respectively, whereas those in Tanzania and Malawi were $500 and $570 respectively. In terms of current dollars, the gap is in the region of 100 or 400 to 1. In current dollars, 1999 per capita incomes were $38,380 in Switzerland, $32,030 in Japan, and $31,910 in the USA, while they were $100 in Ethiopia, $180 in Malawi, and $260 in Tanzania.
249. Maddison 1995.
250. World Bank 1991; see also Maddison 1995.
251. See Maddison 1995; World Bank website.

Chapter 3. Institutions and Economic Development: 'Good Governance' in Historical Perspective

1. World Bank 2002 is the most recent example.
2. Kapur and Webb 2000.
3. For a review of these studies, see Aron 2000. The institutional variables are often represented by various 'indices' constructed by consulting firms and research institutes based on surveys of experts or businessmen (for detailed discussions on these indicators, see Kaufmann et al. 1999).
4. Kaufman et al. 1999; Aron 2000; La Porta et al. 1999; Rodrik 1999.
5. E.g., Kapur and Webb 2000.
6. Crafts 2000 is a notable exception, but it only covers the UK experience and is focused on financial and corporate governance institutions.
7. Bardhan 1993, is a concise review; Rueschmeyer, Stephens and Stephens 1992, provides a comprehensive review; see also Przeworski and Limongi 1993.
8. Even Rodrik, who is known for exposing the intellectual weaknesses of the IDPE,

agrees with this orthodoxy and goes as far as to argue that, as the 'meta-institution' that helps us build better institutions, democracy is the only appropriate 'institutional conditionality' that IFIs may attach to their financial assistance (see Rodrik 1999b).

9. Kent 1939.

10. Daunton 1995, pp. 477–8.

11. Clark 1996, p. 64.

12. Ritter 1990; Kreutzer 1996.

13. Garraty and Carnes 2000, pp. 445, 473; Foner 1998, p. 154; Kruman 1991, p. 1,045.

14. Linz 1995; Carr 1980.

15. Nerbørvik 1986, p. 125.

16. Foner 1998, p. 74.

17. See above; see also Therborn 1977; Silbey 1995.

18. For example, in 1814, about 45 per cent of men were already able to vote in Norway (Nerbørvik 1986, p. 119). Compare this with the figure (cited above) for the UK (18 per cent in 1832). See id., p. 125; Kreutzer 1996.

19. Kreutzer 1996.

20. O'Leary 1962, pp. 23–5.

21. Searle 1979–80 and Howe 1979–80.

22. It also involved the manufacture of aliens into citizens with bribery, which was done 'with no more solemnity than, and quite as much celerity as, is displayed in converting swine into pork in a Cincinnati packing house', according to the *New York Tribune* newspaper in 1868 (Cochran and Miller 1942, pp. 159). See also Cochran and Miller 1942, pp. 158–9; Benson 1978.

23. Garraty and Carnes 2000, p. 472. Open sales of votes by them were especially widespread in the 1860s and 1870s. The group of corrupt assemblymen from both parties, called 'Black Horse Cavalry' demanded $1,000 per vote on railroad bills and vigorous bidding drove prices up to $5,000 per vote. The group also introduced 'strike bills', which if passed would greatly hinder some wealthy interests or corporation, and would then demand payment to drop the bill. As a result, some companies created lobbying organisations that bought legislation, sparing themselves from blackmail. See Benson 1978, pp. 59–60 for details.

24. World Bank 1997, chapter 6, sums up the current debate on this from the IDPE's point of view.

25. Weber 1968; see also Evans 1995, chapter 2, for further discussion of this view.

26. See Hughes 1994 and Hood 1995, 1998, for some critical appraisals of the NPM literature.

27. Rauch and Evans 2000, present statistical evidence to support this.

28. See Kindleberger 1984, pp. 160–1 (for England); pp. 168–9 (for France); Dorwart 1953, p. 192 (for Prussia).

29. Anderson and Anderson 1978.

30. Finer 1989.

31. Cochran and Miller 1941, pp. 156–60; Garraty and Carnes 2000, pp. 253–4; Finer 1989.

32. Garraty and Carnes 2000, p. 472; id., pp. 581–3.

33. Anderson and Anderson 1978.

34. Armstrong 1973.

35. Of course, this does not imply that nepotism was the reason for *all* such appointments.

36. Feuchtwanger 1970, p. 45.

37. Armstrong 1973, pp. 79–81. However, the term 'aristocracy', should be interpreted somewhat carefully in this context. Since the days of the Great Elector, Frederick William (1640–1688), it was customary in Prussia to ennoble commoners who had risen high in the royal service (Feuchtwanger, 1970, p. 45–6).

38. Garraty and Carnes 2000, pp. 254, 583 (for USA); Clark 1996, p. 55 (for Italy); Palacio 1988, p. 496 (for Spain); Baudhuin 1946, pp. 203–4 (for Belgium).
39. For further details, see Dorwart 1953; Feuchtwanger 1970; Gothelf, 2000.
40. On the characteristics of the modern 'Weberian' bureaucracy in the context of today's developing countries, see Rauch and Evans 2000; Anderson and Anderson 1978; see also Blackbourn 1997, pp. 76–7, 82–4.
41. Hobsbawm 1999, p. 209.
42. Benson 1978, pp. 81, 85.
43. See Upham 2000 and Ohnesorge 2000 for a critic of the 'rule of law' rhetoric.
44. See Upham 2000.
45. Glasgow 1999.
46. Blackbourn 1997, p. 384.
47. Clark 1996, p. 54.
48. See Aron 2000, table 1, for some examples.
49. De Soto 2000; Upham 2000.
50. E.g., McLeod 1988.
51. Penrose 1951, p. 13; Doi 1980 (for Japan).
52. I put quotation marks around the term 'deficient', because what is deficient at least partly depends on one's viewpoint. For example, some people believe that product patents on chemical and pharmaceutical substances should not be allowed, while others argue that they are desirable.
53. According to Cochran and Miller (1942, p. 14), therefore, the fact that between 1820 and 1830 the USA produced 535 patents per year against 145 for Great Britain was mainly due to the difference in 'scruples'. Contrast this with the argument by Sokoloff and Khan that it was thanks to a 'good' patent system that by 1810 the USA far exceeded Britain in patenting per capita (2000, p. 5).
54. Chemical substances remained unpatentable until 1967 in West Germany, 1968 in the Nordic countries, 1976 in Japan, 1978 in Switzerland, and 1992 in Spain. Pharmaceutical products remained unpatentable until 1967 in West Germany and France, 1979 in Italy, and 1992 in Spain. Pharmaceutical products were also unpatentable in Canada into the 1990s. For details, see Patel 1989, p. 980.
55. See Schiff 1971, for further details.
56. The 1817 Dutch patent law did not require a disclosure of the details of patents. It allowed the patenting of imported inventions. It nullified national patents of inventions that acquired foreign patents. And there was no penalty on others using patented products without permission as far as it was for their own business (Schiff 1971, pp. 19–20).
57. Machlup and Penrose 1950; Penrose 1951.
58. Schiff 1971, p. 85.
59. Schiff 1971; Patel 1989, p. 980.
60. See Chang 2001a, for further details.
61. Shell 1998; Chang 2001a.
62. Gillman and Eade 1995.
63. However, Kindleberger argues that the Bubble Act was 'a device to save the South Sea Company by halting the diversion of cash subscriptions to rival promotions, not an attack on it' (1984, p. 70), as I suggest here. Whatever the motive was behind the Act, the fact that it survived for a century implies that the view that limited liability promotes speculation, whether true or false, was widely accepted.
64. Rosenberg and Birdzell 1986; Chang 2000.
65. Kindleberger 1984, p. 196.
66. Rozenberg and Birdzell 1986, p. 200.
67. Dechesne 1932, pp. 381–401 (for Belgium); Tilly 1994; Millward and Saul 1979,

p. 416 (for Germany); Bury 1964, p. 57 (for France); Volts 1979, pp. 32–5, 46 (for Spain); Mata and Valerio 1994, p. 149 (for Portugal).

68. Garraty and Carnes 2000, pp. 231–2, 244, 362.
69. See Carruthers and Halliday 1998, and Carruthers 2000, on the current state of the debate, especially in relation to the USA, the UK and East Asia.
70. Duffy 1985, pp. 7–9.
71. Duffy 1985, pp. 10–12.
72. Duffy 1985, pp. 16–17; Hoppit 1987, pp. 32–7.
73. Duffy 1985, pp. 52–3; Marriner 1980.
74. Coleman 1974, pp. 6–16, 19–20, 23–6.
75. For more details, see Chang 2000.
76. Amsler et al. 1981.
77. Edwards 1981.
78. Kennedy 1987, cited in Crafts 2000.
79. Crafts 2000, p. 5.
80. Tilly 1994 (for Germany); Norwegian Government Website: http://www.lovdata.no (for Norway); Atack and Passell 1994; Garraty and Carnes 2000, p. 750; Newton and Donaghy 1997, p. 251 (for Spain).
81. See Singh and Dhumale 1999, for a criticism of this orthodox view.
82. Cornish 1979; Gerber 1998, p. 36.
83. Brogan 1985, pp. 458, 464; Garraty and Carnes 2000, pp. 518, 613–14, 622.
84. Cornish 1979; Mercer 1995, pp. 44–6, 49–50, 99–105, 125–6; Hannah 1979.
85. Bruck 1962, pp. 93, 96; 196–7, 222; Hannah 1979; Gerber 1998, pp. 115, 129–31, 134, 147. It is well known that after the Second World War, Germany, together with Japan, was made to adopt a stringent US-style competition law by the American Occupation Authority. However, subsequent modifications of the law, especially in 1953, made collusive arrangements easier, especially among small firms, when they are related to aims like 'rationalisation', 'specialisation' (i.e., negotiated market segmentation), joint export activities, and structural adjustments (Shin 1994, pp. 343–355).
86. Hodne 1981, pp. 514–15 (for Norway); Dahl 1982, p. 298 (for Denmark).
87. Details in the following paragraph are from Kindleberger 1984, unless otherwise specified.
88. Details on Prussia are taken from Tilly 1994; on Sweden, Chang and Kozul-Wright 1994, p. 872; on Portugal, Mata and Valerio 1984, pp. 147–8.
89. Lamoureaux 1994. However, Lamoreaux argues that, given the high degree of competition and low leverage level prevailing in the US banking industry, this practice was beneficial.
90. Munn 1981; Cottrell 1980.
91. Atack and Passell 1994, p. 103
92. Atack and Passell 1994, p. 104.
93. Broagan 1985, p. 523.
94. Clark 1996, pp. 97–9.
95. Tilly 1994 (for Germany); Van der Wee 1987, p. 56 (for Belgium).
96. Grabel 2000, is a lucid review of this debate; Helleiner 2001, is a fascinating review of the history of this debate in the context of developing countries.
97. And indeed this is the line taken by Friedrich von Hayek, when he proposes the scrapping of central banks and argues for free competition among note-issue banks.
98. Quoted in Kindleberger 1996, p. 146. The original source is H Spencer, 'State Tampering with Money and Banks' in *Essays: Scientific, Political, and Speculative* (London: Williams & Northgate, 1891), vol. 3, p. 354.

99. For further details, see Kindleberger 1984; Cameron 1993.
100. Kindleberger 1984, p. 50; Larsson 1993, pp. 47–8; Swedish Central Bank website: http://www.riksbank.se.
101. For the Bank of England, see Kindleberger 1984, pp. 90–2, pp. 277–80; for Banque de France, see Plessis 1994; for the Nederlandische Bank, see 'T Hart et al. 1997, p. 4; Jonker 1997, p. 95.
102. Pérez 1997, p. 67 (for Spain); Mata and Valerio 1994, pp. 139–48 (for Portugal).
103. Dechesne 1932, p. 402.
104. Garraty and Carnes 2000, pp. 154–5, 423; Atack and Passell 1994; Brogan 1985, pp. 266, 277.
105. Cochran and Miller 1942, p. 295.
106. Brogan 1985, p. 477. The most telling evidence is the story of Charles E Mitchell, head of the National City Bank and a director of the Federal Reserve Bank of New York. Mitchell, in an attempt to minimise damage on his speculative activities in the run-up to the Great Depression, successfully put pressure on the Federal Reserve Board to reverse its policy of monetary tightening announced in early 1929 (Brogan 1985, pp. 525–6).
107. Singh 1997, provides a powerful critique of this view.
108. Zysman 1983; Cox 1986; Hutton 1995; Dore 2000 provide sophisticated up-to-date discussions of this debate.
109. Banner 1998, pp. 39–40, 101–5, 109–10.
110. Pennington 1990, pp. 31, 38–42.
111. Pennington 1990, pp. 54–5.
112. Banner 1998, pp. 161–3, 170–1, 174–5, 281.
113. Geisst 1997, pp. 169, 228; Atack and Passell 1994; Garraty and Carnes 2000, p. 750.
114. Di John and Putzel 200; Toye 2000 provides a very illuminating up-to-date survey of fiscal issues in developing countries.
115. See Kindleberger 1984, pp. 161–2 (Britain), pp. 168–70 (France); 'T Hart 1997, p. 29, and Kindleberger 1996, p. 100 (the Netherlands).
116. Cited in Cochran and Miller 1942, p. 48.
117. di John and Putzel, 2000.
118. Booney 1995, pp. 443–5; Deane, 1979, pp. 228–9 (Britain); Mørch 1982, pp. 160–1 (Denmark); Garraty and Carnes 2000, pp. 408, 468; Carlson 1991, p. 540 (USA).
119. Cited in Bonney 1995, p. 434.
120. Hobsbawm 1999, p. 213.
121. Mørch 1982, pp. 160–1 (Denmark); Baack and Ray 1985; Carson 1991, p. 540 (USA); Baudhuin 1946, pp. 113–16 (Belgium); Meta and Valerio 1994, pp. 186–92 (Portugal); Larsson 1993, pp. 79–80 (Sweden); Carr 1980, p. 101 (Spain).
122. See Chang and Rowthorn 1995, chapter 2; Rodrik 1999 takes a similar view.
123. Pierson 1998, pp. 106–7.
124. Pierson 1998, p. 105, table 4.2.
125. Blackbourn 1997, pp. 346–7; see Balabkins 1988 for details on the German Historical School.
126. Basu 1999a is a comprehensive and sophisticated review of the debate. Basu 1999b is a more user-friendly version. Engerman 2001 provides a comprehensive review of the history of this issue.
127. Hammond and Hammond 1995, p. 169 (Britain); Lee 1978, p. 466 (Germany); Montgomery 1939, pp. 219–22 (Sweden).
128. Garraty and Carnes 2000, p. 227, n. 1.
129. Garraty and Carnes 2000, pp. 229, 600.
130. Blaug 1958; Marx 1976, p. 390; Hammond and Hammond 1995, pp. 153–4.

131. The following details are from Marx 1976, pp. 390–5 unless otherwise specified; see also Mathias 1969, pp. 203–4, for further details.
132. Hobsbawm 1999, pp. 103, 634–5, 636, n. 47.
133. Lee 1978, p. 467; Engerman 2001.
134. Hadenius et al. 1996, p. 250; Montgomery 1939, pp. 225–6.
135. Mørch 1982, pp. 364–7.
136. Nerbørvik 1986, p. 210; Engerman 2001, appendix 1.
137. Soto 1989, pp. 702–4 (for Spain); Engerman 2001, table 1(for Holland and Switzerland).
138. Dechesne 1932, pp. 494–5; Blanpain 1996, pp. 180–2 (for Belgium); Clark 1996, p. 137 (for Italy); Serrao 1979, p. 413 (for Portngal) .
139. Engerman 2001, table 5.
140. Garraty and Carnes 2000, pp. 607, 764. I thank Stanley Engerman for bringing the 1919 legislation attempt to my attention in a personal correspondence.
141. Cochran and Miller 1942, p. 245.
142. Lee 1978, pp. 483–4 (Germany); Pryser 1985, pp. 194–5 (Norway); Hadenius et al. 1996, p. 250 (Sweden); Mørch 1982 (Denmark).
143. Marx 1976, p. 394.
144. Marx 1976, pp. 395, 398–9; Hobsbawm 1999, p. 102.
145. Garraty and Carnes 2000, p. 607; all the information in the rest of the paragraph comes from ibid., pp. 607–8.
146. Garraty and Carnes 2000, p. 607.
147. Kuisel 1981, p. 4 (France); Engerman 2001, appendix 1 (Scandinavian countries); Clark 1996, p. 137 (Italy); Soto 1989, p. 591 (Spain); Dechesne 1932, p. 496 (Belgium).
148. Soto 1989, pp. 585–6 (Spain); Norborg 1982, p. 61 (Sweden); Mørch 1982, pp. 17–18 (Denmark); Blanpain 1996, pp. 180–2 (Belgium); Garraty and Carnes 2000, p. 764 (USA).

Chapter 4. Lessons for the Present

1. Of course, what these higher-value-added activities are will depend on the country and the period concerned. So, to take an extreme example, the manufacturing of wool cloth, which was *the* high-value-added activity of fourteenth and fifteenth-century Europe, is now one of the low-value-added activities. Moreover, high-value-added activities need not even be '(manufacturing) industries' in the conventional sense, as is implied by the term 'infant industry promotion'. Depending on where technological advances are happening, the high-value-added activities could be some of those that are officially classified as 'services'.
2. See Chang 1994, chapter 3; Stiglitz 1996; Lall 1998, for reasons why there may be such discrepancies. Very often, the problem is that the private sector entrepreneurs, whose cost-benefit profiles the state should be trying to influence, are missing altogether. This is, for example, the reason that Frederick the Great had to use (successfully) a small number of bureaucrat-entrepreneurs to develop his industries in Silesia or that many developing countries have had to use (in many cases unsuccessfully) public enterprises following their independence after the Second World War.
3. Shafaeddin points out that List also regarded tariffs and subsidies as only two of many policies for industrial development (2000, pp. 9–10).
4. For further details, see Evans 1995; Stiglitz 1996; Chang and Cheema 2002.

5. One plausible argument is provided by O'Rourke 2000, pp. 474–5. He cites some studies by Jeffrey Williamson and his associates which argue that, in the nineteenth century, tariff protection raised investment by reducing the relative price of capital goods, given that capital goods were rarely traded at the time. Then he goes on to argue that in the twentieth century, capital goods are more widely traded, and that there is evidence that protection increases the relative price of capital goods and thus slows down investment. However, he admits that the result for the nineteenth century is very sensitive to the sample and is associated with a completely implausible correlation that investment share is negatively related to growth in an augmented Solow model. The argument, he admits, remains at best inconclusive.

6. Weisbrot et al. 2000 do not define 'developing countries' as a category, but I (somewhat arbitrarily) define them as countries with less than $10,000 per capita income in 1999 US dollars. This means that countries like Cyprus, Taiwan, Greece, Portugal and Malta (rankings 24th to 28th) are included in the developed countries category, while countries like Barbados, Korea, Argentina, Seychelles, and Saudi Arabia (rankings 29th to 33rd) are classified as developing countries.

7. The only two developed countries where growth accelerated between the two periods are Luxembourg and Ireland. The 13 developing countries where growth accelerated were Chile, Mauritius, Thailand, Sri Lanka, China, India, Bangladesh, Mauritania, Uganda, Mozambique, Chad, Burkina Faso, and Burundi. However, in the case of Burundi, what happened was a deceleration in income shrinkage rather than any real growth acceleration (25 per cent shrinkage vs. 7 per cent shrinkage). Also, growth acceleration in at least three countries – Uganda, Mozambique, and Chad – can be largely explained by the end to (or at least a significant scaling-down of) a civil war, rather than by policy changes. In this context, there were really only nine developing countries where there was a growth acceleration that can in theory be attributed to a shift to 'good policies'. Of course, even then, we should not forget that improved performance in the two biggest of these nine economies, that is, China (from 2.7 per cent p.a. to 8.2 per cent p.a.) and India (from 0.7 per cent p.a. to 3.7 per cent p.a.) cannot be attributed to 'good policies' as defined by the Washington Consensus.

8. Stiglitz 2001b. In the ascending order in terms of growth rate (or rather the rate of contraction, in all cases but Poland), they are Georgia, Azerbaijan, Moldova, Ukraine, Latvia, Kazakhstan, Russia, Kyrgyzstan, Bulgaria, Lithuania, Belarus, Estonia, Albania, Romania, Uzbekistan, Czech Republic, Hungary, Slovakia, and Poland.

9. The 16 countries are Australia, Austria, Belgium, Canada, Denmark, Finland, France, Germany, Italy, Japan, the Netherlands, Norway, Sweden, Switzerland, the UK and the USA.

10. Marglin and Schor 1990; Armstrong et al. 1991; Cairncross and Cairncross 1992.

11. Another reason behind this faster growth is that the world economy as a whole was growing faster thanks to the rapid growth in the developed countries, which account for the bulk of the world economy. I thank John Grieve Smith for raising this point. It should, however, be noted that, as pointed out above, this rapid growth in the developed economies also owed to the improvements in their institutions. On the role of world demand in the growth of developing countries during the 1960s and the 1970s, see Kravis 1970; Lewis 1980.

12. The figures in the two tables are not strictly comparable, as the category of 'developing countries' is comprised of slightly different sets of countries in each table.

13. This will be a growth rate that is more similar to those in the NDCs in the early-to mid-nineteenth century (when they had very few of the institutions recommended by the IDPE these days) than the ones in the late nineteenth and early-twentieth centuries (when they had seen major improvements in the quality of their institutions).

14. Another piece of evidence that 'good institutions' are not enough to generate growth is the fact that the major Asian developing economies remained virtually stagnant during the first half of the twentieth century, despite the fact that many modern institutions were introduced under (formal or informal) colonial rule. According to the estimate by Maddison 1989, the average per capita GDP growth rate for the nine largest Asian developing countries (Bangladesh, China, India, Indonesia, Pakistan, the Philippines, South Korea, Taiwan, and Thailand) during 1900–50 was 0 per cent p.a.. During this period, Taiwan and the Philippines grew at 0.4 per cent p.a., Korea and Thailand at 0.1 per cent p.a.. China grew at -0.3 per cent p.a., the South Asian countries and Indonesia at -0.1 per cent. These countries were, however, able to generate much faster growth after the end of colonial rule. The average per capita GDP growth rate for the 1950–87 period for these countries was 3.1 per cent p.a.. Part of this was, of course, due to improvements in the quality of their institutions, but the more important change was that they were able to pursue the 'right' policies, that is, activist ITT policies. See Amsden 2001 for a further exposition on this point.

15. A rather sad anecdote that supports my point here is that, right after the collapse of socialism in Mongolia, the US government provided a large sum of money to Harvard University to train dozens of bright young Mongolians as stockbrokers – money that could have been used for a lot of useful developmental purposes.

16. Chang 1998a.

17. Of course, this does not necessarily imply that everyone will benefit from this. For example, some workers in developed countries may suffer as a result of an increase in investment opportunities in developing countries, which, unless there is an appropriate internal income transfer mechanism, results in the transfer of certain production activities to these developing nations.

Index

This index covers the main body of the text but not the notes or references. It is written in word-by-word order, where a space files before a letter, for example, 'trade unions' files before 'trademarks'.

References to tables are given by the letter t.

DATE DUE

8 SEP 2011			
5 SEP 2013			
4 SEP 2014			

Demco, Inc. 38-293

Lightning Source UK Ltd.
Milton Keynes UK
03 September 2010

159352UK00002B/23/A

9 781843 310273